BUSHRANGERS

EVAN McHUGH is a journalist who has written for newspapers, television and radio. His previous books include the bestsellers *The Drovers*, *Shipwrecks: Australia's Greatest Maritime Disasters*, *Outback Heroes*, *Outback Pioneers* and *Birdsville*. Evan's book about true crime in the outback, *Red Centre, Dark Heart*, won the Ned Kelly Award for best non-fiction in 2008. He lives with his wife in the Hunter Valley, New South Wales.

BUSHRANGERS

AUSTRALIA'S GREATEST SELF-MADE HEROES

Evan McHugh

PENGUIN BOOKS

PENGUIN BOOKS

Published by the Penguin Group
Penguin Group (Australia)
250 Camberwell Road, Camberwell, Victoria 3124, Australia
(a division of Pearson Australia Group Pty Ltd)
Penguin Group (USA) Inc.
375 Hudson Street, New York, New York 10014, USA
Penguin Group (Canada)
90 Eglinton Avenue East, Suite 700, Toronto, Canada ON M4P 2Y3
(a division of Pearson Penguin Canada Inc.)
Penguin Books Ltd
80 Strand, London WC2R 0RL England
Penguin Ireland
25 St Stephen's Green, Dublin 2, Ireland
(a division of Penguin Books Ltd)
Penguin Books India Pvt Ltd
11 Community Centre, Panchsheel Park, New Delhi – 110 017, India
Penguin Group (NZ)
67 Apollo Drive, Rosedale, North Shore 0632, New Zealand
(a division of Pearson New Zealand Ltd)
Penguin Books (South Africa) (Pty) Ltd
24 Sturdee Avenue, Rosebank, Johannesburg 2196, South Africa

Penguin Books Ltd, Registered Offices: 80 Strand, London, WC2R 0RL, England

First published by Penguin Group (Australia) Ltd, 2011
This edition published by Penguin Group (Australia), 2012

1 3 5 7 9 10 8 6 4 2

Text copyright © Evan McHugh 2011

The moral right of the author has been asserted

All rights reserved. Without limiting the rights under copyright reserved above, no part of this publication may be reproduced, stored in or introduced into a retrieval system, or transmitted, in any form or by any means (electronic, mechanical, photocopying, recording or otherwise), without the prior written permission of both the copyright owner and the above publisher of this book.

Cover design by Laura Thomas © Penguin Group (Australia)
Text design by Cathy Larsen © Penguin Group (Australia)
Front cover photo: The Helmet of Ned Kelly, courtesy State Library of Victoria
Maps © Michelle Havenstein
Typeset in 10/16 Linotype Centennial 45 light by Post Pre-press Group, Brisbane, Queensland
Printed and bound in Australia by McPherson's Printing Group, Maryborough, Victoria

National Library of Australia
Cataloguing-in-Publication data:

McHugh, Evan.
Bushrangers : Australia's greatest self-made heroes / Evan McHugh.
2nd ed.
9780143567301 (pbk.)
Bushrangers – Australia.
Australia –History.

364.150994

penguin.com.au

MIX
Paper from
responsible sources
FSC® C001695

Contents

1	Strangers in a strange land	1
2	Defiance	19
3	The good, the bad and the vicious	40
4	Suspect everyone	83
5	Reap what you sow	101
6	The lust for gold	128
7	Class warfare	142
8	Eugowra	158
9	Bushranging triumphant	168
10	The scum of the earth	210
11	The odd angry shot	266
12	Kelly	271
	A note on references	319

Place me in a forest glen, unfettered, wild and free,
With 50 tried and chosen men – a bandit chief I'd be;
'Tis there when fighting with my foes amid my trusty band,
I'd freely leave this world of woes and die with sword in hand.
(Owen Suffolk, bushranger poet)

'Foolish, inconsiderate, ill-conducted, and unprincipled youths unfortunately abound, and unless they are made to consider the consequences of crime they are led to imitate notorious felons whom they regard as self-made heroes.'
(Justice Redmond Barry, Ned Kelly sentencing, 1880)

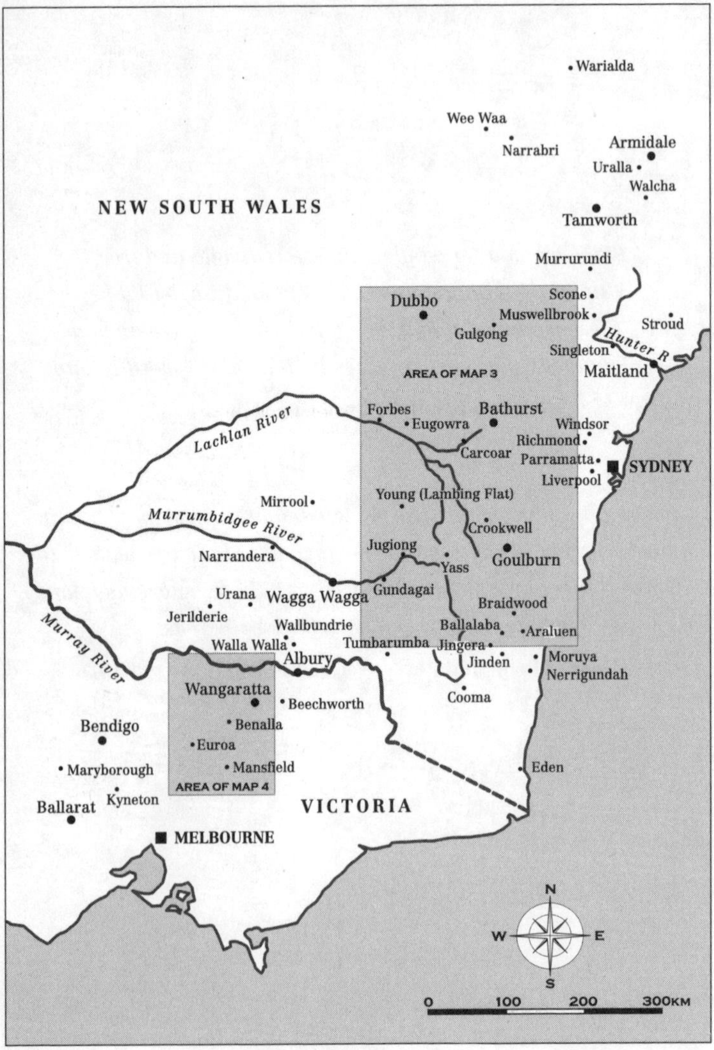

Warialda
Wee Waa
Narrabri
Armidale
Uralla
Walcha
NEW SOUTH WALES
Tamworth
Murrurundi
Scone
Muswellbrook
Stroud
Dubbo
Gulgong
Hunter R
Singleton
Maitland
AREA OF MAP 3
Forbes
Eugowra
Bathurst
Windsor
Richmond
Carcoar
Parramatta
SYDNEY
Liverpool
Lachlan River
Mirrool
Young (Lambing Flat)
Murrumbidgee River
Crookwell
Jugiong
Goulburn
Narrandera
Yass
Urana
Wagga Wagga
Gundagai
Jerilderie
Braidwood
Wallbundrie
Ballalaba
Araluen
Murray River
Walla Walla
Tumbarumba
Jingera
Albury
Jinden
Moruya
Nerrigundah
Wangaratta
Cooma
Beechworth
Bendigo
Benalla
Euroa
Maryborough
Mansfield
Eden
AREA OF MAP 4
Ballarat
Kyneton
VICTORIA
MELBOURNE
N
W
E
S
0
100
200
300KM

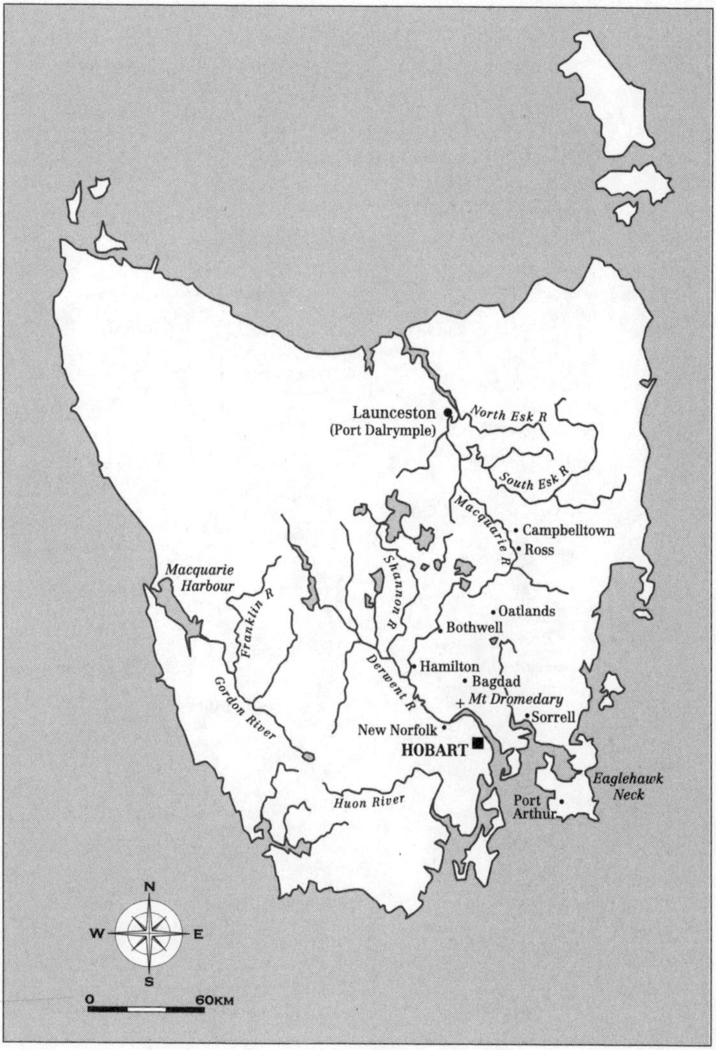

Launceston
(Port Dalrymple)
North Esk R
South Esk R
Macquarie R
Campbelltown
Ross
Shannon R
Macquarie Harbour
Franklin R
Oatlands
Bothwell
Hamilton
Bagdad
Mt Dromedary
Sorrell
Derwent R
Gordon River
New Norfolk
HOBART
Eaglehawk Neck
Port Arthur
Huon River
N
W
E
S
0
60KM

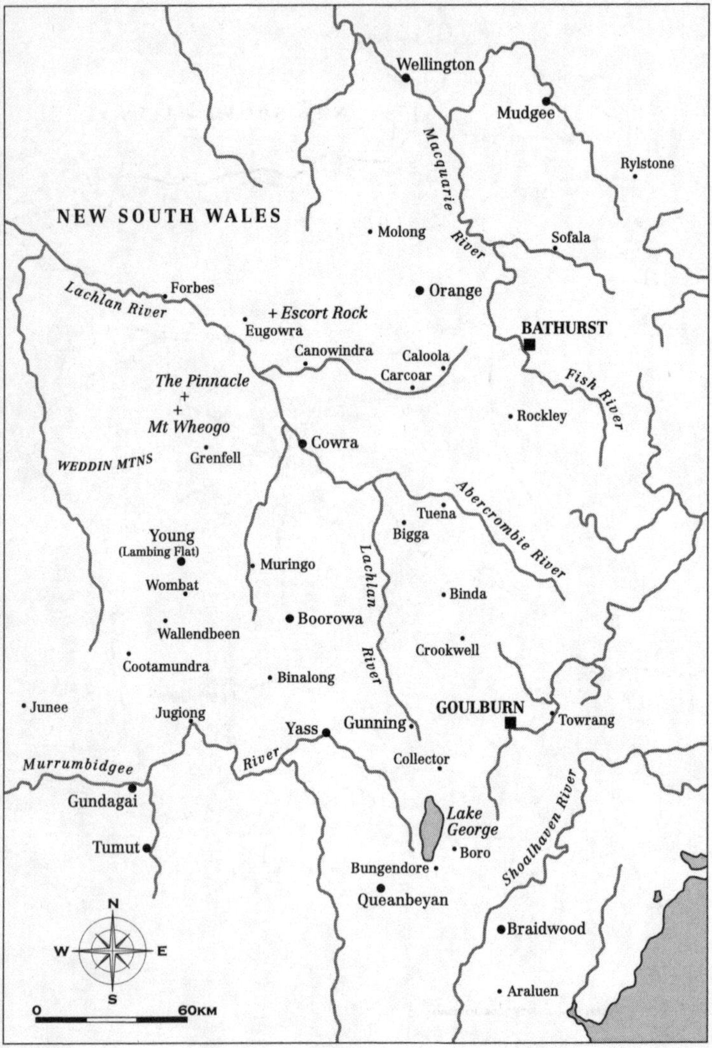

NEW SOUTH WALES
Wellington
Mudgee
Macquarie River
Rylstone
Molong
Sofala
Orange
Forbes
Lachlan River
+ Escort Rock
Eugowra
BATHURST
Canowindra
Caloola
Carcoar
Fish River
The Pinnacle
Mt Wheogo
Rockley
Cowra
Grenfell
WEDDIN MTNS
Abercrombie River
Tuena
Bigga
Young
(Lambing Flat)
Muringo
Lachlan River
Wombat
Binda
Boorowa
Wallendbeen
Crookwell
Cootamundra
Binalong
Junee
Jugiong
GOULBURN
Gunning
Yass
Towrang
River
Murrumbidgee
Collector
Gundagai
Lake George
Shoalhaven River
Tumut
Boro
Bungendore
Queanbeyan
Braidwood
Araluen
N
W
E
S
0
60KM

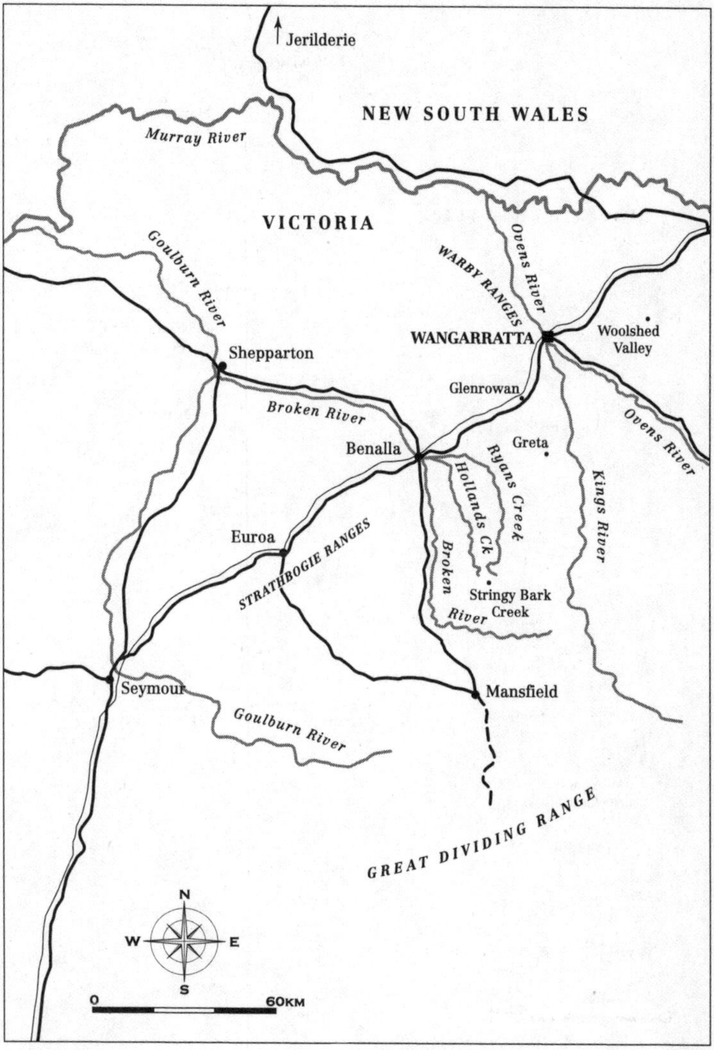

Jerilderie
NEW SOUTH WALES
Murray River
VICTORIA
Goulburn River
WARBY RANGES
Ovens River
WANGARRATTA
Woolshed Valley
Shepparton
Glenrowan
Broken River
Ovens River
Greta
Benalla
Ryans Creek
Hollands Ck
Kings River
Euroa
STRATHBOGIE RANGES
Broken River
Stringy Bark Creek
Seymour
Mansfield
Goulburn River
GREAT DIVIDING RANGE
N
W
E
S
0
60KM

1

Strangers in a strange land

1788–1809

For First Fleet convict John Caesar, hunger was the root of all evil. It gnawed at him during his waking hours. It haunted him in sleep. Seldom, if ever, did he know the pleasure of a full belly. Of all the motivations for crime, stealing food to sustain life is perhaps easiest to understand. It certainly drove John Caesar to become Australia's first bushranger.

He was born probably around 1764 on the island of Madagascar, although he has also been described as coming from the West Indies, where he worked as a slave on a sugar plantation. However, by 1785 he was in England, working as a servant or labourer when he fell foul of the law. On 13 October 1785 he broke into a home and stole £12. He was caught and put on trial early the following year. He was found guilty and sentenced to transportation for seven years. In January 1788 he arrived at Sydney Cove aboard the transport *Alexander*.

Caesar endured a year of hard labour on poor convict rations – his hunger made worse because the rations were calculated as the bare minimum to sustain the diminutive frame of the average working-class Englishman. Caesar, on the other hand, was described by the colony's deputy judge advocate, David Collins, as 'always reputed the hardest working convict in the colony; his frame was muscular and well calculated for hard labour.' Considering he was being measured against the castaways of English society, his reputation for hard work may have been easily won, but it certainly didn't do him any favours. Collins noted that Caesar's appetite was 'ravenous, for he would in one day devour the full rations for two days'.

Collins made no allowance for the fact that Caesar was probably expending so much energy that he might need additional rations. Instead, this member of the English ruling class provided one of the many examples of his sneering contempt for the convicts whose lives were in his hands when he wrote of Caesar, 'In his intellects he did not very widely differ from a brute . . . To gratify his appetite he was compelled to steal from others, all his thefts were directed to that purpose.'

Meanwhile, the colony's failures in agricultural production brought the threat of starvation ever closer. Thefts from the stores, when detected, were punished by death. There was only one exception to the rule: a convict named James Freeman received a pardon for stealing flour in return for becoming Australia's first public executioner. He soon had plenty of work. In March 1789, even six marines were hanged for robbing the stores.

The following month, Caesar and another of the four West Indians in the First Fleet, James Williams (known as 'Black Jemmy'), were caught stealing tobacco. Williams was sentenced to 500 lashes. Caesar had his sentence increased to transportation for life. Caesar's reaction to his new situation was to become typical of many convicts who despaired when faced with the prospect of a lifetime of penal servitude. On 13 May 1789 he took some provisions, stole a musket from a marine and bolted into the bush.

He may have held hopes of living off the land, or perhaps of joining a group of Aboriginal people, but it was only a matter of days before hunger forced him back to the vicinity of the settlement. After stealing food from some gardens, on 26 May he attempted to steal the rations of a convict gang making bricks at Brickfield Hill (in present day Surry Hills) and was almost captured. His escape may have made him more cautious. On 6 June he waited until it was dark before emerging from the bush to attempt another robbery. This time, he broke into the house of assistant commissary for stores, Zachariah Clark. He was attempting to steal some food when he was caught by another convict, William Saltmarsh. If there was any brotherhood among convicts, it didn't apply to Saltmarsh and Caesar. Saltmarsh was able to match Caesar physically and apprehended him.

Under the circumstances, Caesar must have expected a short trial followed by a prompt execution. Collins gave play to his natural prejudices before detailing the condemned man's attitude to his fate:

> He was such a wretch, and so indifferent about meeting death, that he declared while in confinement, that if he should be hanged, he would create a laugh before he was turned off, by playing off some trick upon the executioner.

However, while the situation for the colony was growing steadily worse, for reasons best known to Governor Phillip it was decided that Caesar would not be executed. Perhaps Phillip had realised that the death penalty wasn't a deterrent to people who were dying of starvation. Instead, he ordered that Caesar be sent to Garden Island (a short distance east of the settlement at Sydney Cove) where he would be fettered while he worked in the gardens. Not only that, his rations would be supplemented with vegetables from the garden. The governor appeared to understand the predicament of one of his best workers, even if thuggish underlings like Collins couldn't.

Throughout 1789 the colony's food situation grew steadily worse. Not long after Caesar was sent to Garden Island, convict Elizabeth Fowles was caught stealing food. Her head was shaved and she was forced to wear a canvas cap with the word 'thief' on it. In November convict Ann Davis was caught stealing and became the first woman to be executed in Australia. That month the men's ration was cut by a third.

The following month, Caesar escaped once again. He'd behaved himself well enough to have his leg irons removed and on 22 December, after stealing a week's provisions from his fellow convicts, he boarded the canoe they used to paddle to and from Garden Island and made off. A couple of nights later he returned to steal an iron pot, musket and ammunition. The provisions didn't last the ravenous Caesar long and he was soon prowling the gardens at Rose Hill in search of sustenance. He was spotted and pursued, but managed to escape, dropping the musket as he fled. It proved to be his undoing. Only a few days later, he turned himself in.

William Bradley, first lieutenant on HMS *Sirius*, wrote about Caesar in his journal *A Voyage to New South Wales:*

> When he lost the Musquet he found it impossible to subsist himself, he was then attacked by the Natives & wounded in several places & escaped from a party of them through a very thick brush when he surrendered himself.

Once again it appears Governor Phillip was lenient towards Caesar. In March 1790 he decided to send a large contingent of settlers to Norfolk Island, hoping that increasing farming activity there would take some of the pressure off the settlement in Sydney and Rose Hill. Caesar was included among the 116 male convicts sent with 68 female convicts and 27 children. Phillip also gave Caesar a pardon.

In the same month, two years and two months after the penal colony had been settled and had not seen a single supply ship, the men's ration was cut to half the original allowance. In April, convict William Lane was given 2000 lashes for stealing biscuits. Thomas Halford received 2000 lashes for stealing 1.4 kilograms of potatoes. William Parr got off relatively lightly with only 500 lashes for stealing a pumpkin. The almost certainly lethal punishments seem wildly disproportionate to the crimes committed, particularly considering that in subsequent years the penalty for the serious offence of absconding was usually fifty lashes and an increase in sentence. The sheer number of lashes suggests that flogging can't have been a particularly severe punishment, although records of the experience suggest otherwise. Descriptions of extreme agony, of victims having the skin on their backs reduced to a bloody pulp, of flogger and flogged spattered in gore, of the ground around the flogging frames soaked in blood and of victims being flogged to death abound. The use and abuse of this brutal form of punishment was one of the many motivations for the incidents of bushranging (in its simplest form taking to the bush and engaging in criminal activity) detailed in this volume.

Many convicts carried the scars of their floggings for the rest of their lives. Where 500 or more lashes were involved the chances of survival must have been extremely low, and the victim's best hope was to be rendered insensible as quickly as possible.

On 13 May 1790, two months after Lane, Halford and Parr were flogged for stealing food, convict Joseph Owen, an elderly man in poor health, was the first to die of hunger. Fortunately for the colonists, the vessels of the Second Fleet began arriving the following month.

Meanwhile, on Norfolk Island, the governor's indulgence with regard to John Caesar seemed to have paid off. By the middle of 1791 Caesar was supporting himself on a plot of land and was issued with a pig. In January 1792 his holding was increased to nearly half a hectare. He had formed a relationship with a convict woman, Ann Power, by whom he had a daughter. However, for reasons unknown, he left his holding and young family and returned to Sydney in 1793. It was a bad move, as he was soon in trouble and hunger once again got the better of him. Wrote Collins:

> Caesar, still incorrigible, took up his former practice of subsisting in the woods by plundering the farms and huts at the outskirts of the towns. He was soon taken; but on his being punished, and that with some severity, he declared with exultation and contempt, that 'all that would not make him better'.

Caesar was quiet until December 1795, when he ran away again, and was involved in a confrontation with the Aboriginal warrior Pemulwuy. By some accounts Caesar killed Pemulwuy, but in fact the warrior was only wounded (he was shot dead by Henry Hacking in 1802). Caesar remained at large for more than two months, gathering a band of followers about him, all of them intent on robbing the farms on the outskirts of civilisation.

In January, Governor John Hunter called upon him to surrender, without success. Accordingly, on 29 January 1796 Hunter proclaimed:

> The many robberies which have lately been committed render it necessary that some steps should be taken to put a stop to a practice so destructive of the happiness and comfort of the industrious. And as it is well known that a fellow known as Black Caesar has absented himself for some time past from his work, and has carried with him a musquet, notice is hereby given that whoever shall secure this man Black Caesar and bring him in with his arms shall receive as a reward five gallons [23 litres] of spirits.

The British administration had given such little regard to the financial system of the fledgling settlement that rum had become de facto currency, especially among convicts and workers. In later years the drinking culture of Australia's working class was to be identified as yet another factor that rendered them dissolute and prone to bushranging. Meanwhile, in Australia's early years, those who would eventually bemoan alcohol's pernicious influence were party to its establishment. Hunter's reward was clearly targeted at the convicts and working class, to encourage them to hunt Caesar down or give him up.

David Collins also noted:

> The settlers, and those people who were occasionally supplied with ammunition by the officers, were informed, that if they should be hereafter discovered to have so abused the confidence placed in them, as to supply those common plunderers with any part of this ammunition, they would be deemed accomplices in the robberies committed by them, and steps would be taken to bring them to punishment as accessories.

Caesar, who was one of up to eight men plundering farms, sent word to the authorities that he wasn't about to surrender and that they wouldn't take him alive. However, with the reward on offer, it wasn't long until someone took the bait. On 15 February 1795 David Collins wrote:

> Information was received, that black Caesar had that morning been shot by one Wimbow. This man and another, allured by the reward, had been for some days in quest of him. Finding his haunt, they concealed themselves all night at the edge of a brush which they perceived him enter at dusk. In the morning he came out, when, looking round him and seeing his danger, he presented his musket; but before he could pull the trigger Wimbow fired and shot him. He was taken to the

hut of Rose, a settler at Liberty Plains, where he died in a few hours. Thus ended a man, who certainly, during his life, could never have been estimated at more than one remove above the brute, and who had given more trouble than any other convict in the settlement.

Caesar is now regarded as Australia's first bushranger, although the term wasn't used to describe criminals who ranged the bush until almost a decade later.

Caesar's violent end was to become typical of the fate that awaited many bushrangers over the course of the next century. In detailing the bushrangers' history, it's easy to forget that every death – be it bushranger, victim or police pursuer – represents a human life, with all its potential, aspirations, hopes and dreams. The desire to live long and be free was as strong then as it is now. The premature end of every life, regardless of criminality, class or wealth, is a tragedy. The mixture of desperation, courage, bravado and fear exhibited over the 100 years of bushranging represents one of the most dramatic and tragic aspects of the young nation's genesis. However, dismissing bushrangers as mere criminals doesn't explain why they, unlike other criminals, achieved enduring fame. To the dismay of many, rightly or wrongly some bushrangers achieved a hero status and exerted a fascination that transcended mere crime. Understanding how they did so may say as much about a society in need of heroes (however flawed) as it does about the continued interest in their exploits.

While Caesar pursued his career, he was certainly not alone. As detailed earlier, convicts such as Edward Corbett, executed after absconding with a jacket, were also escaping into the bush. Most bolted in ones or twos. Some returned half-starved. Others simply starved to death, ignorant of the skills required to live off the land and easy prey to an Aboriginal population resentful of their presence. After 1791, with the arrival of a large contingent of Irish convicts aboard the ship *Ocean,* the incidences of absconding rose. Many of the convicts made off into the bush under the mistaken impression that they would be able to escape to China, which they thought to be no more than a few hundred kilometres away.

Not all of them perished. Some, such as John Wilson who had become a free man in 1792 and disappeared into the bush, managed to establish good relationships with the Aboriginal groups that surrounded Sydney, and prospered. However, such relationships were looked on with suspicion by the administration. As always, Deputy Judge Advocate David Collins was dismissive when he described John Wilson as a 'wild, idle young man', and that 'no good consequence' would come of him 'herding with these people'.

Early in 1795 Wilson emerged from the bush to explain to Governor Hunter that the increasing aggression Aboriginal people were displaying towards settlers along the Hawkesbury River, west of Sydney, was in retaliation for the attacks of a small group of settlers. As the situation deteriorated, ex-convicts such as Wilson were regarded as being largely responsible. In February 1796 Collins wrote of Wilson and other ex-convicts:

> They demonstrated to the natives of how little use a musket was when once discharged, and this effectually removed that terror of our firearms with which it had been our constant endeavour to inspire them.

Governor John Hunter took a similar view, and on 13 May 1797 issued a proclamation making Wilson and his colleagues Australia's first outlaws, meaning they were outside the protection of the law:

> Whereas John Jeweson, Joseph Saunders, John Wilson and Moses Williams have at various times and opportunities absconded from the situation in which they have been placed, and from the work which it was then their duty to have perform'd, and are at this time employ'd

in committing depredations upon defenceless settlers and others who live at a distance from any protection: And whereas, in the many robberys and crueltys which have lately been practis'd upon the above defenceless people by numerous bodys of the natives, in depriving them of their live stock, burning their houses, and destroying in a few minutes the whole fruits of their former industry, as well as wounding and sometimes murdering them, there is some reason to believe, from white men having been seen frequently at such times amongst them, that such acts of violence have generally been advis'd and assisted by the abovenam'd deserters, who, having absconded from their duty, can have no other means of living.

This public notice is given from an opinion that it may reach the knowledge of those who are the subject of it. That the said John Jeweson, Joseph Saunders, John Wilson and Moses Williams do not within the space of fourteen days from the date hereof deliver themselves up to the nearest peace officer they will be consider'd as having lost the protection of his Majesty and the aid of the law; consequently, if taken, will be considered not only accessory to the death of those natives who may suffer in the unlawful plunder already mentioned, but as accomplices with them in the mischiefs and cruelty so frequently committed by them, and be liable to be immediately executed without the form of a trial, having by their unlawful conduct forfeited the protection of those wholesome laws under which they have been born and bred.

Not surprisingly, the men didn't turn themselves in by the required date, and it wouldn't be the last time such a proclamation was ignored. Eventually, in November 1797, John Wilson turned himself in. All he wore was a kangaroo-skin loincloth and his body bore the scars of an Aboriginal initiation ceremony.

Wilson (whose life is detailed in the author's *Outback Pioneers*) claimed that he had travelled up to 160 kilometres in every direction from Sydney and discovered the fate of many of the early convict absconders. David Collins documented Wilson's story:

> It was not then to be wondered at, that Wilson, who lately came in from the woods, should, among other articles of information, mention his finding more than fifty skeletons, which the natives assured him had been white men, who had lost their way and perished. This account was corroborated by different European articles which were scattered about, such as knives, old shoes, and other things which were known not to belong to the natives.

Rumours soon circulated that cannibalism was practised among starving escapees. It wouldn't be long before instances occurred in which rumour became fact.

Wherever settlements were established, escapes soon followed, and those who survived their escape became the earliest bushrangers. When a settlement was established for a brief period in Port Phillip Bay in 1803, six convicts escaped under cover of darkness on the night of 27 December. Two were almost immediately captured. A third, Daniel McAllender, gave himself up in the middle of January 1804. When the settlement was abandoned, in February, the remaining three men – William Buckley and two others named Marmon and Pye – were unaccounted for. The fate of Marmon and Pye is unknown. Incredibly, William Buckley survived (as detailed in the author's *Outback Heroes*) until what became Melbourne was settled in 1835, whereupon he emerged from the bush, having lived among the local Aboriginal people for the previous thirty-two years. When it came to ranging the bush, his was the longest reign by far.

It was a similar story with the establishment of a settlement at Risdon Cove, near present-day Hobart, in Van Diemen's Land, also in 1803. No sooner were the convicts landed than they began to escape. To make matters worse, two years later convicts were encouraged to take muskets and live off the land as an acute food shortage saw the whole colony facing starvation. Kangaroos were plentiful and the hunters were able to supplement the colony's food supplies. Thus, sixteen years after starvation motivated First Fleet convict John Caesar to go bush, starvation motivated the government to send convicts there in numbers. It continued to do so until the crisis had passed, in 1807. Unfortunately, when the armed convicts were required to return to their former employment, many stayed in the bush.

The administration was in no position to bring the convicts in, but it also offered little to encourage their return. After a flogging for absconding, most could expect to be returned to whichever master they'd been assigned to. The lucky ones were treated well or found a situation where they could serve out their sentence quietly. However, even there they could face difficulties. If their work was of value to the master, it was a common practice to mistreat convicts so that they would be compelled to run away and thereby have their sentence increased when they were caught and returned. In addition, minor misdemeanours, which wouldn't result in punishment of any kind for non-convicts, could see sentences increased by months or years for those who were. The result was that masters continued to receive free labour at little expense, while some convicts lost all hope of ever being released.

Under the circumstances it was perhaps inevitable that fifteen years after the convict settlement at Sydney was established, the surrounding bush (and that around the newer settlement at Hobart) was well populated with escaped convicts. On 19 March 1803 the third edition of Australia's first newspaper, the *Sydney Gazette*, documented one of the town's most lethal court sittings, when fourteen nascent bushrangers faced a number of charges.

On 14 March Patrick Gannan and Francis Simpson faced a charge of robbing the home of Mr Declamb. According to the *Gazette*, 'The Judge Advocate summed up the evidence, and upon a deliberation of about fifteen minutes, the Court returned a verdict, "Guilty – Death."'

A further eleven men were also indicted for having been present at Declamb's, for having assisted in the robbery and for having stolen goods in their possession, including silver spoons, a pistol and a spyglass. The verdict for three of them: 'Lawrence Dempsey, Michael Woollaghan, and Patrick Macdermot, Guilty – Death!'

The other eight men – John Lynch, Thomas Shanks, John Morgan, Laughlan Doyle, Timothy Malahoy, John Brown, James Conroy and Patrick Ross – were acquitted but faced another charge the next day, of feloniously entering the house of Thomas Neal at Richmond Hill and taking 'one bushel and one peck [45 litres] of wheat. Verdict: The court after some minutes' deliberation, returned a verdict – all Guilty – Death!'

A man named John Taylor stole 21 shillings from the house of Robert Foster and was given a year's hard labour. William Jones and Mary White stole goods from the house of Robert Harley. Both were found guilty. Jones was sentenced to death. Mary White was acquitted.

In reporting the cases, the *Gazette* observed:

> The prisoners who had been capitally convicted (14 in number) were again brought to the bar; and the JUDGE ADVOCATE, after a pathetic admonition to sue for that forgiveness in Heaven, from which the crimes of some among them had precluded them on Earth, pronounced the awful sentence!

Some of those who avoided justice fared no better. In March 1803 James Hughes robbed a house near Sydney and escaped into the bush. A skeleton presumed to be his was found in 1806. Other escaped convicts were caught before they could commit any crimes. In 1803 John Place was given 500 lashes after his first escape attempt. He was sentenced to death after his second attempt.

Most references from this era describe escapees as insurgents or banditti. It wasn't until 1805 that the first references to bushranging occur. On 17 February 1805 the *Sydney Gazette* reported:

> On Tuesday last [12 February] a cart was stopped between this settlement and Hawkesbury, by three men whose appearance sanctioned the suspicion of their being bush-rangers. They had been previously observed lurking about the Ponds by a carrier, who passed unmolested, owing perhaps to his having another man in company: they did not, however, take any thing out of the cart they did stop; nor at this time has any account been received of their offering violence to either passengers or other persons; from whence it may be hoped they prefer the prospect of being restored to society to any momentary relief that might be obtained from acts of additional imprudence that could at best but render their condition hopeless. It is nevertheless necessary, that the settler as well as the traveller should be put upon his guard against assault, and that exertion should be general in assisting to apprehend every flagitious [criminal] character who would thus rush upon a danger from which they can only be extricated by timely contrition and their return to obedience.

This reference may also illustrate the earliest moralising on the vice of bushranging. It continued:

> All that have heretofore devoted themselves to this most horrible state of exile exactly correspond in the narration of vicissitudes to which many have fallen the unhappy victims. How deplorable must be the prospect of terminating an existence under all the accumulated horrors of such an exile! without a friend at hand to administer the last kind offices, or to alleviate affliction by humane condolence! parching with thirst, perhaps, but deprived by famine of the power to quench it! instead of the delightful confidence which Christian resignation can

alone inspire, each succeeding pang embittered with self-accusation and remorse, heightened by the surrounding gloom to all the agonies of deep despair. If conscious impropriety of conduct inspires the fatal resolution of flying to the woods, this second act becomes a second outrage, and by an obstinate perseverance the very doors of mercy may be closed, and every avenue to hope cut off.

It was only the first of many high-blown reflections on the subject of bushranging. And as with subsequent references to the physical and psychological challenges, it fails to understand that many of those who took to bushranging didn't do so by choice. It was their last resort. For all its swashbuckling tales of daring robberies, remarkable horsemanship, wild gunfights and even chivalrous conduct, the tragic reality of bushranging was that for most, once embarked upon there was no going back. It was the same at the very beginning as it was right to the end.

The short career of bushranger John Murphy was typical of many. On 12 October 1806 Murphy robbed a house in the early hours of the morning. He was arrested soon after and faced a charge of breaking and entering. Unlike most defendants, he pleaded guilty. The judge advocate reportedly warned him that he should be careful because his plea would make it unnecessary to provide any further evidence to prove the case against him. This may seem obvious, but Murphy didn't seem to realise, or care about, the danger he was in. Altogether he was asked to enter his plea three times. Each time he answered 'Guilty.' The court proceeded to sentence the unfortunate man to death.

The victims of bushranging come in many forms, but in November 1806 a shepherd became one of the first to die after being mistaken for a bushranger. At the time five escaped convicts were bushranging together around Prospect Hill, between Sydney and Parramatta. They appeared to be targeting the flock of prominent grazier John McArthur, who'd lost five sheep in one night. His shepherds' huts had also been robbed while they were watching the sheep. McArthur increased the number of shepherds, especially at night. Two of them, John Griffiths and an old man named Simeon Donnally, were on watch during the night of 8 November 1806 when their sheep started running about within their fold. It could only mean bushrangers. According to the *Sydney Gazette* of 16 November 1806:

> Griffiths posted his brother watchman as advantageously as possible, while he himself should reconnoitre, as well as the extreme darkness of the night admitted, the movements of their adversaries. No sooner had they separated than Donnally from some unaccountable cause, forsook his post, and went within the fold, not improbably to discover whether any person had introduced himself therein or not. The other, having traversed a considerable part of the circuit, at length descried a human form, and could not possibly suppose it to be any other than a bushranger. He hailed him instantly, and thrice repeated the challenge; but receiving no answer fired upon him, and the charge having taken place he very soon discovered the object of his aim to have been no other than the unfortunate Donnally, who was mortally wounded in the side.

Donnally, it was revealed at the inquest into his death, was hard of hearing and probably didn't hear Griffiths challenging him. It turned out Griffiths and Donnally were good friends, and while Griffiths wasn't held to blame for what had happened, he would forever have the blood of an innocent man on his hands.

Some of the miscreants were brought to justice soon after. While bushrangers tried to provoke Aboriginal people to attack settlers and thereby cause security forces to be diluted, settlers were also trying to enlist Aboriginal people to pursue the bushrangers. In this case, with the assistance of one of them, three convicts employed as stockmen tracked the bushrangers to a camp where five of them were happily dining on a variety of meats, washed down with tea.

Despite being outnumbered, the stockmen rushed them. The motivation for the stockmen was all too clear. There was the possibility of a pardon if they managed to secure even one bushranger. It was a fight for liberty on both sides. On this occasion the stockmen (and quite probably the tracker) managed to take all five bushrangers prisoner. However, when one of the stockmen went to get some stringy bark with which to tie them, the bushrangers attacked the remaining two. The stockmen fought hard until their mate returned, armed with a musket and tomahawk. Three of the bushrangers escaped, leaving two – named Cox and Halfpenny – too badly knocked about to run.

Three others, injured to varying degrees, plus a sixth bushranger appear to have been taken not long after. On 30 November the *Sydney Gazette* reported:

> Yesterday the Court reassembled at 9 and commenced its proceedings with the trial of Henry Kelly, William Gorman, James Sheely, and James and Stephen Halfpenny, bush-rangers, an indictment containing four distinct counts, all of which were of a capital tendency; and charging the prisoners, jointly and severaly with having stolen two cows belonging to Captain ABBOTT prior to the 23rd of November last, and a cow, two ewes, and two lambs, the property of John McArthur, Esq. four muskets, taken from his stockmen's huts during the night time and a chest belonging to Thomas Herbert, flockman [stockman], containing wearing apparel and other property.
>
> Patrick Cox admitted Evidence for the Crown, gave a testimony by which all the parties were criminated, as was likewise Matthew Collins, not yet apprehended; after which several respectable witnesses

corroborated his evidence in many material points. The Court cleared, and after much deliberation returned a Verdict *All guilty* – Death.

In December the brothers Halfpenny were executed. Gorman, Kelly and Sheely had their sentences commuted to life imprisonment. It was hoped the death of the Halfpennys would set an example to others. The purveyors of justice might just as well have attempted to turn back the tide.

2

Defiance

1810–1819

There are essentially two types of bushranger. The first are those whose careers are short, often consisting of a crime, pursuit, capture, trial and execution. The second are those who survive long enough to commit two or more offences, and who may eventually make a name for themselves as a 'notorious bushranger'.

In 1810 the country around Sydney was infested with villains of the first category. However, Van Diemen's Land was about to become the scene of an outbreak of bushranging that for the first time would transcend mere crime. It would place one of its perpetrators on a pedestal of admiration that few in authority could begin to understand.

As mentioned in the previous chapter, the convicts of Van Diemen's Land had been ranging the bush in search of food for some years. And unlike the Sydney convicts who were still hemmed in on one side by the sea and on the other by the cliffs of the Blue Mountains, the Van Diemen's Land convicts were free to roam the sparsely inhabited interior. Their depredations were indiscriminate, as reported by the *Sydney Gazette* on 10 April 1813:

> The natives of Van Diemen's Land continue very inimical, which is mostly attributed to their frequent ill treatment from the bushrangers, who to avoid punishment for their offences have betaken themselves to the woods, there miserably to exist on the adventitious succours which those wilds afford. Acts of cruelty are reported of these desperadoes against the natives, at the mention of which humanity must shudder; and the latter seldom suffer opportunity to escape of wreaking their vengeance upon all persons of the same colour with the lawless wanderers, without discrimination. In order, however, to break up the horde that have resorted to this dreadful course, a Proclamation had been issued by Government, requiring their surrendering themselves up by the 4th of April instant, on promise of forgiveness, and declaratory of a determination to issue a Writ of outlawry against all or any who should not avail themselves of the proffered clemency.

Only some took advantage of the amnesty. The offer was renewed in May the following year by Governor Lachlan Macquarie. On 14 May 1814 his proclamation named twenty-nine men who were at large:

> [Who] had feloniously and wickedly committed many atrocious Robberies and Depredations upon the peaceable inhabitants of the said settlement, by feloniously and violently driving away and stealing their Sheep and Cattle, and feloniously, violently, and burglariously breaking into their houses, and then and there stealing divers of their Goods and Chattels, to the great Damage and Terror of His Majesty's Subjects.

While the governor's pardon listed convicts who were at large at the time, it may have been incorrect to assume they were all together. However, the frequent raids on outlying settlements were carried out by large groups. These attacks were not solely for the purpose of obtaining fresh supplies or money. During an attack at New Norfolk in 1813, wheat stacks and houses were also set alight, suggesting that revenge against cruel masters was also a motivating factor.

Among those named in Macquarie's proclamation were John Whitehead and Michael Howe. They were required to surrender, and would be pardoned all offences except murder. If they didn't, they would be deemed outlaws, effectively meaning they enjoyed no protection under the law and could be shot dead by anyone who saw them, no questions asked.

Whitehead, a former gardener, had been transported in 1801 for seven years for stealing two pairs of pants. Howe had been a sailor in the British navy but after deserting he took to highway robbery. He was caught and sentenced to seven years' transportation, arriving in Australia in 1812.

After Whitehead and Howe both absconded in 1813, Whitehead became the bushrangers' leader. In his *History of the Australian Bushrangers* George Boxall details one of Whitehead's worst excesses:

> The gang captured a half-crazy fellow named John Hopkins and accused him of trying to betray them. As a punishment for this offence a pair of moccasins, roughly made of bullock hide, was fitted on to his feet, and in these were placed a number of the great red ants, commonly known in Australia as 'bull-dog' or 'soldier' ants (*Myrmecia gulosa*). These ants are an inch and a quarter [30 millimetres] long, and of most ferocious appearance. They are the dread of the colonists. They sting quite as severely as a bee or a hornet. But a bee stings only once, while a soldier ant will continue to sting until removed . . . The victim is said to have died in agony.

In Sydney, even the careers of the 'notorious' were short-lived. On 24 September 1814 the *Gazette* detailed the capture of one of them:

Patrick Collins, the notorious bushranger implicated in the murder of Alder, White, and the woman at Hawkesbury, in company with the late Donovan; and, suspected also of many subsequent robberies, was apprehended on Thursday evening by a party of soldiers quartered at Liverpool, conducted by Mr. John Warby, and several natives, by whom his place of concealment near the Devil's Back, had been discovered. In an effort to escape he was speared by one of the natives in the leg and arm, when finding himself immediately overpowered, he was forced to yield, and was brought in yesterday.

However, such reports were eclipsed by events in Van Diemen's Land. The *Sydney Gazette* had much to report on 20 May 1815:

A party of villains, eight in number, and accompanied by a native woman, made a daring attack upon the settlement of New Norfolk [50 kilometres north-west of Hobart] on Monday the 24th of last month, and stripped the settlers of all property they could carry off, together with all arms and ammunition they could find. They had previously visited the Government herds about five miles [8 kilometres] from New Norfolk, and killed a fine cow. When in their course of plundering they had reached as far as the Back River, Mr Dennis McCarthy, who resides about two miles [3 kilometres] distant, received information of their approach, and determined to give them a meeting, without knowing their number, or the manner in which they were armed; for during a late absence from the settlement his house had been plundered by a party of the banditti; and on the present occasion his vessel the Geordy lay near his premises, and contained a considerable property which would have been at the mercy of the plunderers.

McCarthy rounded up nine other men – the *Geordy*'s master, James O'Berne, mate Keith Hacking, a crewman named Tooms who'd been given a conditional pardon after apprehending two other offenders, one of his servants, four friends and a neighbour's son. They armed themselves with five fowling-pieces and a brace (pair) of pistols and confronted the bushrangers who, with twelve muskets, three or four brace of pistols and a sword, were better armed. Despite this:

> Mr McCarthy commanded them to lay down their arms – but received in reply the fire of three of the ruffians, by which five persons fell, one of whom (Carlisle) received a ball in the groin and three slugs in the breast, of which wounds he died in less than an hour after. Messrs Jamott and Triffit were severely wounded on the thigh, Murphy on the lower part of the belly, and Mr O'Berne receiving a ball in the cheek, which perforated the tongue and lodged in the neck . . . The major part of Mr McCarthy's party being thus disabled, the villains ordered him to lay down his arms; to which command he returned a shot. He fired thrice, but without execution, as the bushrangers were positioned behind trees. Two of their balls passed through his coat; his servant Brown behaved with equal gallantry; and with only a broad-sword sprang forward to engage the miscreants hand to hand; but was alone with his master, and was compelled to retire with him.

The badly wounded Murphy was left to the mercy of the bushrangers. At first, despite his serious injuries, they attempted to tie him to a tree and flog him, but the gang's leader, probably John Whitehead, managed to dissuade them. O'Berne died a few days after the attack, when a blood vessel in his neck suddenly ruptured.

The bushrangers were subsequently identified by informants as Whitehead, Michael Howe, Richard McGuire, Richard Collyer, Hugh Byrne, Peter Septon, Dennis Geary, Edward Edwards and John Jones. The native woman was probably Mary Cockerill, Howe's partner. The informants also claimed that the gang was responsible for the burning of haystacks in the area and the robbery of a man named Fisk. However, the nine were held responsible for the murder of

Carlisle, meaning they all faced the death penalty.

By the end of the month, two detachments of soldiers, eighteen volunteers from Hobart and another search party led by Tooms were in pursuit of the gang. According to the *Gazette,* 'All [the gang's] succours must be now necessarily cut off, and they must either deliver themselves up, or perish through harrassing and hunger.'

Lieutenant Governor Thomas Davey took the extraordinary measure of declaring martial law on 25 April 1815, the legality of which was suspect and subsequently repudiated by Governor Macquarie. However, it took until September 1815 before it was repealed. Meanwhile, a reward of £50 (approximately two years' income for the average labourer) was offered for the apprehension of any of the bushrangers. Pardons were offered to offenders who hadn't committed a felony, and rewards offered to convicts. However, it was also clear that the bushrangers were getting help from convicts and former convicts throughout the colony. The governor's proclamation took the unusual step of offering £50 for information leading to the conviction of harbourers as well.

However, the ink was barely dry on the proclamation when the bushrangers struck again. A detachment of the 40th Regiment was guarding properties around Pitt Water, 30 kilometres east of Hobart, seemingly with some success. However, in early May the house of a man named Humphrey at Pitt Water was attacked and stripped of everything of value. A week after that, the house of Mr McCarthy, back at New Norfolk, was besieged. It was guarded by a contingent of soldiers and five of McCarthy's servants, but the bushrangers were undeterred. The *Sydney Gazette* of 2 September 1815 reported:

> The doors of the house were all barred, but the front door was nevertheless forced in, and a fire immediately commenced from the assailants, who levelling their muskets through a long hall that led into the kitchen, wounded a soldier in the thigh. Their reception was

as warm as it could possibly be, and after a brisk interchange of shot that lasted about twenty minutes, the villains went off . . . The conduct of the military party was conspicuously meritorious, and that of Mr. McCarthy's men, as their assistants, was no less entitled to commendation. They had taken the precaution to extinguish all lights, and rifle firing was kept up through the doors and window shutters, which were of course perforated in many places. Whitehead, who as commander of the assailants was dressed in a cocked hat, part of the spoil taken from the house of Mr. Humphrey, was killed in the act of surveying the premises to find an entrance; and upon his fall, which was effected by a soldier who caught his glimpse as he passed, the attack appears to have been abandoned.

The bushrangers stopped at a stockman's hut later that evening and while there said that they had decapitated Whitehead to prevent anyone claiming his head money, literally the reward payable upon presentation of his head for identification.

Some sources suggest Whitehead may have realised he wasn't going to survive and had asked for his head to be taken. The bushrangers also said that since they'd been stopped from robbing McCarthy, the next time they visited the place they'd burn it to the ground.

The *Sydney Gazette* continued the story:

The same night Mr. McCarthy returned home with all possible expedition, and found the headless body at his threshold: he augmented the number of his guard, and conveyed the body down to Hobart Town the same night, where he arrived very late, but found all the inhabitants up, waiting with anxious expectation the report of the result. The death of Whitehead (whose person was identified in that of the deceased), was a subject of general satisfaction. The body was next morning hung in chains.

Throughout May the bushrangers were hunted, with little success. One of their huts was found, along with a number of hunting dogs, a cache of weapons and ammunition. Two bushrangers were at the hut but they ran off. They were prevented from rejoining the rest of the gang and were pursued down one of the banks of the Derwent.

The bushrangers, later identified as Richard McGuire and Hugh Byrne, attempted to bribe a settler to get them a boat. While they waited for him to find a vessel, the hunters closed in. When the bushrangers discovered they were surrounded they levelled their muskets and prepared to fight. Reported the *Sydney Gazette*:

> Serjeant Beaufort, who commanded the party, immediately on perceiving this, fired upon them and wounded Byrne in the hip. They were then both secured, and tried a few days after by a court martial, who sentenced them to be executed and hung in chains, which sentence was carried into effect accordingly.

The *Gazette* believed the remaining bushrangers couldn't last long:

> The condition of those miscreants is now hopeless, and the more they are in consequence to be dreaded. If totally deprived of dogs, they must resort to the flocks more than they have done, and by thus necessarily approaching the various settlements, fall more frequently within the power of the inhabitants. Without the means of leaving a country, in which their own misconduct has rendered them obnoxious, the sea coast can afford them no prospect of relief; and, if they fail of ammunition, their condition will be completely wretched. The dread of treachery will then become the stimulus to mutual treasons, particularly with those who have been less remarkable in deeds of desperation than their more marked companions – and who are no longer useful to society than by their miserable example to warn others from entering into their unhappy courses.

It was a forlorn hope. The gang had certainly suffered a major setback and during the course of the next year it was reduced to only five – Howe (now the gang's leader), Septon, Geary, Jones and Collyer. By August 1816, eight convicts had joined the bushrangers, rebuilding the gang's numbers to thirteen. As winter gave way to spring, they renewed their activities. The *Hobart Town Gazette* of 16 November 1816 detailed their latest attack, with more than a hint of frustration:

> We are again truly sorry to acquaint our Readers that another most audacious and outrageous Robbery to a large amount, has been committed on the premises of DAVID ROSE, Esq. on the evening of the 7th inst. by the Bush Rangers. Their conduct during this attack was accompanied with circumstances peculiarly aggravating; they even demanded the wearing apparel of Mr. Donald Sutherland, his Wife and child (who lately arrived from Ceylon as a Settler), and who resides in the house . . . Notwithstanding the numerous depredations these villains still continue to commit, it is surprising they elude all search of their pursuers.

The report further added that two more men had joined the gang, one of whom, Dennis M'Caig, was a free man.

A week later the *Hobart Town Gazette* of 23 November 1816 reported that the gang not only robbed a group of travellers, but they'd been told the group was coming:

> The party were alarmed by the appearance of the Bushrangers, headed by Michael Howe & his gang of 8 runaways, who seemed well informed of the intent of their journey; and requested to know the reason of Mr. S's delay, observing, he ought to have been there the day previous.

During the attack, the bushrangers' conversation revealed that they had good knowledge of the efforts of the authorities to apprehend them. They also knew who was departing from Hobart and Port Dalrymple (now Launceston) and when. Clearly, they were being fed a steady stream of information by sympathisers in both locations.

The police, meanwhile, seemed less than enthusiastic about coming to grips with the gang. The *Hobart Town Gazette*'s report added:

> Previous to the attack at Mr Hayes, MR JOHN WADE, Chief Constable (being on his way to inspect his flock at Stony Hut Valley), accidentally joined the party at Mr H's, but suspecting the approach of the Bushrangers, from the noise he heard while in the house, he made all haste off the premises; his escape was very fortunate, as from the threats they made use of, serious consequences might have followed his falling in their way.

The threats against Wade were confirmed by John Yorke, a traveller who fell in with the bushrangers at Scantling's Plains on 27 November 1816. He identified Howe and Geary as men he knew personally and in sworn evidence given to a police magistrate the following month, Yorke said:

> [They told me] to inform MR. HUMPHREY [a magistrate] and MR. WADE [the Chief Constable] to take care of themselves, in they were resolved to take their lives, and to prevent them from keeping stock or growing grain, unless there was not something done for them – that Mr. Humphrey might reap what grain he liked, but they would trash more in one day, than he could reap in a year; they said they could set the whole country in a fire, with one fire stick.

Yorke also stated that he subsequently met two stockmen who'd been forced to render down a large quantity of beef fat at a location called Murderer's Plains, which the bushrangers referred to as the Tallow Chandler's Shop. The cattle used to make the beef fat were thought to be stolen from two graziers named Stines and Troy who had mustered their property and found only 160 cattle out of 200 to 300.

The attacks of Howe's gang continued into 1817. They seemed to be able to strike with impunity, despite the large contingent of soldiers who were scouring the country for them. Even when members of the gang were shot or captured, there were more escaped convicts to take their place.

The soldiers did have some success. On 19 March 1817 Ensign Mahon reported a somewhat hesitant encounter to the lieutenant governor:

SIR

I have the honour to acquaint you, that the party dispatched on the 25th of February by your orders, under my command, after a banditti in the woods, commonly called bush-rangers, on the 15th day of March discovered three of them (armed) laying in ambuscade, close to a place called Scantling's Plains. Being then within musket shot of them, I called on them to surrender, or that I should fire on them; they made no answer, but immediately ran away when I ordered a pursuit after them, & still called on them to surrender, but the hindmost, Chapman, turned round with great deliberation, and snapped his piece at the guide, William Cresswell.

Finding all efforts to take them alive fruitless, and that they would inevitably have escaped, I ordered three of the soldiers to fire, when one of the banditti named Parker fell; but I should suppose could only have received a slight wound, as he rose again in a few seconds and started towards the thickest part of the wood, turning round the second time and firing at the soldier who pursued him; the soldier again fired and wounded him between the shoulders, but the place being thick with brush, he concealed himself and evaded the search we made for him.

Another of the banditti, Elliott, whom I was in pursuit of myself, placed himself behind a tree, called me by my name, presenting his piece, and swore if I approached him he would blow my brains out. In my own defence I was then obliged to fire at him, when he fell and expired instantly, with his finger put in the posture of pulling the trigger. Chapman still continued running forwards, and again snapped his piece, when one of the soldiers shot him through the back – he expired in about twenty minutes after. Thinking it might be necessary to produce their heads, I ordered them to be cut off before I had the bodies interred. The few articles found with them have been returned to the different claimants.

By this time, people travelling between Hobart and Port Dalrymple were escorted by an armed guard. Meanwhile, the efforts of various parties of soldiers to capture the bushrangers continued. On 10 April 1817 Captain Nairn and a company of the 46th Regiment made contact. According to the *Hobart Town Gazette* of Saturday, 12 April 1817:

After a diligent search in the woods the party at Jericho perceived Michael Howe, accompanied with a native black girl, named Mary Cockerill, with whom Howe cohabited. On the approach of the party Howe darted into a thicket, and effected his escape, after firing at the native girl, who, from fatigue, was unable to keep pace with him in his flight, and was taken. Howe being so closely pursued, threw away his blunderbuss and knapsack.

Hell may have no fury like a woman scorned, but they tend to react badly to being shot at as well, even if the shot may have been aimed at the pursuers. The *Hobart Town Gazette*'s report continued:

The native girl then led the party to the Shannon River, a distance of 11 miles [17.6 kilometres] from Jericho, where they found four huts, which they burnt. While thus employed, they perceived three of the bushrangers (Howe, Septon & Geary) at the side of a high hill, contiguous to the river. On the appearance of the party, they were not in the least alarmed, for being in an advantageous position on the other side of the river, they by their gesticulations put them at defiance, and afterwards made off. The party then forded the river, and for two days, continued eagerly their pursuit, accompanied by their native guide, till all traces of them were lost; still their exertions were not in vain, for she led them to the discovery of 56 sheep, the property of different individuals which had been driven into the woods by the runaways . . .

The native girl has since been repeatedly examined; and we have no doubt, some important information may be derived regarding the numerous depredations of the bush-rangers.

Clearly it was a bad move for Howe to try to put a bullet in his girlfriend. Meanwhile, some sections of the community may have derived enjoyment from the information that the bushrangers 'by their gesticulations put them at defiance'. Exactly what those gesticulations were is best left to the imagination.

The word 'defiance' may also have resonated with those who lived in a state of subjugation. Some historians have noted that many convicts couldn't read and that newspaper reports may not have gained much circulation among them. However, the ability of oral communication to 'telegraph' information can't be discounted. In the case of such sensational events, the story probably spread like wildfire, while Michael Howe's reputation grew with every telling.

The story took a new twist early in May 1817 when Howe surrendered himself to Captain Nairn, of the 46th regiment. He had sent a letter to Lieutenant Governor Sorell 'From the Governor of the Ranges to the Governor of the Town' offering to surrender on condition that he was given a free pardon. Despite the presumption in the address, the offer appears to have been accepted, subject to the approval of Governor Macquarie. Howe surrendered and was taken into custody in Hobart, where he soon enjoyed considerable notoriety. The governor faced a major obstacle in giving Howe a free pardon. Howe was suspected of being involved in at least four murders of Europeans and an unknown number of Aborigines. Was the governor willing to pardon murder?

While Howe awaited a decision, he was lodged in Hobart Gaol but allowed to walk around the town in the company of a police constable. He initially spent his time giving depositions on his activities to police magistrates. He spent almost three months waiting to hear his fate, during which time he may have learned that the governor was unlikely to confirm the pardon bestowed by Lieutenant Governor Sorell. In any case, towards the end of July he 'absented himself from the gaol'. It was far from the most daring escape in the annals of bushranging history. He simply walked away. As the *Gazette* reported:

> On the [Monday] evening above named the constable who ought to have kept Howe in charge, left him outside of the gaol for some time. As Howe was informed, that the Governor in Chief had promised to obtain his pardon, his disappearance is the more unaccountable. It proves, however, that a man long habituated to the life of a robber & an outlaw is incapable of setting any value upon being restored to society, and relieved of his crimes; or upon anything that mankind in general deem the blessings of life; that all lenity towards such men is thrown away, and that while they continue to live, they must be a pest and a disgrace to their species.

Howe disappeared from view, while his colleagues continued their activities. However, on 10 August they committed a robbery at Clarence Plains and ended up getting so drunk that they fought with each other. They were so hung-over and knocked about after the fight that they were all caught within the next week, two of them by a party of the 46th regiment assisted by Mary Cockerill and another woman, who were working as trackers.

On 6 September 1817 Lieutenant Governor William Sorell proclaimed a £100 reward for the apprehension of Michael Howe. A month later, the offer almost saw results. The *Hobart Town Gazette* of 11 October 1817 reported:

> This morning the notorious bushranger, George Watts, was brought into Town wounded. The corpse of a man of the name of William Drew (commonly called Slambo) was brought in at the same time, he having been found dead in the bush near Burne's farm.
>
> The account given by Watts is as follows:- That he and Drew having met Michael Howe they contrived to secure him, and had brought him 8 miles [13 kilometres] on the road towards Town with his hands tied; that by means of a knife concealed about him, Howe disengaged his hands, and immediately robbed Watts with the knife, who fell and dropped his gun, which Howe at the moment seized and shot Drew. Watts states that he made his way to Burne's house, while Howe was loading his gun to shoot him. The whole of this account resting upon the narrative of Watts, is of course not to be relied upon. It seems that when he reached Burne's house yesterday evening, he said nothing of Drew's death, nor did Watts mention him till he was in the cart coming to Town. He then said that Drew was dead in the neighbouring bush and Burne, Waddle, and others, after a search of some hours, found it. He had been shot directly through the body.

Drew was a shepherd working at New Norfolk. Watts had convinced him to attempt to capture Howe for the reward.

Shortly after, the Lieutenant Governor increased the reward for the capture of Michael Howe. Sorell held out the offer of a free pardon and passage back to England to any Crown prisoner 'who shall be the means of apprehending the said Michael Howe'.

Howe's gang was now well and truly broken up, yet he was still able to elude capture. In mid-November 1817 the only other member of his gang who was still on the loose gave himself up at Pitt Water. Howe managed to keep a low profile until June 1818 when the *Hobart Town Gazette* reported:

> That great murderer Michael Howe, with whose enormities our Readers are so well acquainted, within these few days made his appearance to the stock-keepers of Mr. G. W. Evans, Deputy Surveyor General, at a place called Blinkworth's Hunting Ground. He took what provisions the men had, and two fine Kangaroo dogs. What is astonishing, he had plenty of ammunition, and was well armed. His beard is of a great length, and his appearance, connected with the idea of his horrid crimes, is altogether terrific.

He was sighted again on 19 September 1818. He had just robbed a stockman's hut on the Clyde River, known at the time as the Fat-doe River, when he was chased and forced to discard everything he was carrying. He also lost the two kangaroo dogs.

Among the items in his knapsack was a scrap of paper that recorded some details of his existence. It transpired that the Aboriginal people in the bush were attacking him on sight. They had almost caught and killed him on more than one occasion. He was now reduced to living on whatever scraps of food he could find. His papers made no reference to the Governor of the Ranges.

On 21 October 1818, five years after Howe had escaped from custody, Private William Pugh of the 40th Regiment, convict Thomas Worrall and a kangaroo hunter named Warburton managed to corner Howe. There are several accounts of his capture, which vary widely in detail. Worrall subsequently gave his version of events in *The Military Sketch Book*:

> The plan was this: – Pugh and I were to remain in Warburton's hut, while Warburton himself was to fall into Howe's way. The hut was on

the River Shannon, standing so completely by itself, and so out of the track of anybody who might be feared by Howe, that there was every probability of accomplishing our wishes, and 'scotch the snake', as they say, if not kill it. Pugh and I accordingly proceeded to the appointed hut. We arrived there before daybreak, and having made a hearty breakfast, Warburton set out to seek Howe. He took no arms with him, in order to still more effectually carry his point, but Pugh and I were provided with muskets and pistols. The sun had just been an hour up when we saw Warburton and Howe upon the top of the hill coming towards the hut. We expected they would be with us in a quarter of an hour, and so we sat down upon the trunk of a tree inside the hut calmly waiting their arrival. An hour passed but they did not come, and I crept to the door cautiously and peeped out. There I saw them standing within 100 yards [91 metres] of us in earnest conversation; as I learned afterwards the delay arose from Howe suspecting that all was not right; I drew back from the door to my station, and about 10 minutes after this we plainly heard footsteps and the voice of Warburton. Another moment and Howe slowly entered the hut – his gun presented and cocked. The instant he espied us he cried out 'Is that your game?' and immediately fired, but Pugh's activity prevented the shot from taking effect, for he knocked the gun aside. Howe ran off like a wolf. I fired but missed. Pugh then halted and took aim at him, but also missed. I immediately flung away the gun and ran after Howe; Pugh also pursued; Warburton was a considerable distance away. I ran very fast; so did Howe; and if he had not fallen down an unexpected bank, I should not have been fleet enough for him. This fall, however, brought me up with him; he was on his legs and preparing to climb a broken bank, which would have given him a free run into the wood, when I presented my pistol at him and desired him to stand; he drew forth another, but did not level it at me. We were then about 15 yards [14 metres] from each other, the bank he fell from being between us. He stared at me with astonishment, and to tell you the truth, I was a little astonished at him, for he was covered with patches of kangaroo skins, and wore a black beard – a haversack and powder horn slung across his shoulders. I wore my beard also as I do now, and a curious pair we looked. After a moment's pause he cried out, 'Black beard against grey beard for a million!' and fired; I slapped at him, and I believe hit him, for he staggered, but rallied again, and was clearing the bank between him and me when Pugh ran up and with the butt end of his firelock knocked him down, jumped after him, and battered his brains out, just as he was opening a clasp knife to defend himself.

Michael Howe had managed to put himself beyond the reach of the law for more than five years. It makes him one of the most successful bushrangers of any era in terms of longevity. However, his violent death was typical of most bushrangers, regardless of the length of their careers.

Howe's head was taken from his body, and the body was buried near the hut where he died. The head was taken to Hobart and put on public exhibition. The *Hobart Town Gazette* initially promised an extensive outline of the bushranger's career. However, it proved so extensive that it was decided to publish the account in a separate pamphlet. *Michael Howe: The Last and Worst of the Bushrangers of Van Diemen's Land* was written by Lieutenant Governor Sorell's secretary, T. E. Welles, and in 1818 it became the first general work of literature to be published in Australia. At the time the title was correct, but it wouldn't stay that way for long.

Howe, the man, was a thief and a murderer. Howe, the myth, was a symbol to an entire class whose lives were spent in servitude, chains and misery. He was both infamous and famous, antihero and hero. It isn't what he did that gave him his place in history, it's what he represented. He called himself the Governor of the Ranges, but he was the first bushranger prince. With blood on his hands and a reign of terror in his wake, his exploits as he bestrode the landscape nevertheless exerted a powerful fascination that endures to the present day.

Another bushranger who lurked in Van Diemen's Land during its years as a destination for convicts was an Aboriginal man from Sydney who had been involved in tracking Howe. Known to European settlers as 'Musquito', in 1805 at the age of twenty-five, he'd been arrested for his part in the ongoing hostilities between the local Aboriginal population and the British settlers. He was sent to Norfolk Island for eight years and then exiled to Port Dalrymple in 1813. There he earned a reputation for his ability to track bushrangers, including Michael Howe.

In 1817, after Musquito had completed several years of service, Lieutenant Governor Sorell approved his return to 'his native place' but a year later had failed to make good on his promise. Disillusioned, Musquito went bush, where he soon became involved in reprisal raids by the local Aboriginal tribes.

He was implicated in violence in 1824, upon which the *Hobart Town Gazette* reported on 2 April:

> We are sorry to learn, that another stock keeper has been speared by the natives, and that the poor man's life is despaired of; his name is James Taylor, servant to Mr. John Cassidy of the Old Beach. It does not appear that Musquito or Black Jack were seen with this party, though there is reason to believe they must have been near the spot, from the circumstance of the natives having been, with one or two instances only excepted, entirely harmless, until these two blacks have lately appeared among them.

A week later the paper reported that a search party had returned without success after pursuing Musquito for five weeks. He remained at large until August 1824. On 6 August the *Hobart Town Gazette* reported that Musquito had speared a man at Pitt Water:

> The man it seems was enticed from his house by Musquito cooying [cooeeing] till he brought him within his reach, when he drove the spear into his back, while returning to get him some bread. The weapon broke in the wound, and the unfortunate man has in consequence suffered much in having it extracted.

The government was spurred to action, and within days there was news of Musquito's capture. The *Hobart Town Gazette* reported on 20 August 1824:

> Musquito was taken with two female Aborigines, near Oyster Bay, by a black native boy, about 17 years of age, named Tegg, who, on the promise of reward from the Lieutenant Governor in the event of his being successful, volunteered to go out for the purpose. This boy, in three days after his leaving town, came up with Musquito in the woods; he was accompanied by two Europeans, named Godfrey and Marhal, who secured the women while Tegg shot Musquito. They had no spears with them, when taken; Musquito ran a considerable distance after he was wounded, and while leaning against a tree from weakness, took up a stick and threw it at Tegg who appears to be a very acute and sharp youth.

Musquito and a companion named Black Jack were tried for murders committed in 1823. When they were found guilty and the death sentence was passed, Musquito is reputed to have replied, 'Hanging no bloody good for blackfellow . . . Very good for whitefellow, he used to it.' He and Black Jack were executed in February 1825.

In a subsequent editorial the *Hobart Town Gazette* bemoaned the fact that Van Diemen's Land was being used as a dumping ground for many of the worst criminals from New South Wales, and blamed the practice for many of the colony's bushranging problems. However, the sheer brutality of the convict system was not put forward as a possible cause. It doesn't appear to have occurred to any of Australia's rulers that bushrangers were escapees from that brutality who resorted to crime because they had no other means of survival.

While the idea of reforming criminals was slowly taking root back in England, in the Antipodes the only response to crime was harsher and harsher punishment. Thus, while the convict system endured, so it seemed would bushranging.

3

The good, the bad and the vicious

1820–1829

In 1822 Lieutenant Governor Arthur claimed in a despatch to his masters in England that he had managed to suppress bushranging throughout Van Diemen's Land. In the same year, thirty-four bushrangers were hanged in Sydney. Yet, for all the Lieutenant Governor's puff, Van Diemen's Land was about to unfold a bushranging tale that would eclipse all that had gone before.

In 1819 Alexander Pearce was charged in England with stealing shoes and sentenced to seven years' transportation. After repeated escapes from penal institutions in New South Wales and Van Diemen's Land, he was sent to Macquarie Harbour, on the west coast of Van Diemen's Land. He was almost continually in trouble there, and when faced with yet another sentence of fifty lashes began plotting his escape.

Just as Australia was regarded as the penal colony of Britain, Hobart was regarded as the 'penal settlement' of Sydney, and Macquarie Harbour the penal settlement of Hobart. The almost impenetrable wilderness that surrounded the harbour meant the prison was virtually escape-proof. Convicts who ran away simply had nowhere to go. The real walls of the prison were the 100 kilometres of cold, damp forest that was shunned even by Aboriginal people. Yet in September 1822 Alexander Pearce was one of eight convicts who seized axes, food and cooking utensils and fled into the bush.

After seven days the cold, wet escapees fully understood why Macquarie Harbour was considered escape-proof. They were starving.

'I'm so hungry, I could eat a piece of a man,' convict William Kennerly reportedly said as the men bedded down for the night. Their food was all gone and as they tried to sleep, the pangs of hunger gnawed at them throughout the night. Kennerly may have been joking, but the following morning the subject of cannibalism came up again.

'I've seen the like done before,' Robert Greenhill said. 'It tastes very like pork.'

Another of the men, John Mather, protested, 'It would be murder to do it. And then perhaps we won't be able to eat it.'

'I'll warrant you,' said Greenhill, 'I will eat the first part myself, but you must all lend a hand that we may be equally guilty of the crime.'

The men spent another day without food as they trekked slowly onward, at times reduced to crawling through the thick scrub on their hands and knees. That night, as they camped once more without food, Greenhill's eye fell on fellow escapee Alexander Dalton. He accused him of flogging other prisoners. Dalton, Kennerly and another convict named Brown sensed what was coming and camped apart from the others – to no avail. At 3 a.m., as the men slept, Greenhill crept up to Dalton and killed him with a single blow of an axe.

There followed a grisly scene as Dalton was stripped, disembowelled and decapitated. Three of the convicts – Mather, Travers and Greenhill – put his heart and liver on the fire but were so hungry they took them off again and began eating them raw.

They offered pieces of Dalton to the other convicts, but none of them could face it – for now.

As the group prepared to set off the next morning, the now-cooked Dalton was carved up and distributed among them. It was too much for Brown and Kennerly. They waited for a chance to slip away, and fled. They managed to return to Macquarie Harbour, but were so emaciated by their ordeal that both perished not long after.

The five remaining convicts – Pearce, Bodenham, Mather, Travers and Greenhill – continued on their journey, feeding on the unfortunate Dalton as they went. They travelled for a further two weeks, hoping to reach the settled eastern side of Van Diemen's Land. By 15 October 1822 they were again starving, having long since eaten all of Dalton that they could carry. They decided to cast lots to see who would die next. When Thomas Bodenham drew the short straw, he made no protest. He only asked for a moment to make peace with his God. Greenhill again filled the role of executioner.

The cycle of cannibalism, famine, murder and cannibalism continued across the uninhabited western region of Van Diemen's Land. Around the end of October, Mather was the next to die. Four days later, Travers was bitten by a snake and when he became too ill to travel (a week later), even his close friendship with Greenhill couldn't save him.

Finally, there was only Greenhill and Pearce. When starvation again assailed them, they spent days watching each other warily. Exhausted from lack of sleep, Greenhill eventually nodded off and Pearce saw his chance. He later confessed, 'I instantly seized the opportunity, took the axe from under his head and struck him with it and killed him. I cut off part of his thigh and arm which I took with me.'

Pearce eventually managed to reach the eastern settlements near Hobart's Mount Wellington. He was barely alive, but had become the first person to escape from Macquarie Harbour. He had the good fortune to fall in with a convict shepherd named McGuire who cared for him 'with the tenderness of a saint'.

When he was well enough, Pearce moved on. Around December 1822 he fell into company with a pair of bushrangers, William Davis and Ralph Churton, who were in the business of trading in stolen sheep. Unfortunately, their career was short-lived. They were surprised by a patrol of the 48th Regiment that was part of the government's efforts to suppress bushranging and were forced to abandon their sheep, provisions and weapons.

Two days later, the trio was asleep under a tree when they were surprised again. Davis managed to run, but was shot in the thigh and arm. Churton and Pearce were taken where they lay. In Hobart, Churton and Davis were tried for sheep-stealing, found guilty and sentenced to death.

Pearce confessed to everything that had transpired since his escape from Macquarie Harbour, but the authorities found his horrific tale so far-fetched that they didn't believe him. They suspected he'd concocted the story to discourage the search for those convicts still at large.

Pearce was sent back to Macquarie Harbour, but in mid-November 1823 evidence emerged to prove he was telling the truth. Pearce escaped again, in company with another prisoner, Thomas Cox. This time they headed north, hoping to reach Port Dalrymple, near present-day Launceston. Once again, they ran out of food and were soon starving. Unfortunately, when they reached the King River, Pearce discovered that his companion couldn't swim. In a rage, Pearce attacked Cox with an axe, and left him for dead.

'For mercy's sake,' Cox reportedly groaned, 'come back and put me out of my misery!'

Pearce returned and did as he was asked, with one last blow of the axe. He then cut off a piece of Cox's thigh, cooked and ate it. He carried off more of Cox's remains to sustain him on his journey. However, only a few days later he realised he had no chance of reaching Port Dalrymple. He managed to signal a passing boat and was taken back to the penal settlement.

There he again confessed what had happened and a search quickly uncovered the remains of Cox. Thomas Smith, coxswain to the commandant at Macquarie Harbour, later testified, 'The head was away, the hands cut off, the bowels were torn out, and the greater part of the breech and thighs gone, as were the calf of the legs, and the fleshy parts of the arms.'

When asked how he could do such a thing, Pearce replied, 'No person can tell what he will do when driven by hunger.'

Pearce was put on trial for murder on 20 June 1824. The *Hobart Town Gazette* was the first publication to reflect on the morbid fascination the case exerts to this day:

> The circumstances which were understood to have accompanied the above crime had long been considered with extreme horror . . . We confess, that on this occasion, our eyes glanced in fearfulness at the being who stood before a retributive Judge, laden with the weight of human blood, and believed to have banqueted on human flesh!

Pearce was found guilty and executed the following month.

It had long been suspected that escaped convicts preyed upon each other when hunger overtook them. The story of Pearce the cannibal not only confirmed this, but also provided the inspiration for the likes of Charles Dickens and Marcus Clarke, who included cannibal convicts in *Bleak House* and *For the Term of His Natural Life* respectively.

The conditions that produced Alexander Pearce were not restricted to Macquarie Harbour. The case of William Yems shows that New South Wales had equally brutal penal settlements. Yems was a private in the 3rd Regiment of Foot when he ran away to join a group of bushrangers in the Sydney region, late in 1824. Yems is one of several bushrangers who came from the ranks of the military, where it seems low pay, harsh discipline or simply boredom led some to desert. However, the 23-year-old, who was reputedly from a good family, was soon apprehended, court-martialled and sentenced to death. The *Australian* of 24 February 1825 recorded the events on the day of his scheduled execution:

> At half past five in the morning the prisoner was put into a cart, in which was placed a coffin; he was then drawn to the place of intended execution about three miles [5 kilometres] on the South Head Road . . . The sentence of the Court Martial was read, and after the prisoner had been led through the ranks, tidings were communicated to him that his sentence, on account of his former good conduct, had been commuted to transportation for life to Port Macquarie. On hearing this he expressed his wish rather to be shot than sent to Port Macquarie.

Yems appears to have endured the notorious penal settlement on the New South Wales mid-north coast for nearly four years. He then escaped, joined another band of bushrangers and was caught again. He was tried in April 1829, found guilty of putting three persons in bodily fear, and was again sentenced to death. This time he would receive no mercy. On 27 April he and an accomplice were hanged along with six other criminals. The following day, the *Sydney Gazette* noted:

> The spectacle of eight human beings deliberately hurried out of the world is appalling, but the unfortunate state of society in the Colony, and the manifold increase of crime, renders a striking example a most imperious necessity. May it have the desired effect.

In New South Wales, the inevitable consequence of what we might now call 'getting tough on crime' was that the convicts absconded in droves. And escaping was no great challenge as the Australian bush closed in on all sides – thick, silent and perfectly suited to frustrating any search. Similarly, it made the perfect place to wait in ambush for unsuspecting passers-by.

So common did convict bushrangers become that on 19 January 1825, Governor Sir Thomas Brisbane introduced *An Act to Prevent the Harbouring of Runaway Convicts and the Encouraging of Convicts Tippling or Gambling*. The fine for harbouring was 'not less than five dollars, nor more than $50, for every such offence; and a further sum of one dollar for each and every day he, she or they shall so harbour or employ such person, whether knowing or not knowing him or her to be illegally at large.'

A mounted police force was also organised by Governor Brisbane for the specific purpose of hunting bushrangers. It began with two officers and thirteen troopers, but under Governor Ralph Darling, who took office later in 1825, it rapidly expanded until a decade later it numbered over 160.

Among the bushrangers of the mid-1820s one figure stands out: Matthew Brady. He was convicted of forgery in 1820 and transported after his sentence of death was commuted. In 1821, after a series of misdemeanours and an escape attempt, he was sent to Macquarie Harbour. There, on 7 June 1824, he and James Bryant, John Bains, James Crawford, James McCabe, Patrick Connolly, John Griffiths, George Lacy, Charles Rider, Jeremiah Ryan, John Thompson, Isaac Walker, James Tierney and George Saxon stole a whaleboat and rowed for the open sea. They managed to navigate the treacherous waters around the south of Van Diemen's Land and after a nine-day voyage eventually reached the Derwent, near Hobart, on 18 June. There, Brady and the other escapees went bushranging, robbing travellers and unprotected homesteads. Rewards of £10 were offered for their capture.

From the first, Brady was the leader of the gang. At the time he was twenty-six years old, and described as being 165 centimetres tall, with dark brown hair and blue eyes. The spare details were later embellished to include striking good looks, and an almost princely demeanour.

The gang's successful raids saw them pursued relentlessly. In an early encounter with soldiers led by Lieutenant Gunn, five were captured. Later, at the farm of a man named Taylor, Crawford and Bains were captured. In mid-September 1824 Captain Innes of the Buffs (the 3rd Regiment of Foot) came close to completely disbanding the gang. Near the River Styx he and his men apprehended three of the bushrangers, including Bryant. At that point it was thought that only two of the bushrangers remained at large – Brady and McCabe. In 1825 they continued holding up travellers on the road from Hobart to Port Dalrymple, and robbing farms and huts. Gradually they were reinforced by newly escaped convicts or those who were already at large.

On 14 April 1825 Lieutenant Governor Arthur increased the reward for Brady and McCabe's capture from £10 to £25, plus a conditional pardon, and by some accounts a large quantity of rum. Brady responded in terms that mirrored the governor's proclamation:

Mountain Home, April 20, 1825.
It has caused Matthew Brady much concern that such a person known as Sir George Arthur is at large. Twenty gallons of rum will be given to any person that will deliver his person unto me.
M. Brady.

Under Brady's leadership some of the gang's robberies had an air of a social call rather than a crime. When they stuck up Robert Bethune's house on Friday, 25 November 1825, they bailed up the family and remained there until Bethune Senior and Captain Bannister returned from the city in the evening. They, too, were taken prisoner by Brady, who said to one of his men, 'Take the gentlemen's horses to the stables and see that they are cared for.' Brady then sat down to dinner with the Bethune family while his men ate dinner at their posts. As they prepared to leave, Brady thanked Bethune for his hospitality and kind reception.

Brady's conduct may be regarded as gentlemanly, but to a modern criminologist it can be seen as savouring the opportunity to exercise power over the victim and prolonging that experience as long as possible. Under normal circumstances Brady would have been thrown out of the Bethunes' dining room. Surrounded by armed and dangerous men, he was treated as an honoured guest.

While at the Bethunes' home, Brady also announced his intention to bail up the nearby town of Sorell and free the prisoners in the gaol. When the bushrangers got there they found the soldiers stationed in the barracks cleaning their guns after a long, damp day searching for them. With their weapons in pieces, the soldiers were in no position to fight, and were quickly overpowered and imprisoned.

The gaoler managed to escape, and ran to the residence of the town's doctor, Dr Garrett, where he found Lieutenant Gunn, the local commander. The doctor and Gunn (armed with a double-barrelled gun) returned to the gaol. The doctor was immediately seized. Gunn attempted to fire at the bushrangers but was shot in the right arm, which was badly mutilated below the elbow. The bushrangers then robbed the entire town at their leisure. Gunn eventually had his arm amputated.

During the robbery Brady reputedly told an assigned convict to join his band, but the man refused, whereupon Brady filled a glass with rum and told him to drink it. The man again refused, saying he never took strong liquor.

'Well, you will this time,' Brady said, and pointed a gun at the convict's head.

The man drank the rum and immediately became intoxicated, much to Brady's amusement. However, the man was so unused to strong liquor that he died of its effects the following day. When Brady heard of it he expressed contrition for his actions.

While Matthew Brady was emerging as a dashing, gentlemanly bushranger, at the same time others were achieving fame for their pure savagery. Thomas Jeffries certainly qualifies as one of those bushrangers whose career was so brief that it should barely rate a mention. However, during the six weeks that he was at large, from mid-December 1825 to late January 1826, he did more than enough to make himself famous for all time.

Jeffries was originally transported for life in 1819, but was repeatedly in trouble after arriving in Van Diemen's Land. He was employed as the flogger and watch-house keeper at Launceston Gaol when he decided to escape, on the night of 11 December, in company with three or four other men. One of them was reported to have been an escapee from Macquarie Harbour who had been found wearing moccasins made from human skin.

It later transpired (as reported in the *Colonial Times* on 20 January 1826) that the escape plan was 'fully known to the police; and instead of *preventing crime* by immediately securing these men, Mr. Mulgrave, the Police Magistrate, personally (with some others) placed themselves in ambuscade to detect them in the act of breaking out [and the] ruffians escaped . . .'

Jeffries was eventually found to be in company with two men, John Perry and Edward Russell. By Jeffries' own subsequent admission, as quoted in the *Hobart Town Gazette* of 28 January 1826:

> On Christmas day he fell in with two men on Mr. Sutherland's grazing farm, one of whom ran away, but the other exchanged a few shots. He was at last wounded by Jeffries, in the thigh, and his brains blown out by one of the party.
>
> About a week after this he went to Mr. Tibbs' house, and led captive Mr. and Mrs. Tibbs, their child, and a stock keeper a few miles

into the woods, when one of Jeffries' associates shot the stock keeper, and the other fired at Mr. Tibbs, who instantly fell and was expected to have been mortally wounded [the stockman died, Tibbs survived]. Mrs. Tibbs was obliged to proceed with them farther into the woods, but not walking so fast as Jeffries wished, in order to lighten her load he took the child from her and dashed out its brains. The next murder he committed was that of Baker, of George Town, whom he had compelled to carry his knapsack, and whom he deliberately shot as he was proceeding with it on his back.

Some time after this they fell short of provisions, and cast lots who should die. The lot fell upon Russell, but he did not believe his companions to be in earnest; and, therefore, in a convenient place, lay down and composed himself to sleep. Jeffries took advantage of his defenceless condition and shot him through the head, and he and his remaining associate lived on his flesh for four days. When they arrived at a stock-keeper's hut, where they killed two sheep, they had about five pounds of his flesh remaining.

Early in January, while Matthew Brady was robbing the home of a man named Haywood, he told his victim that Jeffries had tried to join his gang, but Brady had rejected him. It's likely that Brady was unaware at the time just what a monster Jeffries had become.

Jeffries and Perry were nearly captured on 21 January 1826, and in their flight they became separated. On 22 January three search parties, comprising a dozen men, were breakfasting at a hut when an Aboriginal youth exclaimed, 'There is Jeffries!'

Fortunately, Jeffries hadn't seen them and they managed to keep themselves hidden until he was within range of their muskets. A man from Mr Davies' search party and one from Mr Wedge's rushed him, whereupon Jeffries took cover behind a tree. When he saw that he was facing a dozen armed men, he asked if there was any quarter. One of Wedge's men replied, 'Yes, lay down your arms.'

Jeffries surrendered without a fight and was seized by a convict named William Parsons. He was taken into Launceston, where an extraordinary scene ensued. The *Colonial Times* on 27 January reported:

> It clearly showed that Jeffries stands alone, unequalled, unparalleled among the human race. Men, women and children, free and prisoners, joined in their personal execrations against this monster. The town was literally glutted of its inhabitants; there must have been upwards of 500 persons crowding round the cart . . . their shouting reached the remotest parts of the town. It was with the greatest difficulty imaginable the people were prevented from tearing him to pieces.

A later report in the *Hobart Town Gazette* stated:

> Several attempts were made by the people to take him out of the cart that they might wreak their vengeance upon him, and it became necessary to send into Town for a stronger guard to prevent his immediate despatch. He entered the Town and gaol amidst the curses of every person whomsoever.

Perry was captured only a few days later. He and Jeffries were held for the next six weeks, pending their removal to Hobart for trial.

By March 1826 Brady's gang seemed to have become invincible. A letter dated Monday, 6 March (one of several published on 10 March in the *Colonial Times*) revealed how, since the previous Saturday, they had the town of Launceston and the surrounding region in a state of paralysis, as they ran rings around the military who were hunting them:

> [The bushrangers] sent [a carrier named] Watson into Launceston to say they would that night rob Mr. Dry, and would go to the Gaol in

Launceston, and take out Jeffries, torture him, and then shoot him. It was treated with derision! A man who escaped from Mr. Dry's, came into Launceston at 10 o'clock, P. M., to say the banditti were there. Colonel BALFOUR instantly started with 1 sergeant and 10 soldiers, and some volunteers. They surrounded the house just as [the bush-rangers] had packed up their booty, when a brisk fire commenced; the bush-rangers were forced out of the house into the back yard, and kept firing into the house; it was quite dark, and the banditti were thought to have gone, when Colonel BALFOUR proceeded with half the soldiers to defend the town (rendered the more necessary, as a part of the banditti under Bird and Dunn had been previously dispatched by Brady to attack Launceston.) On his going away, the banditti went up to Mr. WEDGE'S hut, (adjoining one of the out-buildings) and began to plunder; when the soldiers, with Dr. PRIEST, proposed to charge. The bush-rangers heard it; and fired a volley, by which Dr. Priest's horse was shot dead, and himself shot in the knee. The soldiers, not above five in number, with some volunteers, fired and charged, but owing to the darkness, the banditti escaped.

The *Colonial Times* went on to castigate the commander of the troops, Mr Mulgrave, for his ongoing failure to deal with the bushranging crisis. However, the reaction from the authorities proved to be swift.

On Tuesday, 7 March 1826 Lieutenant Williams of the 57th Regiment, aided by 'private information', led a force of fourteen soldiers and four armed convicts to Paterson's Plains, near Launceston. There they found Brady and six other bushrangers. There was an exchange of gunfire and the bushrangers fled. The gang split up and while Brady (who was thought to have been wounded) and four of his men escaped, two others were pursued and one, named Bryant, was captured. On Thursday another member of the gang, Goodwin, was captured.

Then, on Saturday night, a party of armed prisoners led by John Batman (who subsequently helped settle Port Phillip Bay) noticed a camp fire on the Watery Plains. As they approached, all but one of the bushrangers fled. Brady, who had been wounded in the leg, attempted to escape but was tracked and captured by Batman. Some accounts suggest he'd only been able to run 20 metres.

When Batman called on him to surrender, Brady reportedly asked, 'Are you an officer?'

'I'm not a soldier,' Batman replied. 'I'm John Batman. If you raise that gun I'll shoot. There is no chance for you.'

Brady then said, 'You're a brave man and I yield; but I'd never give in to a soldier.'

The *Colonial Times* described the scene when he was brought to Launceston:

> As might be expected, the whole population of Launceston crowded to see him. He deported himself in a firm and determined manner, and rode well, although badly wounded in the leg. He had no hat – an handkerchief was bound round his head.

Brady, Bryant, Goodwin, Perry and Jeffries were taken to Hobart by ship, where they were again met by a crowd of spectators 'anxious to behold the personal appearance of wretches who had so long disturbed the tranquillity of the island, and committed such daring outrages on the settlers'. The *Hobart Town Gazette* further reported that Brady 'suffers much from the wound in his leg, and was carried from the vessel to the cell in a chair'.

Brady was put in a common cell with Jeffries. However the *Colonial Times* of 28 April 1826 reported:

> Brady, on Tuesday night, told Mr. Dodding, one of the turnkeys at the gaol, that if Jeffries was not taken out of the cell, 'he would be found in the morning without his head'. Jeffries was consequently removed to another cell. He [Brady] voluntarily gave up two knives, which he

had concealed about his person, either to carry his former threats into execution, or to cut his irons, in attempting to escape. McKenny, whose leg was trodden upon by a horse, and who goes with a crutch, and Bryant, are in the same cell with Brady, who we understand has received many little comforts while in the gaol, from a very respectable Gentleman, whose humanity is proverbial.

The bushrangers were tried on a number of charges ranging from arson and stock theft to armed robbery and murder. Brady pleaded guilty to many of his charges and eventually told the court that he would plead guilty to anything the Crown wanted to pin on him.

Most of the trials were brief and the verdicts swift. The exception was the case of Jeffries and the murder of the child of Mr and Mrs Tibbs. The terrible scene where Mrs Tibbs testified against the two men was described in the *Sydney Gazette* of 29 April 1826:

When Mrs Tibbs came into Court, and her eye glanced on the insatiate murderers of her babe, she was so affected as to be [un]able to stand. Her situation powerfully excited the commiseration of every one present. The bare recital of the dreadful journey which the monster had compelled her to take with him in the woods, was a painful addition to her sufferings. When it was necessary for her to look at the prisoners, in order to prove their persons, the suddenness with which she withdrew her eyes, and the tears with which the effort was accompanied, was an instance of detestation more strongly depicted than any assembly of spectators perhaps ever witnessed. The child was proved to have been taken away from the arms of the mother, and killed by Jeffries and Russell, and its remains were discovered about a week afterwards in a decayed state, and mangled by the carnivorous animals in the woods. When Mrs. Tibbs had asked Jeffries, who called himself Captain, and was dressed in a long black coat, red waistcoat, and kangaroo skin cap, to point out the place where she might find the body, he said 'it was no odds it had not suffered a moment's pain in leaving the world', and he and Russell, who was afterwards shot and partly eaten by the monster, expressed themselves as regarding the life of a child as nothing.

In all, a dozen men were found guilty and sentenced to death. The executions were set down for the following week. On the Saturday before the men died, Lieutenant Governor Arthur visited the men at Hobart Gaol. Brady reportedly told him 'a future state was the last of his thoughts, being bent entirely on endeavouring to escape'. In fact, he and the men in his cell had made an escape attempt the previous night. To thwart further attempts they were chained to a ring and bolt fastened to the floor.

The executions were carried out in two groups the following Thursday and Friday. Brady and Jeffries were executed in the first batch. Accounts published long after the event claim Brady had protested that he had to share the scaffold with the monster Jeffries, but the accounts of the time make no mention of it.

One of the last remaining men from Brady's gang still at large was Patrick Dunne. His most notable crime was the murder of an Aboriginal man whose wife he wanted as a sexual partner. He then found that the woman wouldn't leave the body so he cut off the head and hung it around her neck. After the woman escaped from Dunne, she was seen with a group of Aboriginal people who were attacking a white settlement, urging the warriors on. Later that year Dunne, too, was captured and in November 1826 faced charges of cutting, maiming and stealing. He was hanged on 8 January 1827.

While Van Diemen's Land had its genteel bushranger in Matthew Brady, Sydney had a lesser-known but equally gallant bushranger in Charles Patient. Aged in his early twenties, and described as having hazel eyes and flaxen hair, he absconded in 1824 and became the leader of a gang called the Cumberland Bushrangers. Throughout 1825 and into 1826 they committed a number of house robberies on the outskirts of Sydney. However, it was the manner of their operations that was remarkable.

Peter Cunningham described them in his book, *Two Years in New South Wales* (published in 1827):

> The captain of the gang . . . would take his station among the ladies who might be in the house, and remain in their company while it was ransacked by his party, soothing their fears, on first entering, by assuring them that not an improper word should be uttered, or the slightest violence offered to their persons by any individual under his command; and he invariably kept his promise.
>
> This Don Rolando was quite a literary character besides, never failing to rummage the library, and select what works pleased him best; and when reminded once of the inutility of carrying off Scott and Byron, seeing nobody dared buy them of him, 'Oh!' said the romantic hero, 'books are very instructive, and very amusing, too, in the bush when we have nothing to do;' and he forthwith bore off his literary gems.

That wasn't all. When a member of the gang, Thomas Robinson, was captured, he agreed to give evidence against the others. Among other things he revealed 'that they had resolved among themselves, not to commit murder, but intended to surrender without opposition, whenever they found themselves opposed by a superior force'.

It hardly seemed believable, but when constables from Parramatta surrounded the gang in a hut, the heavily armed bushrangers did indeed attempt to surrender when called upon to do so. However, the bushrangers' pacifism wasn't matched by the police. The *Australian* reported on 16 February 1826:

> As they passed, each constable levelled his piece at his man, but without

effect [rain had dampened the priming, making most of the weapons useless], with the exception of the old watchman, who aimed at Nelson, and shot him dead. Upon this the bushrangers fired their muskets and pistols in the air, and challenged the constables to fight. They declined, and decided it prudent to make off, thinking the bushrangers were strong enough to overpower them.

Not surprisingly, the next time they were cornered, the bushrangers knew they could expect no quarter and fought like tigers. On 2 February 1826 eight constables attacked them in another house near Parramatta. In the battle that ensued one of the bushrangers was disembowelled; Patient was hacked about the head with a cutlass before he finally surrendered.

He and three other bushrangers stood trial for robbery and putting persons in bodily fear. All four were sentenced to death, as were three other gang members.

A number of people were also convicted of receiving stolen property from the bushrangers. On 6 March 1826 the government ordered that they would be forced to witness the execution of the bushrangers and then 'be immediately removed to the Phoenix hulk, under a military escort, and be forwarded from thence, by the first opportunity, to Norfolk Island, there to be confined during the period of the sentences'.

In mid-1825 Patrick Riley and Patrick Clynch in the Hunter Valley formed Jacob's Mob, one of the first bushranging gangs in that region. The name was due to Riley originating from the service of Lieutenant Vickers Jacob. They were also known as Mr Jacob's Irish Brigade.

Riley's road to perdition was typical of many convict bushrangers. On 1 July 1825 he was prosecuted by his master for neglect of duty and losing four sheep. He was sent to Newcastle to receive fifty lashes as punishment, but escaped en route. He stole some horses from Rosebrook estate then convinced three fellow convicts from Jacob's – Laurence Cleary, Aaron Price and Patrick Clynch – to join him. They robbed a number of farms on 5 July and 8 July but were captured on 2 August. However, two days later, they managed to break out of Maitland Gaol. In doing so, they also managed to get hold of guns and ammunition.

They immediately resumed their bushranging activities, robbing a number of farms in the lower Hunter Valley and occasionally exchanging gunfire with pursuing police. On 18 August they burned down the house of James Reid, a landowner at Rosebrook. The attack was thought to be in revenge for Reid's treatment of convicts, including Riley.

Meanwhile, it seems other landowners were deliberately spared. In his book *Two Years in New South Wales,* surgeon Peter Cunningham wrote that Jacob's mob 'never molested the premises of a friend of mine, on account of his having come out as passenger in the ship in which one of them was a convict – into whose goodwill this gentleman had so far ingratiated himself, that his unknown friend declared he would forsake the gang if Mr. G.'s house were assailed.'

Cunningham also makes one of the earliest references to the glorification of bushranging, at least in some circles: 'The vanity of being talked of, I verily believe, leads many foolish fellows to join this kind of life – songs being often made about their exploits by their sympathizing brethren.'

According to Cunningham, Riley boasted that regardless of what happened to him, he would long be spoken of in fear by his enemies and admiration by his friends.

As their bushranging spree continued throughout August and September 1825, rewards were offered for their capture. It also became apparent that they were enjoying the support of a number of former convicts. Nevertheless, on 3 October 1825 their luck ran out. At Hexham, the gang was confronted by Magistrate James Reid (the man whose house they had burned down) and three soldiers from the Buffs regiment. Riley was shot dead, Price surrendered, Cleary and Clynch escaped but were captured the next day. The surviving gang members were tried in November 1825 and sentenced to death. Clynch's sentence was commuted to transportation to Norfolk Island for life.

Clynch was involved in a breakout and mutiny on the island in September the following year, after which he remained at large for twelve months. He then burst from hiding to attack the commandant, Captain Wright, but Wright managed to escape. The next day Clynch attacked the overseer. The following night, 20 October 1825, he was detected lurking around the prison camp. He was captured and killed in the process, although another account suggests 'a Bushranger at Norfolk Island, named Patrick Clynch, after he had been captured by the Constables, and was in safe Custody, in lieu of being sent to Sydney for Trial, was ordered to be shot to death'. The shooting, if it occurred, constituted an execution without trial.

In September 1826 a long-running furore over harsh or illegal sentences handed down by New South Wales magistrates came to a head when a British parliamentary enquiry found that the practice had been going on intermittently at least from 1815 to 1823, particularly at Parramatta. Among the magistrates found to have erred in the application of the law was the Reverend Samuel Marsden. His harsh sentences had been mentioned as early as 1822. In 1826 the *Sydney Monitor* cited a case where a convict shepherd was given 500 lashes and a further seven years on his sentence by Marsden for arguing with his master and making threats. One convict is said to have remarked, 'May the Lord have mercy on you, for his reverence will have none.' Marsden's nickname was 'the Flogging Parson' and the *Australian* newspaper reputedly went so far as to claim that he was 'helping to manufacture bushrangers'.

One of the more enterprising bushrangers of the 1820s was Patrick Geary. On 20 May 1826 the *Sydney Gazette* reported:

> A reward was offered for his apprehension, and a day or two previous to the opening of the Quarter Sessions in that town, a person who was known to be on terms of intimacy with him, surrendered him to justice and received the reward. The opinion prevails, that the prisoner, believing nothing serious would be the consequence of his offence, practised this scheme in order to obtain a share of the profit arising from his own capture.

He soon escaped again and robbed at least three homes. He was recaptured and tried for the robberies on 15 November 1826. He was sentenced to death, but the sentence was commuted to transportation for life. He was one of sixty-six prisoners, many of them bushrangers, who were put aboard the brig *Wellington* (John Harwood master), which sailed from Sydney on 11 December 1826, bound for Norfolk Island.

The prisoners' accommodation aboard the ship was outrageously small, even for the times – a space measuring 4.8 × 4.2 metres. In the heat of summer the sixty-six men were piled on top of each other, covered in their own filth. They endured the conditions for a fortnight, but when they saw an opportunity, on 21 December, they overpowered the minimal guard and seized control of the ship. With a cry of 'liberty or life' the bushrangers became pirates.

The cry 'death or liberty!' and its variants had first been used during the convict rebellion at Castle Hill in 1804. It became a catchcry for some bushrangers, particularly when they knew their capture would lead to their execution. Bushranger John Tennant had the motto carved on his gun. Another motto on the gun read, 'Liberty is Sweet'.

The convicts turned the ship for New Zealand, where they hoped to obtain more water, but were apprehended by two whaling ships and returned to Sydney, where ten ringleaders (including Geary) were executed, despite having shown mercy to the rest of the convicts and captured crew.

As increasing numbers of convicts served their sentences and became part of wider society, the situation where a ruling class enjoyed free labour from the virtual slaves of the convict class began to change. While the relationship between master and convict was governed by a set of rules, the increasingly common relationship between master and paid workers was less clearly defined. Thus, in 1828, the New South Wales government passed the *Masters and Servants Act*. As most legislation tends to put the interests of the legislator first, the *Masters and Servants Act*, written by a master for masters, was in some ways a crude attempt to entrench the working conditions embodied in the convict system in the open market as well. The title says much about its intent.

If that wasn't enough, in rural districts, where the lack of professional magistrates meant that upright members of the community still filled the role, disputes under the act were usually heard by 'magistrates' who were themselves masters. Not surprisingly, their interpretations and rulings favoured their own interests, much to the disadvantage of the servants.

At the time the act was passed, convict absconders still made up most of the bushrangers. However, the injustices of the employment system were to sow the seeds for succeeding generations of bushrangers to come from a new section of society – an entrenched rural poor.

Meanwhile, the proliferation of bushranging was helped by the fractured nature of policing. In 1828 New South Wales had no less than six police forces – the Sydney police, mounted police, water police, border police, native police and rural constabulary. In the same year, the colony was also handed responsibility for the maintenance of the convicts still being sent from England, much to the growing anger of colonists attempting to create a law-abiding society.

Out in the rural districts, the constabulary were part-timers, summoned as required and paid a retainer. Called to pursue bushrangers, they occasionally declined due to work commitments. As for the quality of those in the regular force, police were paid less than labourers, less than £30 a year, which is as little as $15 000 in modern values.

Nevertheless, police still displayed extraordinary courage in apprehending bushrangers. In March 1828 John Ball, John Newman and another man were suspected of a number of robberies around Windsor, 100 kilometres west of Sydney. On the morning of 10 March district constable John Cobcroft was sitting at his door when he saw three men he suspected were the bushrangers. Despite the odds against him, he decided to attempt an arrest. When the men tried to escape, he gave chase and fired at one, but his gun misfired. His pistol was fitted with a bayonet, so still armed, he continued his pursuit. The *Sydney Gazette* of 14 April 1828 detailed the ensuing melee:

> He pursued another of them (Ball) and with difficulty overtook him. This prisoner was daring, and would not surrender, vehemently using the most horrid threats. Cobcroft attacked him — the prisoner was determined — they wrestled together some minutes — both fell. The prisoner wrested the pistol from the Constable, and uttering the most awful imprecations, made seven or eight stabs at his body, but which were warded off, and one stab only entered the palm of his right hand, without doing any serious injury . . .

> While they were thus fighting together on the ground ... a third person, Patrick McManus, a prisoner of the Crown, luckily came up, struck the prisoner a blow with a stick, and thus, as may be truly said, providentially prevented the perpetration of murder.
>
> Cobcroft handcuffed the prisoner to McManus, who is his assigned servant, lodged him in the Windsor gaol, a distance of four miles [6.5 kilometres], gave evidence against him in the Court the same day, immediately returned to his duty, and searched after the others who had escaped ... [He] continued his exertions, and in a few hours came up with, captured, and lodged in Windsor gaol, a second of the three runaways, viz. John Newman.

Cobcroft received a reward of £5 and two head of cattle from the government herd. McManus received a ticket-of-leave (a remission of his remaining sentence dependent upon good behaviour and other conditions).

While Matthew Brady was the bushranger par excellence of the mid-1820s, it was a New South Wales bushranger who bestrode the latter years of the decade. Two years after the establishment of the mounted police, he would lead them on a manhunt that would call into question their effectiveness, and give Sydney's three newspapers – the *Sydney Gazette*, the *Australian* and the *Sydney Herald* – rich pickings when it came to brickbats to throw at a seemingly impotent Governor Darling.

The bushranger's name was John 'Jack' Donahue. He was born in Ireland in 1806 and sentenced to transportation for life in 1823. He was little more than a boy when he arrived in Australia in 1825 at the age of nineteen – short at 162 centimetres but athletic, with flaxen hair and blue eyes. Initially he was assigned to a settler in Parramatta (John Pagan), but misbehaviour saw him assigned to one of the dreaded road gangs. He was then assigned to the estate of Parramatta surgeon Mr Major West.

It was common among assigned servants to go 'fox-boxing', foraging for food at night among the orchards and vegetable patches of their farms to supplement the miserable food that formed the prisoners' ration. Richer pickings, however, were to be had from vehicles transporting goods along the colony's roads. Thus on 14 December 1827 Jack Donahue and two assigned convicts from nearby farms, William Smith and George Kilroy, hid themselves by the Richmond Road armed with two horse pistols (convicts were often armed for protection against attacks from Aborigines and bushrangers) and a cutlass. Soon three carts approached from the direction of Sydney. Moving slowly, they were an easy target.

The three would-be bushrangers burst from cover. Kilroy and Smith rushed the first cart, driven by George Plomer, and demanded money. Donahue confronted the following carts, driven by George Brown and an unnamed third person. While Plomer was parting with the meagre sum of 4 shillings, Donahue climbed into Brown's cart and discovered a 22.75-litre keg of brandy. Taking the brandy, the three men fled. However, the three convicts hadn't finished for the night. Shortly after they'd robbed the three carters, they set upon another highway traveller named William Browne, robbing him as well.

The carters went straight to the police station at Windsor, near Richmond, to report the highway robbery. George Brown had recognised Kilroy and with Windsor's Constable Edward White he headed to the farm at the junction of Breakfast and East Creeks where Kilroy was employed.

'I see I am sold,' Kilroy reportedly said when the policeman and witness arrived. It didn't stop him selling out his fellow felons. The *Australian* stated: 'It was he who informed of Donahue and his coadjutor, and had them apprehended.'

All three were aware they were facing a death sentence, but Kilroy hoped his identification of the others might earn him a reprieve. However, all the people who had been robbed were just as able to identify them as he, and on 4 February 1828 all three went to trial for the robbery of George Plomer. They were found guilty. Then they were tried for the highway robbery of William Browne: guilty again. Three weeks later, all three were returned to the Supreme Criminal Court for sentencing, and all were condemned to death. There was no hope for any of them, or so it seemed. Exactly what happened isn't clear, but after the prisoners who'd been taken to court for that day's hearings were returned to gaol, heavily ironed and guarded, one of them was found to be missing – young Jack Donahue.

He disappeared without a trace. Two months later, on 1 May 1827, a reward of £20 was offered for the 22-year-old whose time under the southern sun had left him with 'a brown-freckled complexion' and 'a scar under the left nostril'. By then Kilroy and Smith were already dead. The hangings went badly. Before a large crowd Smith's rope broke and he fell, unconscious, to the ground. When he was revived, it was to have the hideous spectacle of Kilroy and another criminal, murderer William Johnson, swinging above him – this while the broken rope still hung around his neck. One of the attending priests took off the rope and leaned the close-to-fainting man against the nearest support. Unfortunately, it was the coffin that was waiting to receive his body. Smith became extremely distressed and the sheriff and another priest rushed to Government House to plead for clemency. The plea fell on deaf ears and the sentence was promptly carried out.

Donahue lay low for six months. Then, near Yass, 300 kilometres south-west of Sydney (the very outskirts of European settlement at that time), he joined a band of eight others in a series of attacks on remote outstations.

James, Samuel and Jonathan Hassall held large tracts of land at Bolong, and supplied their workers by using lumbering bullock wagons that were particularly vulnerable on the lonely bush tracks. In an account given by one of the Hassall brothers to the *Sydney Gazette* a week after the event, in August 1828, shots were exchanged between the nine bushrangers and three men guarding a hut full of stores on one of the outstations. Finding themselves fired upon, the bushrangers forced other workers nearby to advance on the hut's door, providing them with cover. As the human shields shuffled forward, the bushrangers dared those inside to shoot at their own men.

Disregarding the danger to their men, the guards in the stores hut did just that, the bushrangers returning fire. One of their shots splintered the lintel above the door, the wood striking one of the human shields, Tom Williams. Another shot narrowly missed his elbow. One of the men in the hut almost hit one of the bushrangers, the bullet passing through the brim of his hat. Eventually the men in the hut were overwhelmed by the bushrangers' superior numbers. They were then stripped naked, in preparation, they were told, for being shot. Instead, the bushrangers spared them as they set about plundering the stores of clothing, linen, food, tobacco, weapons, saddles and bridles, even books and razors. They also made off with two sheep and two horses.

After the alarm was raised, a hunt was organised from the nearest police station, at Bathurst, 120 kilometres to the north. Led by Sergeant Wilcocks it comprised six police, landholder James Hassall and a colleague, Mr Walker. The search party also included six trackers. It was they who found the bushrangers' tracks and followed them for the next four days. In choosing to prowl the farthest fringes of settlement the bushrangers had made themselves particularly vulnerable to the highly refined skills of the trackers. Innocent citizens didn't stray far from the tracks between settlements or much beyond the cattle runs they worked on. Thus a band of nine criminals escaping cross-country left a trail that offered scant challenge to the trackers.

It was on the Cunningham Plain, between Jugiong and what is now Young, that the trackers found the bushrangers' camp. Two of the bushrangers were at the camp fire, playing cards while a pot of mutton simmered on the fire. The first they knew that they'd been discovered was when the police ordered them to stand and surrender. Instead, they ran.

They didn't make it out of the camp. As they fled the police opened fire. Both men were shot in the legs, fell and were captured. Evidently, the sound of gunfire didn't alert the other bushrangers to the police presence. An hour later they returned to the camp with two bullocks (later found to belong to the Hassalls) and more spoils from another station store they'd just held up.

'There's the bloody sergeant!' the leader of the bushrangers, Parsons, reportedly cried on sighting the party deployed around his own camp. 'Come and get us – we are ready!'

Sheltering behind rocks and trees, both parties exchanged shots for the next two hours. In the course of the gunfight one of the bushrangers was shot dead. Three more were injured before night fell. In the ensuing stand-off the police maintained their watch while also eating the bushrangers' dinner that had been prepared on the fire. They taunted the bushrangers, lurking in the cold and dark, to come and join them.

After the police had finished their meal the fire was doused. Wilcocks ordered his men to positions behind the trees, and told them not to talk or sleep. He did allow them to smoke some of the tobacco that had been recaptured. During the night, they heard the bushrangers calling out to them, but by dawn the villains had departed.

The police followed their tracks and only a short distance away came upon the bushrangers' leader, Parsons, shot in both legs and trying to crawl away into a swamp. Having by their count shot, killed, injured or captured seven of the nine bushrangers, the police returned to the Hassall's Bolong station.

They set out again two days later, in three groups of two, each group accompanied by trackers. It wasn't long before one of the parties picked up the trail of two men. They hadn't followed it far when Corporal Prosser and a private saw Donahue and another bushranger, Phillips, lying on the ground taking aim at them with their muskets. Prosser, however, opened fire first and promptly shot Phillips dead. Donahue fled on foot, the mounted police in pursuit on horseback, but the rough ground and thick scrub defeated them.

Donahue managed to elude them while continuing to engage the police in gunfire as he retreated. In one of the exchanges of fire, one of the trackers thought Donahue might have been hit. He told the police that after one shot the bushranger's arm had dropped in a peculiar manner. Shortly after this, Donahue ran off and promptly disappeared. Despite a concerted search by the trackers, who combed the area for the rest of the day, there wasn't a sign of him. In the ensuing days, searches found no trace of him anywhere, not even a rumour of his whereabouts.

Donahue again lay low, this time for three months, perhaps recovering from his bullet wound, and presumably sheltered and cared for by persons unknown. Then, in November 1828, he commenced a series of highway robberies in the Nepean district, on the western outskirts of Sydney, in the company of a fellow Irishman, Jacky Underwood. Their first victim was a man named Chilcott, who was held up at Colo. On 11 February 1829 George Forbes was robbed on Mulgoa Hill of his watch, money and coat. The same night a man named Reeves, groom to George Cox, was robbed of hat, jacket, boots and saddle. Two weeks later Mr Fitz and Mrs Melcham were held up at the same spot.

In March, however, one robbery went badly wrong on the convict-built Great Northern Road. As the *Sydney Gazette* reported on 2 April:

On Thursday last [March 26], Mr Clements, a settler at Hunters River . . . was stopped by two armed men, one of whom, as Mr Clements was about to draw a pistol from his side, fired at and killed him on the spot. The robbers then plundered him of what property he had on his person, part of which consisted of a silver watch of his own, and a gold one, belonging to a Mr Liddle, of Hunters River, which he was bringing to Sydney to be repaired. Extraordinary to relate, the unfortunate deceased had two companions with him, who suffered the robbers to escape, as it appears, without making any effort to secure them.

The identity of the bushrangers can't have been known, as a reward of £10 was offered for information leading to the capture of the murderers, while Donahue already had £20 on his head. The notice offering the reward also referred to Clements as an overseer, a fact which may have contributed to his death. Many overseers had well-earned reputations for cruelty, and it provided a motive for revenge among the convicts. However, this tends to overlook the assertion that Clements was reaching for a weapon when he received his fatal wound.

The robberies continued. In June Major Innes was robbed, then the cleric who had a reputation as 'the flogging parson', Samuel Marsden, was held up on the Western Road and relieved of £4. On 12 June George Wood was robbed at Pentland Hill, just west of South Creek, on the road to the Nepean. On that occasion two men burst out of a quarry, one with a musket, the other with a horse pistol. Wood was robbed of rings, money, silver pencil case, penknife, pistol, papers and cigars. When he asked if he could keep his cigars as he would need a smoke in the evening, he was told, 'We will smoke them for you.' The bushrangers took his watch, missing £3 tucked at the bottom of the fob pocket. They took his black silk neckerchief and handkerchief.

'Now we shall have his body,' one reportedly said.

'No, let him go,' said the other. 'Go on,' he added, thus sparing his life. Wood readily complied.

The account of this robbery in the *Australian* notes that the ruffians 'were both tolerably clad, sporting comfortable jackets, and looked cleanly'.

A few weeks later the son of a magistrate, Mr N. Lawson, was robbed of clothes and gold rings. Then Mr Faithful of Richmond and his son were held up, the description detailed in the *Sydney Gazette*. Two men, armed with a pistol and a carbine, leapt from behind bushes and were at their horses' heads in a moment. As Faithful's son reported, 'My father said he'd be damned if he would be robbed . . . The tallest, who had the carbine, said by the H-- G-- if he resisted he would blow the contents of this through him.'

Both men were then robbed of money and goods. However, when Faithful's son asked twice for his knife to be returned, as it had belonged to his uncle, the bushrangers relented. They also took a bundle of linen, but returned some papers and medicine that were rolled up inside. They then asked for the young Faithful's coat, whereupon, as the *Australian* reported, he replied, 'No, you shan't have that. I think you have done very well.'

The young man's father, who had been incensed from the commencement of the robbery, now lost his temper and cried, 'I'll be damned if you shall have his coat. I'll lose my life first, and if I had my pistol you should not have robbed us so easily.'

To which one of the bushrangers replied, 'It would have been no use to you, for I would have blown you as far as it would have taken a hackney coach to fetch you back in a fortnight; but you're a game old cock, it's a pity to hurt you.'

Mockingly commenting that it had been a 'good morning's work', the highway robbers then left.

Although they ranged quite widely throughout the Hawkesbury–Nepean region, there's a theory the men were hiding out between raids in the rugged Burragorang Valley. On the Nepean River, 500 metres above its junction with the Warragamba River, there's a cave in the steep cliffs that overlooks the broad expanse of water known as Norton's Basin, which is known locally as Donahue's Cave. The difficult access is made easier by footholds and handholds cut into the rock.

Wherever they were hiding out, the robberies continued. Donahue and Underwood tended to target richer travellers on the roads, leaving the poorer settlers unmolested. Thus their behaviour had a cachet of decency not unlike the reputation enjoyed by the legendary Robin Hood. However, another interpretation was that robbing the rich rather than the poor was simply a matter of maximising their returns. And in that, Donahue and Underwood seemed to have an uncanny knack of knowing when wealthy travellers would be on the road.

Not that the poor were immune. Late in 1829 the pair attacked the home of Barney Hoe and John Dunn, two elderly tenants on the Regentville Estate of Sir John Jamison. The bushrangers gained entry by presenting themselves as Windsor and Penrith constables searching for bushrangers. When the door was opened to them they proceeded to rob the old men of a large amount of provisions. They then forced them to drink rum until they were intoxicated. The old men were then tied up while the bushrangers cooked themselves a meal. Their bellies full, Donahue began building up the fire to such an extent that it risked setting the hut aflame. Hoe became terrified that it was his intention to burn him and Dunn alive and started pleading for mercy. Donahue took no notice until Underwood argued with him and took matters into his own hands by throwing water onto the fire.

Hoe then reportedly asked, 'Why don't you attack the houses of swells, where you would get more valuable property?'

'The swells keep bulldogs [pistols],' the bushrangers answered, which suggested that the bushrangers' marauding behaviour had put the entire district into such a state of alert that their operations were beginning to be hampered.

The attack on the old men didn't go unnoticed. A new reward notice appeared in the *Sydney Gazette*, on 23 September 1829, raising the bounty on Donahue and Underwood to £50 each.

Donahue's crime spree continued, sometimes with Jacky Underwood, but now also with two other felons, William Webber and James Walmsley. In the early months of 1830 one of their prime targets was the Hassall family, with whom Donahue had tangled in the 'New Country'. Some of the convicts who had voyaged to Australia with Donahue were employed on the Hassall estate at Mulgoa and claimed they were being mistreated. That may have been provocation enough in Donahue's eyes.

In February, the bushranger stopped Jonathan Hassall. The *Monitor* reported that Hassall had said he had no money, which a body search confirmed. He and his overseer were then ordered to strip. According to the *Monitor*, 'Mr Hassall remonstrated on their stripping his government man, on which Donahue told the overseer not to strip.'

Hassall noticed a gun on the ground that one of the bushrangers had let drop, and became alert for an opportunity to pounce on it. Then he noticed Donahue. 'He drew up and kept the muzzle of his gun within a few feet of Mr Hassall's head. Mr Hassall refused to pull off his trousers. On this Donahue said he had a good mind to give him a Kildare toss [a fall that he'd never rise from].'

Hassall ended up taking off everything but his shirt and socks; the overseer had his boots taken. The bushrangers then gave Hassall a pair of their trousers and a saddle. When they left, Donahue 'retired backwards' so he could keep watch on Hassall, whom he feared might have a concealed pistol.

The same report in the *Monitor* also made reference to Donahue being involved in the earlier killing of one of Hassall's freed convict servants, Cook, who had captured a companion of Donahue named Story. On the day Story was to have been hanged ('the day Governor Darling arrived', which places the events in 1825), Donahue invited Cook to go kangarooing. Cook's body was found, partially burned, five days later near a fire. The *Monitor* reported that those who found the body believed Donahue had shot Cook in the back. At the time Donahue was an assigned servant in the Parramatta area, and therefore easily arrested, but he was never charged with the crime. As such, the story may show how Donahue's reputation was expanding to encompass many more crimes than he actually committed.

Indeed, when George Hall and his son were robbed of £2 and their personal effects, all the Sydney papers started baying for action. Wrote the *Australian*:

> It is reported that not fewer than ten highway robberies have been committed within the last fortnight in the district of Kemps Creek and the Western Road. What are the mounted police about? These outrages have really got to too great a head to be slurred over any longer. We will venture to say that these fellows are runaways from road and iron gangs. If the 'authorities' will not be active in the business, the settlers must try what they can do themselves to scour the country and diminish in some effective way this active pest.

The reality was that many of the settlers, particularly those with smaller holdings, were helping Donahue and company. Recognising this, Governor Darling introduced the *Bushranging Act*, which gave mounted police unprecedented powers to search for stolen goods, evidence of harbouring criminals and to require anyone they encountered to prove their legal status – convict, pardoned, ticket-of-leaver, free, etc. In the case of convicts with papers this was not a problem, but woe betide anyone caught without them. In the case of the locally born population, who had no convict records or documentation, the act stripped them of almost all legal protection.

While the press railed, however, Donahue committed his most brazen outrage. At the end of March, constables Brown and Hamilton were doing their rounds of Parramatta when they thought they saw someone acting suspiciously near the courthouse. However, as they approached the individual, two more men sprang from the darkness levelling pistols. At gunpoint Brown and Hamilton were forced into the courthouse yard and locked up. The media, already buzzing, were outraged. 'Never so daring as they are now,' they wrote. 'A precious humbug! Rare doings!'

By now many people living on the fringes of Sydney had taken to travelling in large groups. However, two days after the police were locked up, Robert Campbell, a farmer at Harrington Park (near Liverpool) and husband of Ann Hassall, made two mistakes. First, he set out for Sydney on his own. Second, he took £120 with him to settle a debt that was due for payment the next day. On the Liverpool Road he came upon an innocent-looking hobo walking with a bundle tied to a stick over his shoulder. However, when Campbell drew level with him, the hobo grabbed his horse and two other men leapt from the bushes. They searched him with such determination that they seemed to have had advance knowledge of what he was carrying.

The frequency of hold-ups led to confusion over which crimes Donahue had committed, and with whom. Some accounts suggested Underwood, others Walmsley and Webber, and still others referred to a felon named McNamara. The robberies continued throughout April 1830, amid intensifying police operations. Led by Chief Constable Thorne, based at Parramatta, and Mr Hodgson of Windsor, parties of constables were scouring the bush, while patrols operated along the Western and Windsor roads.

Finally at Raby, near Campbelltown, the police had their first success. In the late afternoon of 23 July a party of constables surprised the bushrangers and an exchange of gunfire followed. Donahue was seen to be shot, but took flight with his companions. Mr Riley, on whose estate the shooting took place, joined the mounted police in pursuit. Donahue's trail of blood was easy to follow, and they found two fowling-pieces and a pistol dropped by the fleeing men. Once again, nightfall thwarted the pursuit. After dark the search was broken off.

The next day, a large pool of blood was located just a few hundred metres from where the chase had been abandoned. However, there was no sign of Donahue. Chief Constable Thorne continued the hunt, following the trail of blood. In thick bush they found evidence of the wound being dressed. The next day, at a bark hut in the scrub, they found a stolen key, and nearby a large hollow tree containing basic supplies. Another bark hut was found and here it seemed the bushrangers had been barbering themselves, for the floor was scattered with different-coloured hair. Thorne took samples for analysis. At Parramatta police office a comparison revealed that one of the samples belonged to Jack Donahue – an early example of forensic analysis in Australian criminal investigation.

What may have been Donahue's second gunshot wound did nothing to curtail his activities – a hold-up of several carts just 3 kilometres from Windsor was reported in the *Australian* on 19 August 1830:

> Donahue is represented as being lame in the left arm about the shoulder, but remarkably active nevertheless. On one occasion, rather than go round the cart he put one hand on the horse's rump and sprang to the other side with remarkable ease and agility.

Among the merchandise on the carts was a crate of rum, which Webber reportedly seized upon and began to consume. When Donahue told Webber to curb his thirst, Webber replied, 'I wish I could get some of this when under the gallows.'

Donahue replied, 'I would rather meet my death by a ball than the gallows.'

It was a prophetic comment, for Donahue's flash days were numbered. And they were indeed flash. The *Australian* report detailed Donahue's attire as 'black hat, superfine blue cloth coat lined with silk, surtout fashion, plaited shirt (good quality), laced boots rather worn at the toes and snuff-coloured trousers'. His colleagues were equally well-dressed: Walmsley had a black hat, shooting jacket with double pockets, blue cloth trousers, plaited shirt and laced boots; while Webber wore a black hat, blue jacket, plaited shirt with a very handsome silk handkerchief round the neck, blue trousers and laced boots.

Meanwhile, stung by media criticism, embarrassed by Donahue's exploits and frustrated by his skilful avoidance of capture, the head of the mounted police, Lieutenant Macalister, decided to switch tactics. As reported by the *Sydney Gazette* of 7 September 1830, he realised that chasing Donahue from district to district was useless. The bushrangers had the bush skills and knowledge to escape with apparent ease. Macalister needed the element of surprise. So he concentrated his forces in the area around Bringelly, which seemed to be the base for Donahue's operations. Regular patrols were costly and arduous but on Wednesday, 1 September 1830, they paid dividends.

Towards evening, just a few kilometres north of Campbelltown in a hollow near a creek that curls around the present-day suburb of Raby, a party of mounted police commanded by Sergeant Hodson of the 57th Regiment were setting up camp. They'd spent a fruitless day scouring the bush and were unsaddling their horses in the setting sun when they noticed three suspicious-looking men leading a packhorse around the side of a hill about 2 kilometres away.

Hodson realised this might be the opportunity the police had been hoping for. He left two men to guard the camp and sent three others towards the approaching bushrangers while he and another constable crossed a small creek in an attempt to cut off their avenue of retreat. The police got to within 100 metres of the bushrangers without being seen.

Constable Gorman testified at Donahue's inquest: 'Suddenly espying us, they made preparations for defence.'

Donahue reputedly shouted: 'Come on, you cowardly rascals, we are ready, if there's a dozen of you.'

As it happened, both sides spent the next half-hour inviting the other to advance and fight, but neither chose to leave the protection of the trees. Gorman maintains that it was then that one policeman opened fire, 'his shot knocking the bark from a tree behind which Webber was situated. I now levelled my piece, which went off at the same moment with those discharged by two of the robbers.'

Another of the mounted police, John Mucklestone, held his fire. He'd chosen his target and was waiting patiently for the right opportunity. He was considered one of the best shots in the force, but at a range of 100 metres, he needed to be. He kept his aim on the tree Jack Donahue was using for protection, and patiently bided his time. Finally, Donahue peeped out, showing just his head and part of his chest. Mucklestone squeezed the trigger.

According to Gorman, Mucklestone's carbine was double shotted – loaded with a carbine ball and a pistol ball. When Mucklestone fired, both found their mark. According to the *Gazette* of 4 September, one ball entered Donahue's left temple (probably the lighter pistol ball), the other struck him in the neck. Gorman says he saw Donahue fall immediately.

The other two bushrangers fled, pursued by the police. Once again, in the gathering darkness the bushrangers Webber and Walmsley made good their escape. When the pursuit was abandoned, Hodson and his constables returned to find Donahue 'in his last agonies'. The mounted police stayed where they were for the night, then took the body and the property found with it to Sydney. There an inquest was conducted, and a jury took just five minutes to return a verdict of 'justifiable homicide'.

Walmsley and Webber didn't remain at large for long. They both continued their bushranging but both were taken alive – Walmsley in November 1830, Webber in early 1831. They were both put on trial. Webber was found guilty of a range of crimes, and hanged on 12 July 1831. To save himself, Walmsley turned informant. He identified twenty-three places where people had harboured Donahue and his gang. He named dozens of people who had received or traded stolen goods.

On 16 June 1831 John Smith, Thomas Sims, Michael Cantwell, Michael and Mary O'Brien, and John, James and Mary Ann O'Hara went to trial in the New South Wales Supreme Court, charged with receiving. All were 'small-acre farmers' and all except Cantwell were found guilty. They were sentenced to 'transportation' for fourteen years, effectively returning them to convict status. The 16-hectare farm of Michael O'Brien was seized and sold, as was the O'Hara's 25 hectares. Although he was acquitted, Cantwell also lost his 12-hectare holding.

On 20 June, another group was tried for 'harbouring bushrangers and receiving their plunder'. It comprised Edward and Daniel Chalker and their mother Elizabeth (the author's great-great-great-great grandmother), Samuel Jones, Thomas Baldwin, James Thompson, James White, William Sconce and Henry Page. The only evidence against them was Walmsley's testimony, but it was damning. For example, Walmsley stated that one of the pistols found by the police after Donahue was shot had been bought for him by Edward Chalker, and that 'at the time we got the rum from Lander's cart we played cards – Donahue and I, in Chalker's home . . . Mrs Chalker used to bring us tea and bread and butter and flour and other provisions.' Walmsley also said that when the police grew suspicious of the goings-on around the smallholders' farms, the bushrangers rendezvoused a short distance from the farm and servants were sent out with provisions.

There was just one problem with Walmsley's evidence: there was nothing to support his claims. As had occurred when Donahue was at large, the police case was hampered by a reluctance among those with information to come forward. Fear of retribution from the bushrangers or their supporters counterbalanced the rising rewards on offer. The smallholders and convict labourers knew their vulnerability to a visit in the dead of night, far from the protection of police. Indeed, in February 1832 the pardoned Walmsley had to be removed from the colony for his own safety due to the strength of feeling against him 'among the native-born Australians' after the O'Hara convictions especially, as reported in the *Sydney Gazette*.

Nevertheless, at this second trial of Donahue's supporters Judge Gurner warned the civilian jury that because the prosecution's case relied entirely on the testimony of a witness hoping to avoid the gallows, a guilty verdict was extremely risky. All the defendants were subsequently acquitted.

What remained unanswered, however, was the question of why the smallholders and others harboured the bushrangers in the first place. As with bushrangers in Van Diemen's Land, the convict versus gaoler factor may have swayed some sympathies. Another element is the oft-quoted aspect of nationality, especially that of the Irish convict opposing the English system. There are also suggestions of loyalties founded on religious persuasion – namely Catholic versus Protestant.

However, among the harbourers and receivers the suggested loyalties are present in some, but not all. In his 1988 masters thesis, *The Wild Colonial Boy*, M. Fitzgerald notes that the main harbourers were the McGlynns (who married into the Chalker family), the Chalkers and Hogans on South Creek (south-east of Penrith) and the O'Briens on the Windsor Road just north-west of Parramatta. Fitzgerald notes that all the harbourers shared a convict background but discounts almost all the other commonly believed reasons for their allegiance. The O'Briens, for example, were relatively wealthy, with total holdings of over 200 hectares. The Chalkers were English Protestants (although this may have been due to a lack of priests to baptise their children as Catholics), as were Walmsley and Webber. However, the key factor that Fitzgerald believes history has overlooked is that the harbourers and bushrangers were all friends before they took to bushranging. Webber was an assigned servant known to the Chalkers and McGlynns. Donahue knew the O'Briens. Thus the taboo against 'dobbing in your mates' may have applied.

Despite this, the facts haven't got in the way of a good story. Indeed, the mythologising of Donahue began even before he was buried. Surveyor-General Thomas Mitchell visited the Sydney morgue and sketched Donahue's portrait in death. Beneath the image he quoted Byron's epic poem 'Mazeppa':

No matter; I have bared my brow
Fair in Death's face – before – and now.

The next year Governor Darling wrote to his superiors in England:

Jack Donahue was one of the most notorious bushrangers of the first epoch in bushranging or highway robbery in New South Wales.

He arrived in the colony as a convict, and during his career committed several murders. After he was shot, a pipe maker was permitted to take a cast of his head showing a bullet wound in the forehead. One of these casts is still extant. The pipe maker made clay pipes, the bowl bearing a facsimile of the cast, and these pipes had a large sale. A song was composed called 'Bold Jack Donahue', and, as this song had an evil influence, its singing was prohibited in any public house on pain of loss of licence.

In 1835, however, Charles Harpur wrote a play about the bushranger, *The Tragedy of Donoghue* [sic], and by then public opinion had turned the bushranger from a villain into a hero. Whatever the reality might have been, the balladeers and storytellers were able to project their own agendas onto the fading memory of the real Jack Donahue.

'Bold Jack Donahue' is the first bushranging ballad known to have engaged in such mythologising. There are many variants, but they share the same tone. 'Come all you gallant bushrangers' they begin, or 'There was a valiant highwayman . . .' They all 'scorn to live in slavery born down by convict chains'. When called upon to surrender, 'I'd rather range these hills around like wolf or kangaroo than work one hour for government, cried bold Jack Donahue.' As for the manner of his death, he fights just as boldly, 'until the fatal ball which pierced his heart with cruel smart caused Donahue to fall'. Never mind that he was actually shot in the head and neck.

Poetic licence notwithstanding, the ballad of 'Bold Jack Donahue' marks a further shift in attitude towards bushrangers, at least in some sections of society. It was soon to be followed by many others as the exploits of bushrangers grew.

History even judged previous bushrangers in a more favourable light, as James Bonwick wrote in 1856 of Matthew Brady:

> This celebrated character had the physical structure, the mental energy and the culture of intellect which eminently fitted him for a leader. Under other circumstances, he might have become a successful explorer in savage lands, a distinguished warrior, or a prominent chieftain in some revolutionary struggle . . . Tall, robust, and handsome, capable of the most withering sneer, or winning smile, he was formed by nature for the control of man and the conquest of woman.

The chapter of Bonwick's book on Van Diemen's Land bushrangers was titled 'Brady, Prince of Bushrangers'. It makes one wonder what definition of 'prince' or 'gentlemen' is being used. Certainly modern victims of hold-ups at gun- or knife-point would not regard escaping with their lives as a sign of their attacker's good nature. That said, when compared to the bushranger that Bonwick titles 'Jeffries, The Monster', the others are saints.

Meanwhile, in the wake of Donahue's bushranging spree the continuation of the *Bushranging Act* gave the general populace ample cause to dislike those who governed them. Even after Darling left, his departure unlamented, his successor renewed the act. Governor Sir Richard Bourke wrote to London, 'It would occasion very great dissatisfaction among the free people of the Colony to deprive them of the protection this law affords.' That is, when they weren't being persecuted by it. Indeed it's tempting to reflect on the social forces that gave rise to Donahue, the *Bushranging Act* and to the bushrangers who followed. In the early nineteenth century there may well have been an emerging division between the haves and have-nots, between the ruling elite and the downtrodden. However, Australia was also a place of opportunity for those who were prepared to 'have a go'. Many freed convicts and their descendants who received land grants prospered without turning to a life of crime. Yet there's no denying the brutality of the system many convicts endured and the harshness of the laws that the authorities applied to the population at large.

Donahue's history can be seen as a reaction to the system he endured, while the fame that followed his criminal exploits may have rebuilt his battered self-esteem. Meanwhile, the song 'Bold Jack Donahue' not only lauded his career, it became an anthem of anti-establishment resistance. Thus bushranging acquired a cachet that wasn't lost on those who followed. Some, indeed, are reputed to have sung the ballad of bold Jack Donahue themselves, Ned Kelly among them. Somewhere along the way, the essential criminality of bushranging was diminished. It may have been hard to justify harbouring a common criminal, but it was easier when it was a bold and brave bushranger engaged in the battle between an emerging 'us' and 'them'. It became a challenge the authorities would take more than half a century to overcome.

4

Suspect everyone

1830–1839

As draconian legislation goes, the *Bushranging Act* was in a class of its own. Clause 1 stated, 'It shall be lawful for any person having reasonable cause to suspect any other person to be a transported felon unlawfully at large to apprehend every such suspected person.' Clause 2 said, 'Every suspected person taken before a Justice of the Peace shall be obliged to prove he is not a felon under sentence of transportation and in default to be detained until it can be proved whether he is a transported felon or free. In every case the proof of being free shall be upon the person alleging himself to be free.'

As noted in the previous chapter, one of the many problems with this crock of legislation was that if you were a convict, there was usually some paperwork to establish the fact. However, if you were a native-born Australian, or a free settler, there was usually nothing on paper. So it wasn't hard to establish your status if you'd at some time been found guilty of a crime, but it was a tricky business if you'd lived a life of innocence.

But there was more. Clause 3 of the *Bushranging Act* stated, in essence, 'Every person who shall be found on the roads with firearms [or other weapons] affording reasonable grounds for suspecting that such person may be a robber, shall be liable to be apprehended. In every case the proof that such firearms were not intended for an illegal purpose shall be upon the person apprehended.'

Many of those arrested under the act found themselves marched back to Sydney from wherever they were arrested, in order for the records to be examined closely to determine their status.

In *Settlers and Convicts,* Alexander Harris wrote of a typical experience:

> A native [meaning an Australian-born person] had once told me he had some time before passed seven weeks out of three months marching in handcuffs under the Bushranging Act. Having been born in the colony he had no protective document whatever. Some busy farm constable arrested him on suspicion of being a bushranger at one of the farthest stations at Hunters River, where he was looking for work. After being taken in handcuffs to Sydney, fully 250 miles [400 kilometres], and discharged, he went to the Murrumbidgee on the same errand, where he was again taken into custody by a soldier and forwarded in handcuffs to headquarters under the same law.

Prisoners were often handcuffed to the stirrups of a mounted police horse and were forced to trot beside their arresting officer. In one instance, the practice and the ability to 'arrest on suspicion' led to the death of an innocent man when the horse he'd been handcuffed to bolted because the policeman trying to mount the animal was drunk.

In 1830 one of the most active gangs was known by something of a catch-all term, the Hunter River Banditti. It comprised more than a dozen men, including at various times Edward Bowen, a part-Aborigine named Coffee, John Donovan, Patrick Feeny, Christopher and Michael Kearney, plus John Jones, Morgan Browne, Patrick Donnelly, a man identified only as Daly, Hugh Duffy, Patrick Finney, John Mason and Charles Westbury. They were all mounted on horses and armed.

Their first attack is thought to have been on the house of a man named Onus, on the Hunter River, on 18 July 1830. They then held up a man named Cameron, at Kingdom Ponds, on 9 August 1830. By then magistrates and troopers were already searching for them and were soon on the bushrangers' trail. Not long after, Magistrate Francis Bingle and his men encountered a body of six or seven bushrangers. Two were captured and a third, Daly, was later shot dead by a tracker named Jemmy the Locust, near Merriwa.

This setback didn't deter further attacks. On 21 August the property of John Towns, at the Goulburn River, was held up and the bushrangers made off with a gun, blanket, calico, a jacket, coat, waistcoat and a tea kettle. Again, the attack brought the forces of law and order to follow the bushrangers' trail. Four days later Corporal Quigley and a troop of mounted police encountered the escaping men. After an exchange of gunfire, one of the bushrangers, Edward Bowen, was captured.

The gang was quiet until 20 September, when they held up the station of John Rotton. The gang was again followed and nearly all of the bushrangers were captured. The efforts of the police were assisted by one of the bushrangers, John Jones, who turned informer and named half a dozen of his colleagues.

Just two months after they'd begun their rampage, most of the Hunter River Banditti were captured and the remainder driven from the district. When their lair was discovered in the Warrumbungle Mountains north-west of the Hunter Valley it turned out to be a 'regular settlement'. The banditti were growing crops and had a herd of 130 cattle, plus ten horses, farming implements and, of course, a dazzling array of weapons.

Browne, Mason, Bowen, Westbury, Duffy, Finney, Donnelly, Coffee and Donovan went to trial in January 1831. All were found guilty of some or all of the offences mentioned above. Mason, Bowen, Duffy and Finney were sentenced to death. The sentence was handed down on Wednesday, 12 January. The executions were carried out the following Saturday.

The *Sydney Gazette* detailed yet another botched execution:

> The caps were then drawn over their eyes, and their spiritual attendants shook hands with them and departed. They continued for a few moments, loudly and spiritually ejaculating, 'Oh Lord! Receive my soul! Oh, Lord Jesus, have mercy upon me. Oh, good people, beware of our fate,' etc., in the midst of which, the executioner withdrew the bolt, and the unhappy men were launched into eternity. Three of them died almost instantaneously without struggling but the fourth (Finney) was not so fortunate. The rope by some means became entangled with his arm, and he was suspended thereby till the hangman went up the steps and disengaged it. The fall having been broken, the neck was not dislocated and he remained for a considerable period of time suffering all the horrors of protracted strangulation.

John Donovan, Patrick Donnelly, Morgan Browne and Charles Westbury were tried in June 1831. Donovan was found guilty and sentenced to death, but the others were acquitted, possibly because the case against them rested on the evidence of the informer Jones. The Kearneys and some of the other banditti managed to escape, as detailed by Governor Darling in a letter to his masters in England dated 5 October 1830:

> A Party of from 12 to 15 in Number, lately assembled at Hunter's River,

plundered the Settlers of Horses, Arms, etc., and with difficulty were driven from that part of the Country, it having been impossible to come up with them after the first Skirmish, in which three Men were Killed, from the Circumstance of their being all well Mounted. They directed their Course across the Country towards Bathurst, and I am sorry to add that the Men belonging to one of the Establishments in that District, about 13 in Number, have recently risen, and, proceeding to the neighbouring Farms, plundered them of what was necessary for their Equipment.

Michael Kearney certainly reached Bathurst, and soon was one of the 'Ribbon Boys' in what became known as the Bathurst Insurgency.

It began, according to some accounts, with the crime of skinny-dipping. Ralph Entwistle was a lifer transported for stealing clothes. A brickmaker by trade, he was assigned to Bathurst landholder John Liscombe and went to work as a bullock driver. It was while thus employed that he succumbed to the heat of late spring 1829 and with a mate went for a swim in the Macquarie River. Unfortunately, Governor Darling happened to be passing at the time and one of his entourage, Thomas Evernden, who'd been promoted from the Buffs to become police magistrate and superintendent of the Bathurst police, happened to see the naked men. He had them arrested, gave them fifty lashes and cancelled Entwistle's pending ticket-of-leave. Entwistle supposedly burned with the desire for revenge.

In fact it wasn't until September 1830, the same month that the Hunter River Banditti were disbanded, that Entwistle and at least five other men absconded from Liscombe's farm, taking with them weapons and food. As they passed other properties they picked up more recruits. On 23 September 1830 they went first to Woodstock station where they obtained more weapons and recruited all the assigned convicts. They then headed for Bartlett's Farm, the property of Evernden (the site of the town of Wimbledon, 20 kilometres south-west of

Bathurst). The gang now numbered as many as fifty, with Entwistle at their head wearing a white ribbon on his hat. The ribbon signified his leadership and may also have been a reference to the Ribbon Men, a rebel Irish organisation, although Entwistle was in fact English. In any case, the gang soon became known as the Ribbon Boys.

They reached Bartlett's Farm on the morning of 23 September. The gang now included Entwistle, William Gahan, Peter Gleeson, Thomas Dunn, John Shepherd and Hunter River Banditti member Michael Kearney. After plundering the station the Ribbon Boys called on the assigned convicts to join them. Most agreed, but the overseer, James (John in some accounts) Greenwood refused.

The Ribbon Boys reportedly warned him, 'It would be much better for you to come, as we'll shoot you if you don't.'

'You're not game enough to shoot,' Greenwood replied and bared his breast to them. It was a foolish provocation. Entwistle and Gahan both shot him, almost simultaneously.

'Oh, Lord!' Greenwood cried and staggered back into his hut. He was still at the door when Michael Kearney also fired at him, hitting him in the back. Greenwood got as far as the fireplace, where he lay down and soon after died.

The killing prompted the Ribbon Boys to voice their sentiments against Greenwood, whose conduct as overseer during the previous six months was known to have been harsh. As Gahan reloaded his weapon, he is reported to have said, 'Who is the next man to say he will not go?'

None dared, and now numbering seventy or eighty, the Ribbon Boys proceeded from station to station throughout the afternoon, robbing as they went. That night, however, several of Evernden's servants and many others took advantage of the cover of darkness to steal away from the gang.

The plunder continued the next day, Friday, 24 September 1830. A writer to the *Sydney Gazette* detailed their activities:

They had collected about 80 men when they arrived at my farm. They took all my men except one, whom they left with the sheep, as they stated that they had no wish to injure me, as I was not a bad master; they took a little tea, sugar and tobacco, and my blankets, but did me no other injury at all.

They then marched, on horse and foot, to Mr. Icely's place, Wandorama, where they feasted, but did not do any great injury. They proceeded after that to Mr. Bettington's station, where they took some horses. At this place they found that no reliance could be placed by them on the men they had forced, as they were leaving them on every possible opportunity; they therefore formed the resolution, on the Saturday, of releasing them altogether, and took to their horses to the amount of 13, well armed and resolute. On Monday (the 27th ult.) they were doing damage about 30 miles [40 kilometres] off – no outrage, only collecting food and ammunition.

At least one harsh overseer saw the sense in making himself scarce when the Ribbon Boys came calling. On Sunday, 26 September 1830, Captain John Brown sent his overseer away before the Ribbon Boys reached his property on Dunn's Plains, just east of the town of Rockley, as the *Sydney Gazette* put it, 'in consequence of information that there was a bad feeling existing against him [the overseer] on the part of the bushrangers. The overseer not being there, they proceeded to take what articles they wanted, and left the farm without offering violence to any person there.'

The gang now comprised Entwistle, William Gahan, Michael Kearney, John Kenny, Peter Gleeson, Thomas Dunn, John Shepherd, Robert Webster, James Driver, Dominic Daley (all of whom ended up facing trial) and three others (who were killed before capture).

While the Bathurst police, under Lieutenant Brown, continued their efforts to pursue the gang, on Monday, 27 September 1830, a dozen volunteers (and their 'men' from the Bathurst Hunt Club) were selected to assist. William Suttor (who told Entwistle's story in *Sketches of Country Life* some years later) was made their commander. When they received news that another station, owned by a man named Arkell, had been robbed, they set out that night. Suttor obtained the assistance of two Aboriginal trackers and caught up with the Ribbon Boys an hour before sunset the following day, at a gully between Trunkey Creek and the Abercrombie River.

Suttor attempted to surround the gang, but one of his men stumbled on rocks and alerted them. They immediately started shooting. The Ribbon Boys assumed Evernden was leading the attack, and were heard shouting that they intended to kill him. Entwistle was seen with 'a profusion of white streamers about his head'.

One report of the ensuing gun battle was that Mr Arkell and a ticket-of-leave man named Yates managed to drive the Ribbon Boys back from their camp and seize most of their ammunition but were forced to retreat when Suttor and the others refused to advance to support them. The Ribbon Boys then managed to drive the attackers off. Suttor was subsequently ridiculed in the Sydney press.

On 29 September 1830 a second contingent of volunteers, under the command of Lieutenant Delaney, set out when it was learned that a station on the Lachlan had been attacked. The news having by then reached Sydney that up to eighty convicts were on the rampage, a contingent of the 39th Regiment was also despatched. Mounted police from Goulburn, under Lieutenant McAllister, were also sent north. There were now up to 200 police, soldiers and armed volunteers in pursuit of the gang.

There was a skirmish between Lieutenant Brown (and possibly Suttor's or Delaney's men) and the Ribbon Boys at the Lachlan River on 30 September or 1 October. The gang escaped and headed for caves in the vicinity of the Abercrombie River.

Several contingents of law and order gathered near the caves, and presented an overwhelming force to the hard-pressed Ribbon

Boys. After a pitched battle at Grove Creek Falls, the gang fled but were soon captured by the contingent from Sydney, under Captain Walpole, on Monday, 4 October 1830. By then three of the Ribbon Boys had been killed. Four of their pursuers, including Lieutenant McAllister, had been wounded. The Bathurst Insurgency had lasted less than a fortnight.

The ten survivors were put on trial on 30 October 1830. Entwistle, Gahan, Kearney, Gleeson, Dunn and Shepherd were found guilty of the murder of John Greenwood and were sentenced to death. Daley, Driver, Kenny and Webster were found guilty of robberies at two stations in the district and also sentenced to death. Their executions were carried out in Bathurst – the first in the town. The site of the execution is known as Ribbon Gang Lane.

The difficulties of life for bushrangers were highlighted with the arrest of Daniel Hickey and Joseph Walker, two otherwise unknown men who were captured by the mounted police and stockmen on the road to Bathurst. They were carrying a compass, two muskets and a fowling-piece.

The *Sydney Herald* described Walker's condition:

Walker had been in the bush about eighteen months, and is tattooed in various parts of his body like an Aboriginal black. This man is suffering severely from the effects of a ball or slug which he received in his neck during a rencontre with the military some time ago, and which has not been extracted. When taken, he was in a state bordering on starvation, and the policemen told our Reporter that he was actually eating grass like a brute! Walker and Hickey are both charged with capital offences; and to fill up the dread climax of their miseries – they expect to die on the gallows. Such are the wretched consequences of bushranging.

The settlers of Port Phillip Bay (pastoralists Edward Henty in 1834, and John Batman and John Fawkner in 1835) may have felt that the fledgling colony's freedom from the convict stain would insulate it to some extent from bushranging (never mind that their illegal squatting on Crown Land constituted theft on a scale the average bushranger couldn't begin to contemplate). However, it took just two years for bushrangers to appear on the scene, although deranged psychopaths who happened to be in the bush is a description that is closer to the mark.

George Comerford – tall, slim and 'mild looking' – was in the army and aged only nineteen when he struck his sergeant and was transported for seven years, arriving in Sydney in 1835. He was assigned to work at a property near Penrith, west of Sydney, but absconded after eight months. He changed his name to William Cooper and went to work for Charles Ebden as a shepherd on his property in the Port Phillip district. In May 1837 he left Ebden's station with two assigned servants, Joseph Dignum and a man named Smith. They were joined by three men assigned to Mr Howey and three of Ebden's men who were already at large.

They headed west, towards Portland and South Australia, but along the way one of the men, known as the Shoemaker, told Dignum and Comerford that the other men intended to murder them. Exactly why they would do so isn't clear, but some accounts suggest their supplies were running low and the sacrifice of a few would increase the chances of the many. According to a confession Comerford made some time afterwards, Dignum and the Shoemaker beat them to the punch. One night, while everyone was sleeping, Dignum rose and managed to kill four of the group with a tomahawk before any of them woke. The remaining two men may have stirred, whereupon Dignum and the Shoemaker shot them both dead – Comerford watching on. The bodies and bloody blankets were then burned. In the morning the three men broke up the bone fragments that remained, built up the fire and burned what was left.

Dignum, according to Comerford, also had his suspicions about the Shoemaker. A couple of nights later the latter woke to find Dignum murdering the Shoemaker. Dignum then reassured Comerford that he didn't intend him any harm. They then went to work at the station of a man named Agar, but they were recognised within a fortnight by Ebden, who had them arrested for absconding from his property. Nothing was known at the time about the multiple murders one (and quite probably both) had committed in the bush.

Incredibly, while they were being held, they managed to get hold of a key that could open their handcuffs and escape. This time, though, they robbed Ebden's house and stole his horse. Not long after, they held up a man named McLeod and took his horse as well. They then went on a crime spree while avoiding the pursuit of the fledgling Port Phillip police force.

An account by overlander Alexander Mollison suggests they may have ranged quite widely. While boating stock over the Murray River, he wrote in his *Overlanders Diary* on 1 July 1837:

> Mr Hooson, Chief Constable at Port Phillip, with two soldiers and the assigned convict, came to our camp at sunset yesterday. They had been eight days out from Mr Ebden's station beyond the Goulburn, in pursuit of three men who had robbed Mr Ebden and Mr Burton with arms. Three men, corresponding in appearance with those described by Hooson, crossed the Murray while I was ferrying our sheep. They were armed and had a horse and said that Mr Ebden had sent them for cattle.

The third person referred to was probably Fred Hallam, another of Ebden's men, who absconded with them when Comerford and Dignum robbed the station of Mr Bunny as they travelled north.

Comerford's suspicions about Dignum were confirmed some time after when he heard the click of a pistol and turned to see that

Dignum had attempted to shoot him. According to a report in the *Sydney Herald* of 31 May 1838, Dignum told Comerford that it was 'well there was no priming', as Comerford was the only man he was afraid of.

Comerford managed to escape and gave himself up, his confession painting Dignum as a cold-blooded killer and himself as an innocent led astray.

When Dignum was captured, shortly after, the New South Wales attorney-general sent Comerford to Port Phillip to obtain corroborative evidence of the seven murders Dignum was supposed to have committed. He was accompanied by constables Partington and Thompkins. In Melbourne they were joined by Sergeant Chinn and a private of the 80th Regiment.

Comerford took the men to the scene of the deaths of six of his colleagues and was taking them to where the Shoemaker had been killed when he showed a side of himself his guards were clearly not expecting. The *Sydney Herald* of 1 February 1838 detailed what occurred:

> When they arrived in the place where they intended to breakfast, about the 12th day from their departure, it was discovered that the tea and sugar was lost off the pack-horse, and Partington and the soldier returned to look for it, leaving Comerford in [the] charge of Thompkins and the Sergeant, who busied themselves in making preparations for the meal, incautiously leaving their arms within reach of Comerford, who appears to have been neither handcuffed nor ironed.
>
> Comerford watched his opportunity, and picked up one of the muskets; Thompkins, who was standing near, said, 'What are you going to do, John [sic]?' To which Comerford replied, 'Stand off, I don't want to hurt you, Thompkins.'
>
> Thompkins, however, made a rush towards Comerford, intending to seize him, when Comerford levelled the gun and fired, and the ball

passed through his chest and right arm. The Sergeant then ran up, but as Comerford had possessed himself of the other loaded musket, he desired the Sergeant to stand off, and made his escape. Partington and the other man shortly afterwards returned, and found Thompkins in a dying state, and as he earnestly entreated them not to leave him until he was dead, as he was afraid of being eaten alive by the birds and native dogs, they waited for him about three hours, when he expired, and they buried him where he was lying, and the whole party then went in pursuit. In the meantime, Comerford made his way to Mr. Howey's farm, where he told the men he had murdered the whole party . . . The men, it is said, took Comerford into custody, and detained him until the arrival of Partington and his party. (We have also heard that he was apprehended by a stockman in the bush, and taken to Mr. Ebden's, but we cannot say which story is true.) He was then taken to Melbourne, where he was committed to take his trial for the murder of Thompkins.

The trial was actually conducted in Sydney, where it was widely suspected that Comerford was involved in not one but probably all eight of the murders he and Dignum had committed between them. He was found guilty and sentenced to death.

Despite the seemingly overwhelming evidence against him, Dignum couldn't be tried for murder. The only witness against him was Comerford, but because he was already a convicted murderer, his evidence was inadmissible. He could, however, be tried for the robbery at Ebden's and for horse-stealing.

He was found guilty of the robbery, which was a capital offence, but because there had been no violence he was sent to Norfolk Island for life.

Comerford was executed on 30 May 1838. On his way to the gallows he didn't utter a word except to respond at the appropriate points in the religious service associated with his demise.

As the 1830s came to a close, the *Bushranging Act* was clearly not working. Bushrangers were active in Van Diemen's Land, New South Wales had two bushranging hot spots – Bathurst and the Hunter Valley – and even Victoria now had its bushrangers.

Early in 1839 a new expression entered the language. The term 'bail up' was probably in use among bushrangers for some time before then, but the *Colonist* of 27 February 1839 appears to have first used it in print when it reported:

> About three weeks ago, I met the postman that conveys the post bags from the Hume to the Ovens . . . He informed me, that the celebrated Black Police of Port Phillip had run away from that settlement; having taken away the fire arms and ammunition which the local authorities of Melbourne had placed in their hands to protect the whites from the aggressions of the savages: – that on their arrival at the Goulburn, they proceeded to the station of Mr. John Rutledge, where they bailed up the inmates, among whom was the postman, my informant.

The term appeared again in the *Colonist* of 4 May 1839:

> It appeared that about one o'clock in the morning of the 18th of January, an attack was made upon Woods' house by a party of men, who fired through the door and broke open the window. Upon the door being opened by Woods, one of the men struck him a violent blow on the head with a musket, and then made all the persons who were in the house come out and what is called 'bail up'; that is, they were all placed together and made to lie with their faces on the ground.

One of the women in the house, Ann Hamlin, wasn't bailed up. She was taken from her husband's side and raped by five of the bushrangers.

In his *History of the Australian Bushrangers,* published in 1899,

George Boxall gave an explanation of the term's origins:

> The first supply of horned cattle for Australia was obtained from Cape Town, South Africa, big-boned, slab-sided animals, with enormous horns. The animals are much more active than the fine-boned, heavy-bodied, short-horned, or other fine breeds, but they can never be properly trained. It is always unsafe to milk one of these cows unless her head is fastened in 'a bail', and her leg tied. When driving the cows into the bail it was the custom to order them to 'bail up'. It was also usual for bullock drivers yoking their teams to call 'bail up' to the bullocks, although no bail was used for this purpose. The words were in constant use all over Australia, and were adopted by the early bushrangers in the sense of 'stand'.

The Hunter Valley was again the setting for an outbreak of bushranging in the late 1830s. Edward Davis was the leader of what became the Jewboy Gang, a confederacy of bushrangers whose numbers varied with capture, death and the recruitment of absconding convicts.

Their activities began on 12 January 1838 with the robbery of a servant on a road near Tamworth, north of the Hunter. The gang then headed into the Hunter Valley itself. The *Sydney Gazette* of 3 April 1839 detailed their ensuing spree:

> The country between Patrick's Plains [now Singleton] and Maitland has lately been the scene of numerous outrages by bushrangers. A party of runaway convicts, armed and mounted, have been scouring the roads in all directions. In one week they robbed no less than seven teams on the Wollombi Road, taking away everything portable. They also went to Mr Nicholas's house, and carried away a great quantity of property after destroying a great many articles which they did not want. Mr MacDougall, late Chief Constable of Maitland, and a party of

volunteers, set out in pursuit. The Wollombi district constable is a tailor by trade, and he refused to leave his work to accompany the party on the plea that it would not pay him.

Such were the difficulties that beset the police force based in the outlying districts.

Meanwhile, the robberies continued. Travellers were robbed on the roads, and huts and homesteads were plundered from Maitland to the Upper Hunter. In mid-June the gang robbed the home of Lieutenant Caswell. Caswell refused to submit to the bushrangers and was about to be shot when his wife pushed the barrel away, and the bullet missed him. The family was then robbed of money and property worth £400.

The gang then took control of the road to Maitland and robbed everyone who passed. They moved on to Maitland itself and committed two more robberies.

On 15 June 1839 the bushrangers were so confident that they sent a message to the homestead of a man named Fleming, near Murrurundi, asking him to have his horses ready for them in the morning. Fleming was fortunate that the assigned convicts on his property were prepared to help him defend the place. When four of the gang arrived, accompanied by an Aboriginal woman and boy, Fleming and his men rolled out the lead carpet. A letter from Murrurundi, dated 17 June 1839, provided details:

> Finding [the bushrangers] were taking possession of a hut belonging to Mr Marshall, Mr Fleming attacked them in it. They, however, refused to surrender, and fired upon his party, which was returned; after firing ten rounds, Mr Fleming, finding they would not surrender to his party, sent a man fourteen miles [23 kilometres] for the Mounted Police who happened to be there, while he and his party kept them besieged seven hours, at the end of which time they surrendered . . .

> It appears that the black gin was taught to load their guns, bail up and stand over men, while the others were robbing huts, &c, and having been a long time with the gang, had become a complete adept in robbing. There are yet a great many bushrangers out in that direction. These are mostly young men, one is said to be free (Thomas Maguire); they are all dressed in clothes taken from gentlemen, which they have been sporting in great style.

The rest of the gang continued to commit robberies over the course of the next year and a half. On 14 December 1840 the *Sydney Herald* carried a letter that gave details of another of their robberies, near Dungog, and of the gang itself:

> Their attire was rather gaudy, as they wore broad-rimmed Manilla hats, turned up in front with abundance of broad pink ribbons, satin neck-cloths, splendid brooches; all of them had rings and watches. One of them (a Jew I believe) wore five rings. The bridles of their horses were also decorated with a profusion of pink ribbons. The leader was formerly an assigned servant of Edward Sparke, Esq., of the Upper Hunter, and another (named Shea) was lately an assigned servant of Mr Coar, the third, I believe, was a Jew named Davis, a very wary, determined fellow.

Having taken several people into their custody, including the local doctor, the gang spent a pleasant evening eating, drinking and relaxing with their 'guests'. The doctor said 'he was treated in the most gentlemanly manner by them, and that he never spent a happier night in his life'.

After the doctor had eaten his fill of eggs, beer and damper, the gang cleared a sofa for his postprandial nap. They spread their greatcoats over him to keep him warm. It was noted that the pockets of the coats were stuffed with ball cartridges and buckshot.

On 21 December 1840 the bushrangers attacked the home of Captain Horsley, at Hexham, on the Hunter River 10 kilometres from Maitland. While one bushranger stood guard over Horsley and his wife, the house was plundered of nearly everything of value.

After they left, Mr Edward Denny Day and a party of soldiers set out in pursuit. They followed a trail of sightings, robberies and another murder up the Hunter Valley for over 100 kilometres, finally cornering the bushrangers at Doughboy Hollow and wounding three before the rest of the gang surrendered. Edward Davis, John Everett, John Shea, Robert Chitty, James Bryant and John Marshall were all taken prisoner. Richard Glanville escaped the gunfight, but was apprehended the following day.

At the subsequent executions of six of the men, on 16 March 1841, the reporter for the *Australian* was struck by how young they all were:

> In health, and strength, and energies, to all which the buoyancy of almost youth, scarcely arrived at the prime of manhood, the six unhappy men saw placed before them their coffins, and suspended from the beam of the scaffold, the ropes ... How marked the contrast this, to the levity they displayed on their trial, when even the assumption of the black cap, awful prelude to a frightful tragedy, failed to make an impression!

5

Reap what you sow

1840–1849

As the 1840s began, bushranging continued to flourish, fed by an ever-increasing supply of convicts and former convicts. The violence that accompanied bushranging was increasing as well. Paradoxically, this may have been due to more enlightened sentencing back in England. Fewer convicts were being sent to Australia for petty crimes such as stealing a loaf of bread. More were being sent for serious crimes that a few decades earlier would have been punished by death. In addition, the brutal convict system was producing brutalised, bitter people then letting them loose on the wider population. The result of getting tough on crime was tougher criminals.

To illustrate the point, the 1840s were ushered in by a gang whose crimes rank among the bloodiest in the history of bushranging up to that time. The nucleus of the gang formed around Thomas Whitton and another man named Thompson, who went by the alias Scotchie, both of whom absconded from the station of Dr Redfern, near Bathurst, around 1837.

Their early career extended over three years and may have involved one murder, at the Redfern property, but it wasn't until they were joined by a bushranger named Russell (in September 1839) and Bernhard Reynolds (in December 1839) that the gang came to prominence. Operating from the then remote and inaccessible Weddin Mountains, near present-day Grenfell, by 1840 the gang was believed to have robbed nearly every settler in the Lachlan River district. The bushrangers were reportedly boasting that the police were afraid to face them and were deliberately avoiding them.

Certainly in January 1840 they commenced a crime spree that mixed the urge to plunder with the desire for revenge against settlers who stood up to bushrangers. It began on 18 January 1840 when Reynolds and John Monaghan assaulted and robbed Thomas Tropers. The next day, Scotchie, Whitton, Russell and Reynolds went to Oak Park, near Crookwell. They were looking for Francis Oakes and his brother, who they intended to shoot. They found Francis with thirteen other people harvesting wheat.

'Here they are,' the bushrangers reportedly cried, and immediately started shooting at anyone they could see. One of the convicts working in the field, John Blackburn, later testified:

I saw four men coming on horseback; I was forty yards [35 metres] off them; first I thought they were policemen – the moment after they said something about bailing up to the fence, and then a shot was fired; I saw Mr. Oakes running through the wheat; all the men ran except three men and myself; the bushrangers called out to them to stand, or they would shoot them; they fired from twelve to fifteen shots; they fired so quick, I could not count the number of shots; I thought all the men that lay down in the wheat were shot; I saw [assigned convict] John Hawker fall; he turned round to where the shot came from, and dropped – he died next morning – the wound was in his back, and the ball was close to the skin under the right breast; I did not see the prisoner so that

I could know him in the field; but I saw him at the burning of the house, about an hour after; the house was in flames; the four bushrangers were sitting at the end of the kitchen taking their dinners; they were dressed the same way as the men who were in the field; the prisoner was one of the men; he told me to tell Mr. Oakes that he was one of the Bathurst mob, and he would make him surrender the firearms that he took from a man named Marshall, a bushranger, from whom Mr. Oakes had taken some firearms a short time before. The bushrangers spoke to other men of ours, and said they would burn down the barn; they spoke to the men as friendly; either I or one of my fellow servants, said, that will do you no good; they then said they would not do it, as it would hurt the country; they said they would remain three or four days in the neighbourhood until they shot Mr. Oakes; they said they would make the bloody settlers submit . . . when they had done firing, and before they went to the house, they desired the men to sit down by the fence, or they would blow their brains out; they did sit down; the bushrangers said they would set fire to the paddock, and burn every one in it, dead or alive . . .

The gang didn't carry out that threat but instead demanded horses. It proved impossible to bring the frightened animals near the blazing house. They did manage to steal one valuable horse, worth £80.

The following day there was more violence and bloodshed. The gang appeared at the homestead of John Cooper, at Gunning, and commenced their plunder. A neighbour, John Hume (brother of the explorer Hamilton Hume), heard gunfire and with some of his assigned convicts went to investigate. As he approached he was spotted by three of the bushrangers. One of them demanded to know who he was. Hume demanded the same thing of them but the only reply he got was a bullet that hit him in the torso. He fell to the ground, still alive, but the bushranger, realising he wasn't dead, put two more bullets into him, killing him.

Hume's servants appear to have been of no help in the confrontation and allowed the bushrangers to escape. It was noted at the time that Hume was mourned by a wife and eight young children.

Meanwhile, the bushrangers moved on to Narrawa, a property at Fish River owned by Dr Gibson, vowing to kill the manager there, Oliver Fry, whom they believed had shot a bushranger dead and captured another during a highway robbery.

According to some accounts, Scotchie, Whitton, Russell, Reynolds and a fifth bushranger (possibly Opossum Jack) caught Fry outside his hut.

'Is your name Fry?' Whitton reportedly asked.

'Yes, it is,' the overseer replied.

'Well, then,' Whitton replied, 'we've come to fry you in your own fat.'

The bushrangers immediately began shooting at Fry, who ran for his hut. It was a miracle that he got inside, where he barred the door and armed himself. He may have been assisted by an old shepherd, Dorney Jack, who helped load his pair of double-barrelled guns. The bushrangers took cover behind an adjacent stable as Fry returned their fire. Neither of the wooden buildings afforded much protection as the bullets tore straight through the bark and timber slabs. The gun battle went on for close to two hours.

Finally, a shot from the bushrangers sent splinters of wood into Dorney Jack, who cried out, 'My God! I'm shot!'

Scotchie heard the cry and thinking Fry was hit, rushed the house. Fry was ready for him and, firing at close range, he couldn't miss. When Fry fired, Scotchie reeled back, bleeding profusely.

Seeing one of their leaders shot was enough to force the other bushrangers to retreat. Taking Scotchie with them, they fled the scene. When Fry realised they'd gone, he ventured outside. He found a pool of blood where Scotchie had been hit. The trail of blood was followed to Fish River. There the body of Scotchie was lying in the water, left by his comrades. Apart from the gunshot wound inflicted by Fry, there was another bullet wound to the head. He had either chosen 'death or liberty' by his own hand, or one of his gang had ensured he wouldn't be taken alive.

At the time, Sergeant Freer, a trooper of the mounted police, a tracker and volunteers Thomas McGinnis (who had shot the companion of the bushranger Edward Hall a year earlier) and Francis Oakes were on the trail of the gang. They caught up with them on 24 January, in the early evening. Freer later testified:

> Whitton was about getting on his horse when I saw him, but dismounted, and the whole party went behind trees for shelter; Russell was thirty yards [32 metres] off; I was taking up my covering when he fired, and wounded my horse in the head, and wheeled to the left; he then fired at either Mr Oakes or Mr McGinnis; then I got a shot at him, when he fell backwards; I mounted my horse again, and rode after the other two; they both fired and missed; I advanced upon Whitton with my empty carbine, and ordered him to lay down his arms; he did so, and I marched him up to where Mr Oakes, Mr McGinnis, and my two troopers had surrounded Reynolds; the bushrangers had three double-barrelled fowling pieces and five pistols.

Only Whitton and Reynolds were taken prisoner. As he lay on the ground, suffering from the wound inflicted by Freer, Russell took out a pocket pistol, put it to his head and became the second member of the gang to choose 'death or liberty'.

Even though Russell was dead, as his body was being carried to Goulburn, strapped on a packhorse, he still managed to escape. During the long journey the straps came loose and he slid from the horse unnoticed. When it was realised he was missing, the police turned back and started searching for him. They travelled nearly a kilometre before they found the escapee at the foot of a small hill.

The remaining members of the gang were taken to Sydney, where they were to stand trial. On 23 February 1840, the day before their case went to court, Reynolds asked to see Whitton so they could work on their defence. They talked for more than two hours then Reynolds returned to his cell.

At five o'clock that night the turnkey was doing his rounds when, as reported in the *Sydney Gazette* of 25 February 1840:

> The inner door of Reynolds' cell was found difficult to open, and when forced, he fell to the ground. On examining the body it was found that he had strangled himself by hanging, and that he must have been dead for some time, being perfectly cold. The ingenuity and cool determination displayed in the whole affair is almost without a parallel.
>
> It appears that his sister had sent him that morning a new silk handkerchief and two clean shirts to wear at his trial. About four o'clock in the afternoon he took one of his blankets and ripped it up, forming a compact roll with one part of it which he fastened to one end of the handkerchief, at the other end he made a running noose, he then threw this roll over the top of the inner door, which was open, then shutting the door upon it jammed it fast. He must have turned the night-tub which was in his room upside down to reach the noose, and by that means effected his purpose of self-destruction. So determined was he that he rolled the remaining blanket round the chains on his legs to keep the noise of his last struggles from being heard by the sentinel.

Whitton had also attempted suicide but failed. The next day he stood trial for the wilful murder of John Hawker at Oak Park. He pleaded not guilty, but the jury took very little time to return a contrary verdict. The prosecution was also prepared to try Whitton for the murder of John Hume, but as he'd already been convicted of a capital offence the attorney-general considered it unnecessary to prosecute. The chief justice then sentenced Whitton to death.

The government decided to make an example of Whitton. He was to be executed at Goulburn, near the scene of his crime, to send a message to other bushrangers in the region regarding the fate they could expect.

As it happened, the 'Bathurst mob' referred to by farmhand John Blackburn weren't easily put off. A letter from Gunning dated 25 February 1840, to the *Sydney Gazette*, stated:

> We have had some hot work at Gunning since I have been here, with bushrangers . . . there has been eight men seen mounted and armed within a short distance from us, and they say they are determined to have revenge for the men that were captured.

Whitton was taken from Sydney in a grim and very pointed procession that travelled down George Street. In modern times, the street is used for processions to honour conquering sportsmen. Not so in 1840. The dray that preceded the one carrying Whitton contained a gallows and his coffin. Whitton was guarded by a gaoler, a sergeant and six troopers of the mounted police. The *Sydney Gazette* of 10 March 1840 reported that 'Whitton displayed a philosophical coolness and determination in his actions and appearance, which we can only attribute to his long familiarity with scenes of blood and guilt.'

Whitton arrived in Goulburn on 14 March. The town's gaol was emptied to make room for its celebrity prisoner and the large contingent of police who were guarding him. He was watched round the clock to ensure he didn't cheat the hangman.

On 19 March 1840, at 8 a.m., seventeen mounted police and Lieutenant Christie of the 80th Regiment formed a guard on either side of the scaffold erected inside the gaol. Nearby, a grave had been freshly dug. A large crowd of men, women and children assembled. At 10 a.m., Whitton was brought out accompanied by a chaplain. They prayed at the foot of the gallows then Whitton climbed the ladder onto the scaffold. He turned to the crowd that now numbered 400. He told the prisoners who were there to obey the orders of their masters. He warned them not to take up arms. If he had done as he recommended he wouldn't be ending his life hanged on the gallows. When he died, Whitton was just twenty-six years old.

At the end of 1840, yet another bushranger began operating in the vicinity of Goulburn – William Westwood. Born in Essex around 1820, in 1835 he was convicted of highway robbery and given a lenient twelve months. In 1837 he was found guilty of a second offence, stealing a coat, and was sentenced to transportation for fourteen years. He was described in his convict records as: 'Aged 16, 5′ 5″ [165 centimetres], ruddy complexion, brown hair, dark grey eyes; errand boy; Protestant; able to read and write.'

He was sent to Gidleigh station, near Bungendore, where by his account he was brutalised and ill fed. He described the station's owner as a 'very hard and severe man'. In April 1838 he was sentenced to another six months' transportation for stealing wheat, but was sent back to Gidleigh.

He absconded in February 1839, received fifty lashes then absconded again in September 1839 and got another fifty lashes plus twelve months in an iron gang. Once more, instead of being worked in chains, he was sent back to Gidleigh. In September 1840 he escaped again and got another fifty lashes. On 13 December 1840 the now twenty-year-old absconded once more, but this time he took to bushranging.

He began his career in company with a fellow escapee, Paddy Curran. Curran had been transported for life in 1834 after trying to stab a corporal. When he took up with Westwood he had been at large for almost a year, having murdered a man near Goulburn in January 1840. Just before linking up with Westwood, and without

Westwood's knowledge, he had raped a woman at Bungendore on 8 December 1840.

The pair kicked off their career with a robbery, where else but at Gidleigh station on 17 December. South of Queanbeyan they robbed 'a gentleman returning from Maneroo', and the Queanbeyan postman. Then they turned their attention to Woden Homestead, in the vicinity of present-day Canberra. It was there that Westwood (calling himself Jacky Jacky) discovered that while he and Curran shared a criminal background, this was all they had in common. As Westwood described it:

> We rode up to the house and stuck them all up. After searching the men we ordered the mistress of the house to get us some refreshment, which she did. After a good snack, and drinking a couple of bottles of wine, I went outside to look at the horses. While outside I heard a scream, and ran inside, where I saw my companion attempting some liberties with the mistress of the house. I checked him at once; he drew a pistol from his belt, and was levelling it at me when I rushed upon him and struck it out of his hand. This led to a row between us, and I resolved to part from such a hot-tempered companion, as two of the same sort were better asunder. I left him there, and mounting my horse I went off by myself.

Curran moved on to the Bathurst district where he was captured in May 1841. He faced charges ranging from robbery to murder and was hanged in October 1841.

After parting company with Curran in January 1841, Jacky Jacky proceeded to rob the Queanbeyan mail and two men from a local station, including its owner, before moving on. He robbed several people on the Sydney Road, was unsuccessful in bailing up the Bungonia mail, and then robbed the Boro Creek store.

His manner during robberies was described by Robert Shirriff, who later testified (as reported in the *Sydney Herald* of 19 April 1841): 'Prisoner asked him who he was, and witness told him; he then said "I don't wish to harm you, but I must have the mare."'

On 13 January he returned to Bungendore and made the mistake of getting drunk. The resident magistrate, Mr Powell, his cousin Frank Nial, Richard Rutledge, William Balcombe and Reverend McGrath seized him, tied him securely and took him to the pub where they put him under guard. He attempted to escape, but was quickly recaptured. He was taken to Berrima under police escort and on 15 April 1841 was found guilty of robbery and sentenced to transportation for life.

If he'd known what was in store at Norfolk Island he might have wished he'd been sent back to Gidleigh. As it happened, he wasn't to find out just yet. While being transported to Sydney for his voyage to the notorious island, he managed to escape from the gaol in Picton. (Curran had escaped from the same lockup a fortnight before, but was recaptured soon after.) Jacky Jacky stole a horse and by 2 May was back in business as a bushranger.

Between Picton and Camden the original line of the Hume Highway crosses a steep hill called the Razorback. It was there that Jacky Jacky not only staged a highway robbery, but also demonstrated his ability as a horseman, galloping down the Razorback, the fine animal he had stolen, reaching the bottom in safety while would-be pursuers baulked at repeating a feat reminiscent of the man from Snowy River's perilous descent.

On 18 May he was reportedly in Sydney. As stated in the *Sydney Herald* of 21 May 1841 the toll keeper at Parramatta claimed he'd received a visit from a man claiming to be Jacky Jacky who'd said, 'I have been in Sydney these three days now and am now just starting again for the interior.' Jacky Jacky then detailed his 'horse trading' in Sydney and said, 'Let me see who will say stop to me while I have these little bull-dogs about me' (pointing to his pistols).

Moving south, he robbed a man named Jones at Bargo, and

Messrs Manning, Roberts and others about 5 kilometres from Marulan. A correspondent at Marulan wrote of the bushranger's exploits there in the *Sydney Monitor* of 26 May 1841:

> The first man he robbed, he stripped, and made him go under a bridge, where he left him when he heard a traveller advancing and he also robbed – and afterwards came others, who happened to be Mr Manning and the Sheriff's bailiff of Goulburn on horseback . . . A foot passenger next appeared and on being interrogated if he had any money the man replied 'no' – 'then be off; you are safe!' Jackey [sic] was last seen in the direction of Goulburn, galloping as if the devil was at his tail.

The *Australian* couldn't hide its admiration for Jacky Jacky's style. It commented on the same robberies in its issue of 27 May 1841:

> Our Berrima Correspondent, whose letter bears date the 19th instant, speaks of several freaks committed by 'Jackey Jackey' whose dexterity in avoiding pursuit is a matter of much wonderment. Notwithstanding the most vigilant exertions of the military, the ordinary police and ticket-of-leave men, this desperado still contrives to remain at large, bidding defiance to one and all . . . The latest account, which our intelligent correspondent in writing gives, is, that on Wednesday morning Messrs. Manning, M'Roberts, and himself, were stopped by 'Jackey Jackey,' about three miles [5 kilometres] from Peter's public house at Marulan, a township in the vicinity of Goulburn. The marauder made bold to seize on the latter gentleman's horse, which being trickey, he took fancy for Mr. Manning's and, sans ceremonie, and with equal nonchalance, returned the first horse and retained the second. The cool intrepidity and daring of this man is astonishing. It is needless to add, that this highwayman is well armed: he is moreover well dressed, assumes all disguises; pays his way as the saying is 'like a gentleman'; and in riding along the road, when from the appearance of the rider, if

in a trotting pace you come abreast, expecting and hoping to join good company, you are presently turned round upon, and in the expected gentleman you find a highwayman, with a brace of pistols levelled at the breast. This 'Jackey Jackey' is certainly a 'Donahue'.

He continued his robberies through May and June and in early July bailed up the man who had sentenced him to transportation for life, Mr MacArthur. The magistrate was on his way home from church in his carriage when Jacky Jacky appeared and took one of the horses.

Jacky Jacky later said, 'I looked back, and had the pleasure to see the coachman leading the one horse up the hill, and Mr. Black Francis pushing the coach behind – a sight that gave me real satisfaction.'

The feeling didn't last. On 13 July he was captured after a brief scuffle at a pub 15 kilometres from Berrima. He was taken to Sydney where, within three weeks, he attempted to escape from Woolloomooloo Gaol. He was flogged and sent to the prison on Cockatoo Island, although the *Australian* of 25 September 1841 noted that he did manage to escape some of this punishment:

> Jacky was not physically able to bear punishment for his late attempt to escape as well as his fellow desperates. He had not received seventeen lashes, when he declared himself unable to bear any more, and when he had received that number, the effect was so serious that the medical officer in attendance ordered the punishment to be stopped.

He next tried to escape from Cockatoo Island and was sent to Port Arthur. He tried to escape from Port Arthur and was given 100 lashes. The commander there noted that 'Westwood made great resistance during his punishment'. More escape attempts saw him sent to Norfolk Island where he reputedly became one of the feared penal settlement's 'Men of Stone'. He led a riot there on 1 July 1846 that left four of the prison's guards dead and led to the execution of several of the bushrangers detailed in this volume. Westwood was executed on 13 October 1846. He was twenty-six years old.

In 1841 the practice of transporting convicts to New South Wales ceased but by then, as George Boxall put it in *History of the Australian Bushrangers*:

> There was a sort of freemasonry among the convicts which impelled them to assist each other in their war against society, and even in cases where it was obviously to their interests to stand by and assist their masters, their sympathies with the bushrangers and their hatred of all forms of authority impelled them irresistibly to take the opposite side.

In many cases it wasn't enough just to catch a bushranger. A letter from a settler living near the Hunter River to the *Sydney Gazette* of 26 June 1841 explained:

> I have great pleasure in informing you that a notorious bushranger named Kelso has been taken by the mounted police at Mudgee, and forwarded down here for trial. He was one of a gang of scoundrels, who in defiance of police and constables, robbed and plundered this neighbourhood for the last twelve months. Kelso, with two others, were captured some time ago near this place, but they all succeeded in making their escape from the lock-up at Patrick's Plains. Now that they have once again got the doubly-dyed villain, I hope they will 'take care of him', though I doubt it very much; the constables are such arrant rogues, and the lock-ups, or gaols, so very deficient in security.

The contempt for the guardians of law and order extended to police magistrates. A letter from 'a subscriber' to the *Australasian*

Chronicle of 6 May 1841 didn't hold back when it came to the escapes of Westwood and Curran and laid much of the blame at the magistrates' doors:

> It is a well known fact, that it is one out of ten of the police magistrates who is fit for the duties inseparable from that office; a great many of these gentlemen being composed of superannuated old ladies, psalm singing half parsons, and attorneys' clerks, who are alike ignorant of horsemanship as they are of loading a gun or pistol. They may do very well upon the bench; they can there hear a case against a man for insolence or for losing a sheep, and award him, on the testimony of a drunken overseer, fifty lashes; but off the bench most of them are worse than useless. Besides this, they are mostly engaged in farming pursuits, contracts, or some other traffic totally unconnected with the duties for which they are paid. It is to be hoped, and the public expect, that the government will appoint some efficient gentleman to go through the different districts at stated times, and whose duty it will be to examine into and report the state of the police in those districts.

The situation may have been even worse than the 'subscriber' realised. Attempts to reorganise the police had been thwarted by self-interested parties, including police magistrates, many of whom jealously defended their patch against any outside interference. There was a preference for appointing 'proper gentleman' from England rather than any of the native-born. Competence and local knowledge were not prerequisites.

The *Australian Dictionary of Biography* lists Martin Cash's occupations as autobiographer/memoirist, bushranger, cattle thief, convict, farmer, murderer, police officer, prison escapee, prisoner and thief. He achieved so much in large part because he managed to do that rare thing among bushrangers – live to a ripe old age. He is also unique because his bushranging career began when he was in his thirties, whereas most bushrangers were in their tearaway twenties.

Martin Cash was born in Ireland in 1808. He was 175 centimetres tall with curly red hair, a blush to his cheeks and 'small blue eyes'. In 1827 he was sent to Australia for seven years for the crime of housebreaking. There he reputedly lived quietly in New South Wales for the next nine years, during which he gained his ticket-of-leave and ultimately became a free man.

By his account he was walking the straight and narrow when he found himself implicated in the branding and selling of stolen cattle. However, various newspapers from late 1836 and early 1837 carried the following advertisement:

> WHEREAS, on or about the 14th day of November last, a man calling himself John Bryan (since discovered to be Martin Cash), came to my Farm with forty-two head of Cattle, stating himself to be a free man, and that the Cattle belonged to him, requesting me to purchase them, which I did for the sum of £100. And whereas I have since had reason to suspect the truth of his statement, I do hereby give notice to all whom it may concern, that the said Cattle are now running on my farm at Taree, where they may be seen at any time, by application to me, or to my overseer. Dated this 23rd day of December, 1836. J. Jones

Cash was by this time living with the love of his life, Bessie Clifford, who had left her husband to be with the charming young Irishman. Facing arrest over the stolen cattle, he fled New South Wales, travelling to Van Diemen's Land with Bessie and arriving there in February 1837 aboard the *Francis Feeling*. His own account of his cattle dealings was that he took the cattle from a man named Boodie who had conned him into branding cattle that were not his in the first place. Cash also claimed that Boodie sold some of his cattle.

In 1839, however, Cash was in trouble again, and after a conviction for larceny he was sent to a penal settlement for seven years. He had no sooner arrived than he escaped, but was retaken within a week. He was given an additional eighteen months on his sentence: nine months in a chain gang and nine months in a road gang. He escaped again, while awaiting transfer back to a penal settlement, and is thought to have remained at large, possibly engaged in honest work for as long as a year, before he got into trouble again.

In early May 1842 Van Diemen's Land newspapers reported:

> On Friday afternoon last, that notorious bushranger, Martin Cash, who has been so long at large, and committed so many depredations, having with his usual recklessness ventured into [Hobart] town, was apprehended in Harrington street, and lodged in custody by constable Kirby and another constable, whose name is, we believe, Williams.

He was sent to Port Arthur, the equal in misery to any of the harshest penal settlements in the Australian colonies. He soon escaped, and to avoid the guard dogs chained across the narrow isthmus of Eaglehawk Neck, swam the adjacent inlet. He then had to cross another narrow land bridge, East Bay Neck, to access the settled lands beyond and be reunited with Bessie Clifford. As it transpired, five days after he escaped, a patrol caught him near the second neck. He was returned to Port Arthur and sent to the stone quarry in chains. There he met two men, Lawrence Kavanagh and George Jones, who had been transported for robbery under arms. They were as keen as he to make another escape attempt.

Kavanagh (sometimes spelled Cavanagh) had been a member of the short-lived Balmain Bushrangers. Balmain is a harbour-side suburb in Sydney that was the site of one of the robberies committed by Kavanagh, Thomas Brown (no relation to George) and a man named Johnson after escaping from Hyde Park Barracks on

27 January 1842. The next night they robbed the home of some fishermen in Double Bay, holding two women and a man at gunpoint. Apart from stealing food and clothing, they also took a boat. It was found on the opposite side of the harbour, near Bradleys Head, on 30 January. They attempted to rob a servant of Alexander Berry, near Berrys Bay, still on the north side of the harbour, on 2 February. On Friday 11 February there were bushranging incidents all over the southern side of the harbour, including Balmain. The *Sydney Gazette* reported that a party riding on the South Head Road was shot at by a gang of bushrangers:

> An old couple residing at Balmain were bailed up in their house by two bushrangers yesterday, who after threatening them severely if they 'split' on them, gathered up what tobacco and valuables they could find, and made off. The same fellows, with another who had joined them, crossed the harbour, and landed in Rose Bay [actually on the same side of the harbour] during yesterday afternoon. They attacked Captain O'Connell on the road to his house, and fired several shots at him, but the gallant behaviour of this officer speedily set them to flight.

The interpretation of what constitutes bushranging may have been broader in 1842, but after all the swashbuckling tales of bushranging in the interior and Van Diemen's Land, the *Gazette* may have engaged in sensationalising crimes in an urban setting by attaching the more dramatic term to them.

A tracker found Kavanagh, Brown and Johnson in a cave near the shores of Elizabeth Bay the following morning. According to the *Gazette* of 15 February, 'The Police Office was crowded to excess, by a number of persons attracted by the hope of obtaining a sight of these marauders.'

All three men were sentenced to transportation for life and sent to Port Arthur.

There, on 26 December 1842, Cash, Kavanagh and George Jones broke their chains, dropped their tools and ran into the bush. A pursuit was organised, but they managed to avoid capture for the next three days.

They made their way to Eaglehawk Neck, sometimes crawling through the scrub on hands and knees to avoid detection. The Neck was swarming with guards, so they waited until nightfall, stripped off their clothes, and took to the water of the inlet with their garments balanced on their heads. However, the inlet was exposed to waves and by the time they emerged from the water, their clothes had been washed away. They travelled on, naked and barefoot, until they reached a work-gang hut used by guards and prisoners.

There was only one man at the hut, a cook, and the escapees took a chance and rushed him. Kavanagh grabbed an axe that was leaning beside the door of the hut and the cook was quickly overwhelmed, not least by the surprise of being attacked by three naked men. Cash, Jones and Kavanagh helped themselves to the abundance of food and clothing.

Knowing that those in search of them were alerted to their presence and would be watching the last barrier to escape, East Bay Neck, they lay in hiding for several days. Search parties scoured the bush the whole time and at one point passed within metres of the escapees without catching sight of them.

Three days after raiding the hut, Cash, Jones and Kavanagh crept towards East Bay Neck at midnight, hoping that at that time there would be fewer guards and that these would be less alert. They took off their boots and crawled past one of the sentry boxes undetected. Passing within metres of the sentries, they managed to cross the open ground of the Neck and reach a field of wheat, through which they crawled until they gained the protective cover of the bush beyond. They were free.

It was January 1843. They quickly armed themselves, obtained fresh clothing and food, and began robbing their way towards the settlements around Hobart. While a reward of £50 and a conditional pardon was offered for their capture, they established a base for themselves at the Dromedary, a conspicuous mountain north of Hobart, and through a friend of Cash sent word for Bessie to join them.

On 14 February 1843 the *Colonial Times* detailed the exploits of the men, referring to them as 'Cash & Co.' On Saturday, Mrs Collies, wife of a smallholder, was robbed of wine, property and £7. They also shot a bottle of spirits out of the hand of a man who ran from them. On Tuesday they robbed Mr Hodgkinson of £4, flour, sugar, ham and tea. The paper reported that Mrs Hodgkinson tried to escape to give the alarm and Cash was about to shoot her when her daughter pleaded for her life. Cash eventually acquiesced.

Cash, in his autobiography published many years later, suggests Mrs Hodgkinson gave as good as she got:

> Still the old lady waged war on my mates and myself, evincing a most determined spirit. She appeared to have been a very masculine person when in the heyday of youth, and from what I could see would be none the worse in appearance by the occasional use of a razor. She remarked that I was some poor woman's hard rearing and in a moment after offered up an earnest prayer that my career would be shortly terminated. I continued, however, to prevent her from doing harm while my mates were making their arrangements, and on leaving the premises she followed us outside, screaming at the top of her voice, but as we could not permit her to follow us any longer I gave her to understand that if she did not return immediately to the house I would not be answerable for the consequences. However, she continued to revile us until we were clear out of sight of the farm.

Meanwhile the *Colonial Times* also took a shot at a man it regarded as incompetent when it added: 'It is said they bent their way towards

Richmond and Pittwater, being informed, no doubt, how securely bushrangers have heretofore enjoyed themselves within the police district of Major Schaw, at Bothwell.'

Based on information from a man named Shone, Mrs Cash was arrested and held in gaol, provoking an angry reaction from Cash. He gave a letter to a man he was robbing to send to Shone: 'Understanding through the public press that Mrs Cash is in custody for some things you have sworn to, we hereby give you notice that if you prosecute Mrs Cash we will come and burn you and all you have to the ground.' He also threatened to visit Government House if she wasn't released 'and beginning with Sir John, administer a wholesome lesson in the shape of a sound flogging; after which we will pay the same currency to all his followers.'

It may have smacked of arrogance, but over the next six months Cash & Co. ran rings around their pursuers, plundered at will and struck fear into all and sundry. The newspapers of the time grew increasingly frustrated at the failings of the police.

Things changed in July, however, when Kavanagh shot himself in the arm while climbing over a log. He surrendered himself at the hut of a settler on 11 July, almost fainting from loss of blood. A month later, amid rumours that Mrs Cash was involved with another man, Martin Cash entered Hobart to try to see her. The *Launceston Examiner* of 2 September 1843 reported:

> On Tuesday evening, the 29th ult., about half past eight o'clock, a man since supposed to be Jones (Cash's companion) accosted two constables who were upon duty in Murray Street, and enquired where a man named Pratt resided. The constable addressed pointed out the house and followed Jones towards the spot. At this time another man was observed standing a little aside, apparently waiting for the information to be obtained by Jones. The constables, who had been for some time on the watch near Pratt's (who cohabits with Mrs. Cash)

residence, suspecting this man to be Cash himself, approached him, when he walked away, but the constables drawing very close he pulled out a pistol and fired at the nearest constable, who returned the fire, both shots however missing the parties fired at. Cash then took to his heels up Brisbane Street, followed by the constables, crying 'stop thief', but the latter having great coats on could not run very fast. When Cash got opposite the Old Commodore public-house, in Brisbane Street, behind Trinity Church, Constable Winstanley hearing the noise ran out to stop Cash, when he was fired at and dropped, the ball entering into his body, and it is feared his death is certain. The delay caused by firing at Constable Winstanley enabled a Mr. Cunliffe to overtake Cash, trip him up, and hold him down until others came to his assistance. Whilst Cash was thus on the ground he drew another pistol from his pocket and fired it, wounding one man in the hand and another person (a schoolmaster) in the face, the ball passing through his nose and lodging in his face, from which it has since been extracted.

Cash was then carried to the prisoners' barracks, where he was held down with difficulty by FOUR men whilst searched by order of Mr. Gunn, and upwards of £47 found upon him, in gold, notes and silver, besides a silver watch. He was then dressed in convict clothing, the necessary depositions taken by Mr. Gunn, heavily ironed, and sent in a cart to the gaol.

Cash was dressed in sailor's clothes and displayed so much strength that he was beaten a good deal about the head before he could be taken to the prisoners' barracks. Jones escaped in the bustle, as he was not identified by the constables, but it is hoped he will soon be captured.

Cash was tried for the murder of Winstanley. Kavanagh was tried for highway robbery. Both were found guilty and sentenced to death. However, public sentiment grew in their favour and the sentences were commuted to transportation to Norfolk Island for life. There Kavanagh joined the prisoners' rebellion in 1846 and was one of the ringleaders executed for the murders of four guards. Cash refused to join the rebellion.

Jones was captured about seven months after Cash. There was nothing gentlemanly in his bushranging during the intervening period. He had deliberately heated a spade in a fire and applied it to a woman's leg to get her to disclose where her money was. He also shot a constable dead and boasted of it afterwards. He was sentenced to death and executed.

Cash was kept at Norfolk Island until 1854, when the penal settlement was disbanded. By then he had married Mary Bennett, a convict on the island. He had been a model prisoner at Norfolk and six months after it closed he was given his ticket-of-leave. He returned to Van Diemen's Land, where he became a constable for the Cascades Agricultural Settlement, perhaps in the belief that to catch a thief, set a thief. He eventually bought a property at Glenorchy where he farmed until he died in 1877, aged sixty-nine. By then he was regarded as a local celebrity – charming, cheerful, a lovable old rogue. He has been described as the only bushranger who died in bed, although others may have died there from gunshot wounds.

Another notable bushranger who would live to see old age was Frank Gardiner, as detailed in several subsequent chapters.

James Wilson, the Little Scotchman, was one of Queensland's first bushrangers. The colony was first settled in 1824 as a penal settlement, but by 1839 it had become the domain of free settlers. In the case of Wilson, bushranging was one of the sins imported from the southern settlements. The first robbery associated with him occurred in New South Wales on 22 October 1843. The *Maitland Mercury* reported that a local publican, Mr Perfrement, was stopped by an armed bushranger near Brown's Springs in the Upper Hunter Valley. 'His horse, boots and everything was taken from him. The robber is well known; his name is Wilson, and he was formerly assigned to Mr. Wightman, of the Page.'

For the next two years the Little Scotchman committed occasional robberies in the Hunter region, but early in 1846 he was on the move north. In March rewards of £30 or a conditional pardon were offered for his capture, the proclamation noting that he 'has made his appearance in the district of New England'.

He may have hoped to escape police by heading into Queensland. It might have worked if he hadn't kept on with his criminal activities. The *Sydney Morning Herald* of 29 April 1846 carried details from its Moreton Bay correspondent:

> The good folks on the Darling Downs have been put into a complete commotion through receiving a visit from the notorious bushranger Wilson, and a mob of six others, who have made their way into this part of the country, the troopers of Mr. Commissioner McDonald having made the New England district too hot to hold them. They visited a station formerly occupied by Mr. Gordon, but now taken up by the Messrs. Hay; the party inside the dwelling house, who were just finishing dinner at dusk, were taken all a-back by seeing half a dozen muskets and pistols presented at their heads, with a polite request from the gentlemen of the road to sit still until they performed a few necessary operations in their line. To the credit of the fellows, they conducted themselves in a quiet, orderly manner, taking the gentlemen's word of honour that none of the desks or boxes contained money.
>
> One of the gentlemen, Mr. Walter Leslie, had his watch returned, and his horse was very politely placed at his service. After remaining some hours at the house, and handing a glass of grog round, they went off, taking with them a small supply of rations – which they weighed out – some double-barrelled fowling pieces, and three horses, leaving a couple of fowling pieces behind them.
>
> Singular to say, Wilson handed over to Mr. Leslie £33 which he stated

he had taken from a poor man in the New England district, giving his reason for having taken that sum from the man, merely that he had refused him a feed when he called at his hut.

The next report of Wilson's activities was of his death.

Mounted police under Sergeant Giles were ranging over a vast area of rugged, mountainous country on the border between what is now New South Wales and Queensland when the sargeant decided to split his force. He sent Corporal Worsley, two troopers and a tracker to the region around the Clarence River, while he travelled north to the Darling Downs, where there was news of another robbery. As it happened, Worsley encountered Wilson, who was in the process of fleeing south. Worsley's report, published in the *Sydney Morning Herald* on 27 May 1846 explained what transpired:

On the 7th May we were informed that the bushranger Wilson and his party, of whom we were in pursuit, had robbed the station of Mr. Bloxome, of Rostion. The next morning we went after them, and took the aboriginal black with us to track. We got on it on the morning of the 9th, and followed them over the mountains and through scrubs so thick that we were obliged to cut our way through them with our knives.

We fell in with them on the morning of the 12th, at half-past eight o'clock; we saw their fire from the ridge where we were. I dismounted the men, as I would have been heard with the horses, from the bank of the creek upon which they were being very hard and scrubby.

As we came up the bank they were prepared. I ordered them to lay down their arms, but they refused to do so. The bushranger Delaney, whom we captured, being behind a tree, five yards from the bank, with a double-barrelled piece, he fired at me, but missed me; when seeing Wilson with a blunderbuss and spring-bayonet attached, presented, and a double-barrelled gun at his knee, I fired at him, but missed, when Delaney rushed on me, and caught me in his arms around the body.

I then ordered trooper Joyce, as he was close by, to do his duty, which he did, and shot him through the shoulder blade. I then, seeing trooper Maher in front of Wilson, without any covering, ran immediately to his assistance, when Wilson fired his blunderbuss at Maher, and shot him in the fleshy part of the thigh, and lodged thirteen buckshot in him, as he was making for cover. Maher then fired his piece and put a ball in his left elbow. Wilson then ran with his double-barrelled piece still in his hand, Maher followed and knocked him down with the butt of his carbine, which broke; he got up again and made an effort to cross the creek; I drew my pistol and shot him through the left side. Trooper Maher not being able to move, I went to see after the other two bushrangers, that we had not seen, as they had got into the scrub when we first challenged. At this time the affray was over, having lasted one hour. Wilson was severely wounded, but lived to half-past three, being six hours and a half.

The following morning, Worsley reached an outstation where he left the wounded bushranger Delaney and trooper and went for help. On 14 May he returned with a dray, only to be informed by Trooper Joyce that one of the escaped bushrangers was lurking nearby. A shepherd was taking him food in an effort to keep him in the area until Worsley returned. Wrote the seemingly fearless Worsley: 'I then rode off, and apprehended him in a gully, about three-quarters of a mile [1.2 kilometres] from the station, with a double-barrelled gun in his possession.'

One victim of bushrangers wasn't about to follow the conventions when it came to being robbed. On 4 May 1843 Thomas Massey of Ellerslie, on the South Esk in Van Diemen's Land, was relaxing on his verandah when a bushranger, John Conway, walked up to him, put a gun to his head and shouted, 'Stand!'

To which Massey replied, 'No, thank you. I'm very comfortable sitting down. What do you want?'

Conway and his accomplice, Riley Jeffs, proceeded to steal two double-barrelled guns, a fowling-piece, shot, powder, tea, sugar, flour and rum. They were caught the next day and tried for the murder of another man they'd robbed. They were publicly executed in Launceston in July, with close to a quarter of the town's population turning out and treating the occasion as a form of entertainment.

In 1846 the prisoners on Norfolk Island mutinied. Martin Cash took no part in the short-lived uprising but several other bushrangers, including Jacky Jacky, joined in and were sentenced to death for their trouble. On 8 October 1846, five days before his execution, Westwood wrote an eloquent condemnation of the system:

> I have been treated more like a beast than a man, until nature could bear no more. I was, like many others, driven to despair by the oppressive and tyrannical conduct of those whose duty it was to prevent us from being treated in this way. Yet these men are courted by society; and the British Government, deceived by the interested representations of these men, continues to carry on a system that has and still continues to ruin the prospects of the souls and bodies of thousands of British subjects. I have not the ability to represent what I feel on this subject, yet I know from my own feelings that it will never carry out the wishes of the British people! The spirit of the British law is reformation. Now, years of sad experience should have told them, that instead of reforming – the wretched man, under the present system, led by example on the one hand, and driven by despair and tyranny on the other, goes from bad to worse, till at length he is ruined body and soul. Experience, dear bought experience, has taught me this.

Westwood's remarks reflected a common thread among bushrangers facing the gallows or long prison sentences. 'The system made me do it,' they said in one form or another. Few admitted that a criminal disposition and poor impulse control may also have been contributing factors, although a few did accept that they were being rightly punished for the things they'd done.

Unfortunately, those grasping the wheels and levers of power weren't about to take note of the comments made by notorious villains regarding the failings of criminal justice in the colonies. Thus the lessons of the previous fifty years had yet to sink in. The colonies still had a lot to learn, and the bushrangers had much to teach them.

6

The lust for gold

1850–1859

In 1850 the governor of New South Wales, Sir Charles Augustus Fitzroy, had much to feel sanguine about in the state of the criminal justice system of New South Wales. Transportation of convicts to his colony, the *raison d'être* of many of his predecessors, had long since ceased and the number of wrong-doers in his care was diminishing rapidly.

The landholders who craved slave labour were to some extent frustrated in their ambitions, while the smallholding free settlers felt that the stigma of being a penal colony was at last being lifted. On 6 January Fitzroy was able to write to his colonial secretary:

> Out of about 60 000 persons transported thither, 38 000 are reformed and respectable members of the community. Of the residue, deaths and departures from the colony will account for the greater part; and I am enabled to state that only 372 out of the whole are now undergoing punishment of any kind.

As convict numbers declined, so did incidences of bushranging – fewer mistreated prisoners translating into fewer absconders. Zealous policing meant any outbreak of criminal behaviour was quickly nipped in the bud. As such, there hadn't been a prolonged outbreak by a bushranger or gang since the mid-1840s. The only significant blemish in the overall peace was a riot in Sydney at the end of 1850 that had led to an attempt to unify the state's fragmented police force. The only thing the attempt succeeded in unifying was the rural magistrates' resistance to change.

However, the discovery of gold in New South Wales in early 1851 soon saw bushranging once again on the rise. By midyear, newspapers such as the *Geelong Advertiser* of 2 June 1851 were warning travellers to be careful on their way to New South Wales because 'large numbers of men – half bushranger, half goldseeker – are travelling along the roads, especially the Sydney Road, robbing all who were unprotected'. Such men were thought to be ex-convicts from Van Diemen's Land flocking to the goldfields.

The bushranging situation in New South Wales improved in mid-1851 when two things happened: first, Victoria achieved statehood (on 1 July); and second, gold was discovered in the fledgling state (miraculously, on 2 July). By the end of July 1851 the discovery of huge quantities of gold at Ballarat and Clunes had turned the traffic headed for New South Wales around, and all roads now led to the Victorian goldfields. In December, gold was found at Bendigo.

Bushrangers followed hot on the miners' heels. Among them was the high-titled Captain Melville. His real name was Frank McCallum. In 1836, aged thirteen, he'd broken into a house in Scotland, was caught, convicted and transported to Van Diemen's Land. He was frequently in trouble and was eventually sent to Port Arthur. From there he escaped in 1851 and headed for Victoria. He committed a number of crimes in 1852, summarised by the *Argus* newspaper's Geelong correspondent on 9 February 1853:

[Government officials] have been publicly warned, and they have received private information besides, that strong reasons exist for supposing this criminal to be the leader of the same gang who murdered Marcus and another man at the Ovens, before they proceeded on their career of robbery by way of Maiden's Punt, the Loddon, the Leigh, and finally Geelong.

Captain Melville's career continued throughout the year. On 18 December he and another bushranger, William Roberts, held up the home of David Aitcheson at 'Wardy Yallock' and stole a horse. However, the following day they hit what seemed to be the jackpot. They bailed up Thomas Warren and his cousin William Madden on the Ballarat Road and robbed them of £40. The amount was more than a labourer's wages for a year, a sufficiently large amount that the bushrangers returned £3 to their victims so they could celebrate Christmas. They were going to steal their horses, but when they spotted Mr Simpson from Port Fairy on a better horse, they stole that instead.

Captain Melville and Roberts proceeded to celebrate Christmas in a Geelong brothel. On Christmas Day police, most likely tipped off by an informant, visited the place and managed to arrest Melville, despite shots being fired.

He was tried on a number of charges of highway robbery and, as the *Argus* suggested, was also suspected of murder. On 3 September 1853 he was found guilty and Justice Redmond Barry sentenced him to thirty-three years' imprisonment. He was initially held in a prison hulk at Williamstown, from which he and others attempted to escape. In November 1856 he asked to see a priest. When they were alone, Captain Melville demanded the man of the cloth strip and swap clothes with him. To his surprise, the priest refused, foiling yet another escape attempt. In August 1857, however, Melville escaped by the only means left to him. He was found dead in his cell, probably killed by his own hand.

In an attempt to deal with the growing problem of bushrangers, in November 1852 the Victorian government took the unusual step of introducing the *Criminal Influx Prevention Act*. It specifically prevented former convicts from landing at Victorian ports. Of course, its effectiveness was limited by the fact that convicts from New South Wales didn't have to pass through any ports. All they had to do was swim or row over the Murray River.

The act barely made a dent in the ongoing crime wave, however, as noted in the *Sydney Morning Herald* of 5 March 1853:

> Several notorious characters have been secured and disposed of lately in Victoria, viz: Captain Melville, the supposed murderer of Marcus at the Ovens; Dalton and Kelly, the Van Diemen's Land villains; 'Black Douglass', once the terror of Friar's Creek and Bendigo, but others spring up in their place. Forest Creek is now honoured with the residence of 'Dublin Jack,' a candidate for the roads or the gallows, who it is said has about forty men under him. The scene of his handiwork on Sunday last was Forest Creek, where it is reported he robbed four or five tents. The police know the man and his residence, still he is at large.

While travellers on their own, small groups and lightly guarded mail coaches had long been easy prey for bushrangers, until 20 July 1853 it was assumed the heavily guarded shipments of gold coming down to Melbourne from inland were too well protected to be vulnerable to attack. Yet they presented a tempting target, laden as they were with a fortune in money and gold.

Such was the case with the McIvor Gold Escort, a privately organised operation that transferred gold from the McIvor diggings to Kyneton, in central Victoria, from where it was then taken to Melbourne by the government escort. The McIvor escort set out every Wednesday, departing precisely at 9 a.m. It was right on schedule on 20 July when it left with Superintendent Warner and Sergeant Duins mounted on horseback, three troopers (Morton, Davis and Reiswetter) inside the coach, and the driver named Foakes.

It had covered just over 20 kilometres when it came upon a large tree that was lying across the road. The coach was forced to deviate around the obstruction and it was at that point that Warner and Duins noticed that on the side of the road a kind of barricade had been erected using six small gum trees with a number of branches threaded between them. They barely had a chance to become suspicious before a volley of shots rang out.

The escort was ambushed. From behind the screen a deadly fire of ball and shot was poured into the coach. The men inside didn't have a chance to return fire from what was later estimated to be fifteen men.

Within moments, Trooper Morton was hit in the shoulder, the ball passing just above his lungs. Davis was hit in the face with swan shot and in the shoulder by a ball (suggesting the bushrangers had double-loaded their weapons with ball and shot). Reiswetter was wounded in the leg (his shoulder was also dislocated), Foakes in the leg and head. The sudden burst of gunfire caused Warner's and Duins' horses to bolt past the barricade, but not before Duins' horse was hit in the rump by two shots from the attackers. When Duins regained control of his mount he turned to see a bushranger taking aim at him with a double-barrelled gun. He fired both barrels, one shot just missing Duins' face, the other passing close to his chest.

The escort was reduced from six able-bodied men to two in the first salvo. Only Morton managed to return the bushrangers' fire, despite being shot. He managed to hit the man who'd shot him, but could then do no more. Hopelessly outnumbered, Warner and Duins had no choice but to escape into the bush. Duins headed to the nearest police station to raise the alarm. Warner attempted to stay close to the scene, hoping to identify the escort's assailants, but was hunted away by some of the bushrangers, while the others set about plundering the treasure that was now at their mercy.

The audacious attack was richly rewarded. A report in the *Argus* of 25 July 1853 (written by McIvor gold agent Bryce Ross) detailed what was taken:

> The gold consisted of forty-six packages, from Nos. 428 ending with 473, weighing 2322 ounces, and £713 10s. in money; but one package of money for Forest Creek, amount £120, escaped the eyes of the robbers. The value of the stolen property, in round numbers, may be calculated at £6360.

In modern values the haul was probably worth around $5.5 million.

By nightfall, up to 400 men (police, soldiers and volunteers) were scouring the bush. Four of the bushrangers' horses were found, as were a number of personal items. Two pannikins were found, one bearing the name Richard Maxfield and the other the initials W.N. However, the initial pursuit only yielded a man who was found trying to lift the wounded troopers into a cart. He was arrested on suspicion of being one of the bushrangers, a curious reward for trying to save lives. As it was, driver Foakes died of his wounds some days after the shootings.

A reward of £500 was issued for information leading to the capture of each of the perpetrators. However, the break in the investigation was, or appeared to be, more straightforward. It involved a stolen gun. According to the *Hobart Courier* of 20 August 1853:

> It appears that a person, when at the McIvor diggings, lent his revolver to another man, who departed without returning it, had gone on board the *Madagascar* for England, and in proceeding on board with the Police for obtaining his property, the arrest of the three banditti was made.

A man named George Francis (under the alias John Murphy) was arrested, with his brother John and a man named George Wilson. George Francis attempted to escape after his capture, while he was being taken in to Melbourne, but the attempt failed. He eventually admitted his involvement in the escort robbery and gave evidence against his co-conspirators. Three more of them turned out to be on the *Madagascar*, which by then had sailed, but another ship, the *Argo*, set out shortly after, hoping to overtake her.

George Francis also fingered William Atkins, George Melville, Edward McEvoy, Robert Harding, George Shepherd, Joe 'Nutty' Grey, George Elson and a man named Billy. While most of the men he named were being arrested, Francis escaped again but was recaptured on 24 August. He then took his own life, using a razor to cut his throat.

Atkins, Melville and Wilson were found guilty of the murder of Foakes and executed on 3 October 1853. A huge crowd gathered to witness the hangings. Wilson forgave the witnesses who gave evidence against him and according to the *Hobart Courier*, said that 'a man now in gaol, charged with the St Kilda robbery, was quite innocent of that transaction'. (He alluded here to Simon Russell. Wilson himself is said to have been involved in the St Kilda affair.) The newspaper also noted that Atkins' wife had been left destitute, and was expecting a child at the time of his death.

At the execution of the three men, Victoria demonstrated that it could bungle a hanging as badly as any other state. Several reports noted that while Atkins and Wilson died quickly, the hangman 'was compelled to draw the legs of Melville down with considerable force before life was extinct'.

In September 1854 Victoria went into recession. Businesses failed, wages fell and unemployment rose. As gold production also dropped away, the government moved to bolster its finances by intensifying its efforts to collect mining licence fees, thus increasing pressure on a group already bitter over the burdens imposed upon it. To the miners, the government was as bad as the bushrangers. As the miners' protests threatened to spill into violence, the police had their hands full maintaining law and order among the general population. It was a golden opportunity for the bushrangers to get up to mischief.

The Ballarat branch of the Bank of Victoria was a juicy plum just waiting to be picked. It was full of money and gold and ideally positioned from a robber's viewpoint. On one side of it there was nothing but bush; on the other side, the nearest building, a bakery, was 50 metres away.

On the afternoon of Monday, 16 October 1854 the only staff in the bank were the manager, Mr Buckley, and the accountant, Mr Marshall. Between two and three o'clock Marshall heard a knock at the door and went to see who was there. As he opened the door four men pushed inside. They had hats and veils over their faces, and all wore similar blue shirts and corduroy trousers. All were armed with revolvers.

The tallest of them reportedly leapt the counter and shouted, 'You b----s! We'll have you this time!' He pulled the trigger of his revolver next to the ear of the accountant. The barrel wasn't loaded, but the man clearly meant business. Two other men snapped their pistols at the manager. Both bank officers were gagged and tied then pushed beneath a stretcher and covered with a sheet to prevent them seeing the bushrangers' faces. Accountant Marshall turned on his side and managed to get a view, but when one of the men saw him, he threw another cover over him, and pushed him further under the stretcher. They then set about ransacking the place.

The haul was enormous – estimated at between £13 000 and £14 300, and between 230 and 330 ounces [6.5 to 9.3 kilograms] of gold, as reported in the *Argus* on 18 and 19 October 1854. The four gunmen disappeared into the bush, unseen and unpursued by the good people of the now much-poorer Ballarat.

Rewards of £200, free pardons and passages to England were offered for any information leading to any arrests, without success.

Then, a month after the robbery, four men answering the descriptions of the bushrangers were found near Warrnambool. They were pursued, whereupon the men revealed they were 'armed to the teeth'. Their pursuers, unarmed, gave up the chase, but three of the men were later captured. Their bush camp was found to contain all the paraphernalia of bushranging, but it transpired they weren't the Ballarat bank robbers. The three gave their names as Jennings, Smith and Balk and if they were bushrangers, they managed to elude any charges.

The first break in the case came with the arrest of Thomas Quinn, a man known to police for his involvement in the robbery of gold worth more than £28 000 from the ship *Nelson* in 1852. He was captured in the Sir Charles Hotham Hotel, in Melbourne's Flinders Street West, on 20 November 1854, by detectives Eason and Powell, from Geelong. A search of Quinn's room revealed 400 ounces of gold, 1200 sovereigns and £400 in notes whose numbers matched those known to be stolen.

Within a week, Thomas Marryatt was also arrested by detectives Cummings and Williams, at a 'house of ill fame' in Melbourne. Marryatt may have been a bank robber, but he also thought a bank was the safest place to hide his loot. Unfortunately, when he deposited £1304 in the Bank of Victoria in Melbourne, they weren't so slow that they didn't check the numbers on the bundle of notes he handed over the counter. They were from the Ballarat bank job. He also deposited £519 at the London Chartered Bank. They, too, checked the notes and found they were from Ballarat.

A third man, John Boulton, went one step further and went to the bank he'd robbed to get a £1450 draft on a London bank. He too covered the draft with stolen notes.

Only one of the four got very far. Henry Garrett made it to London and was leaving his lodgings near Oxford Street when someone shouted his name. He stopped and turned to face Detective Webb, who had followed his quarry all the way from Ballarat. Garrett's hesitation was all he needed to confirm he'd found his man.

Quinn gave evidence against the other men, who were ultimately sentenced to ten years in prison. Garrett was released on a ticket-of-leave in 1861 and went to New Zealand, where he became that country's first bushranger.

The October 1854 Ballarat robbery was rapidly eclipsed by more sensational events on the goldfields. In November 1854 the miners formed the Ballarat Reform League to protest licence fees and a number of other grievances. A radical group then built the Eureka Stockade near Ballarat in defiance of the authorities and the licensing system. It was a red rag to the bull-headed Victorian government. In a drastic overreaction, on 3 December 400 troops and police were sent in to quell the rebellious miners. In the ensuing battle, five police and thirty diggers were killed.

In the wake of the Eureka Stockade, the government was forced to take the miners' grievances seriously. Within a year, they'd got much of what they wanted.

The Victorian police were then able to turn their attention to do the job they were supposed to do, and by 1855 bushranging was in rapid decline throughout Victoria. So successful were the police that the government began to consider decreasing the size of the force, much to the disgust of the miners, who still felt vulnerable to the predation of bushranging.

In May 1855 the miners again took matters into their own hands. Several newspapers carried an extraordinary report from the *Mount Alexander Mail* on the capture of a part-Aboriginal man called Black Douglas and his gang:

The career of this notorious character and his mates in crime has sustained a check at the hands of the Maryborough diggers, whose assumption of the law in this instance is not likely to be condemned. The whole neighbourhood of Simson's [goldfield], from Carisbrook to the Avoca and New Bendigo, has for several weeks past been kept in a continual state of terror and apprehension by the depredations of gangs of scoundrels, whose maraudings gradually increased in violence and brutality as the intention of Government to reduce the police force became more known. The crowning act of the barbarities committed by these ruffians was the murder of a woman at Avoca, as reported elsewhere, and the diggers became sensible that they must themselves take measures for securing their own lives and property. The first intelligence of their active operations for self-protection reached the Camp at Maryborough about 1 o'clock on Sunday, when information was brought that a gang of bushrangers had been captured at the Alma. About an hour afterwards, Lieutenant Shearman took a party of police to the spot, and found a party of 200 or 300 diggers about to sit in judgment on Black Douglas and eight of his companions, whom, after a severe contest, they had succeeded in capturing, and all of whom were known to have been actively engaged in the outrages that had been committed.

Lieutenant Shearman persuaded the diggers to surrender the culprits into the custody of the law, and the whole body marched to the Camp, with their prisoners in a cart, and delivered them with three cheers to the care of the police. The injuries sustained by the gang in their conflict with the diggers, who fought with picks, shovels, &c., are said to be very severe; three especially were very severely handled, and one was so badly wounded that his life is in danger. About 5 o'clock on Sunday afternoon, two more of the gang were captured and taken to the Camp.

After giving the prisoners into the custody of the police, bodies of the diggers proceeded to various tents which were known to be the resort of bushrangers, and gave notice to the owners that, unless they were removed by 4 o'clock on Monday, they would all be razed, and all the people thus warned are said to have decamped. The diggers express their firm intention to rid the country of the rascals by whom it is infested, and are adopting measures for effectually carrying their object into effect.

On Monday the prisoners were examined before the magistrate, and five of them committed for trial on distinct charges of robbery. The others, including the redoubtable Black Douglas, were remanded for further examination. Notwithstanding the reputation which this chief of robbers has obtained, it seems difficult to establish any serious charge against him, and it is thought that he will have to be proceeded against under the Vagrant Act, as a consorter with thieves and vagabonds.

Black Douglas was suspected of killing a digger and wounding three others, but without sufficient evidence ended up being sentenced to two years in gaol. He was released in February 1857 for 'good conduct', after which he appears to have 'gone straight'. He lived to be seventy-five.

Among the many criminals in Victoria during the 1850s was future bushranger Harry Power, who was already displaying horse-stealing inclinations. In March 1855 he was stopped by police while riding an expensive horse near Maryborough. The police asked to see some proof of ownership. Instead, Power pulled out a revolver, arguing the police had no right to stop him. The police tried to arrest Power, who began shooting. One policeman was wounded and Power escaped at a gallop. He was eventually caught and sentenced to fourteen years. As subsequent chapters reveal, after his time in prison he took up bushranging, eventually tutoring the most famous bushranger of all: Ned Kelly.

Towards the end of the 1850s, bushranging in New South Wales, Victoria and Tasmania (as Van Diemen's Land became known after it achieved statehood in 1855) was almost extinct. However, the end of that decade was marked by one of the worst incidents in bushranging history to that date.

On 5 January 1859 a small party travelling from a goldfield in Gippsland to Melbourne passed three men on the road: William Armstrong, George Chamberlain and George Penny. Cornelius Green was a gold buyer and had with him a packhorse loaded with the yellow metal. He was accompanied by a Miss Mutta and escorted by a police constable named Green (no relation). That night, the group stayed at an inn and were joined by a storekeeper named Somes Davis.

The following morning the group of four travelled onwards. However, they had only got started when there was a shot. Constable Green later testified:

> I looked and saw Mr. Green leaning forward in the saddle. I also saw a man on my right armed with a gun. I drew a holster pistol and fired at him, and he either fell or got behind a tree. I was then fired at from a tree on the left side, and was shot through both arms. I did not see the man who fired at me, for the tree was forked with branches interlaced, but he must have been near to me, as several slugs passed through my left arm, carrying strips of my jumper with them. A slug also entered my right wrist, and was held by the skin on the opposite side. Also a slug grazed across my chest. My horse turned suddenly and galloped 60 or 70 yards [55 or 64 metres] and stopped. I was unable to do anything with him, as both my arms were useless . . . I saw a man present a gun in my direction and fire, when my horse galloped away and carried me back to the inn from which we had started in the morning.

The storekeeper and Miss Mutta were thrown from their horses. Cornelius Green, by this time off his horse, slapped the rump of his packhorse, which bolted towards the inn. Davis and Mutta managed to escape and walked back to the inn. Green was not so fortunate. The bushrangers – Armstrong, Chamberlain and Penny – were enraged that he'd denied them their rich prize by sending his packhorse galloping. Near nightfall, despite his wounds, Constable Green led a troop back to the scene of the hold-up, where the gruesome discovery of Cornelius Green's body was made. They found 'his head riddled with slugs, his nose gashed off, and one of his hands nearly severed from the arm by a tomahawk cut, while there was a terrible gash on the left temple'.

Armstrong and Chamberlain were tracked to a shanty 80 kilometres from Omeo and captured. They were found guilty of Cornelius Green's murder on 2 July 1859 and executed on 12 July.

7

Class warfare

1860–1862

Where bushranging was concerned, by the early 1860s all was quiet west of the Great Divide. The bushrangers who'd been lured to Victoria had been shot, hanged or gaoled for lengthy periods, and as the old hands of the convict class aged and died, so did the source of bushrangers. Meanwhile the number of free settlers continued to increase. Some might still be 'sympathetic to those who waged war on society' as George Boxall put it in *History of the Australian Bushrangers*, but the warriors had become few and far between.

Law and order seemed triumphant. The police had perfected their bushranger-hunting skills, knew their areas and everyone in them, and were well aware that when it came to the criminal element, the offer of a reward for information could sway the shaky loyalties of friendship, kin and class.

In the previous decade, New South Wales had been able to sit back and watch as all its bushranging problems headed south of the Victorian border. The police may have congratulated themselves that they'd 'made it too hot' for bushrangers in their own jurisdictions. And as long as gold continued to lure villains south, they could remain complacent.

While the New South Wales districts west of the Great Dividing Range seemed peaceful enough, the reality was quite different. Many of the old hands had settled on smallholdings, where they barely eked out a living for themselves and their families. Others had been forced to sell out and were labouring for free settlers with capital who had been lured to the colony by generous land grants. The result was that free settlers owned 95 per cent of the land. Native-born Australians owned a mere 5 per cent.

The *Masters and Servants Act* of 1828 ensured the free settlers had cheap labour. In 1860 farm labourers were still getting around £30 a year – less in real terms than they'd received twenty years earlier. Then a recession in the early 1860s saw wages fall even further and unemployment rise. Landowners also displayed a preference for immigrant labour, ensuring that difficult times fell hardest on the native-born, specifically the 'convict-stained' children of the old hands.

As they came of age in the 1860s, the rural native-born found themselves in a uniquely disadvantaged position. Many were uneducated, since the government of the time did not see the need to provide schools for a class of people destined to become drovers, shearers and labourers. Few had received the moral education and sense of communal responsibility of a religious upbringing, since churchmen shunned the poorer rural areas. They also had little chance of marrying, since in rural districts in 1861 men outnumbered women by nearly two to one.

It was inevitable that in areas where there were large numbers of unemployed youth, crime started to rise. Many youngsters turned to petty crime to make ends meet. For some, stock duffing was part of life, especially as many property owners didn't see the need to lavish expense on fencing their runs and allowed their stock to wander. Only 30 000 kilometres of fencing had been erected in Australia in the 1860s. In the 1870s the figure had grown to around 1.2 million kilometres.

While landowners had assigned convicts, they could use them to shepherd their herds and have them flogged if any stock escaped. When landowners had to pay people to watch their stock, they cut back on shepherding and turned to the law to punish anyone who helped themselves. It was a reasonably effective measure since in most rural districts landowners also acted as magistrates.

Thus in 1861 New South Wales Governor Sir John Young was moved to note:

> The imprisonment of a young person of from 18 to 25 years, for five, seven, or even more years, for the offence of stealing a horse or a cow of the value of from 1l. to 5l. seems cruel and oppressive; and under all the circumstances of the country, beyond all measure of justice or reason. Instances of this severity are frequently brought before me, while persons in Sydney, stealing property of greater value from a shop or dwelling house, usually get sentences of only two years or less.

On the plus side, when it came to crime, most of the native-born had advantages their convict forebears never knew. Most young Australians could ride and valued horsemanship highly, giving them a mobility their convict forebears lacked and in many cases an advantage if they were pursued by police. They also had a wide circle of support among family and friends. Their networks of 'bush telegraphs', built up through stock duffing, gave them almost immediate information about the movements of the police. Many had also been brought up on tales of legendary bushrangers – Donahue, Brady, Cash and Westwood. Thus, if the opportunity to become a bushranger presented itself, the native-born had distinct advantages compared to absconding convicts. In the 1860s all they needed was a motive.

As it happened, a switch in the fortunes of Victoria and New South Wales provided just that. Throughout the 1850s, Victoria had enjoyed extraordinary gold rushes as phenomenal wealth was discovered throughout the colony. Gold was also found in large quantities in New South Wales, but not in anything like the amounts found in Victoria. However, in the early 1860s the strikes in Victoria tapered off, while in New South Wales gold discoveries were still on the increase.

The divisions in rural communities in New South Wales grew ever wider as more gold was found. On one side there were dirt-poor native-born Australians struggling to get by. On the other were miners and free settlers whose pockets were literally bulging with money. As the native-born were left further behind, they found themselves with both motive and opportunity.

This situation is part of the extensive theorising on what befell New South Wales in the bushranging era of the 1860s. Many researchers regard the period as an expression of social banditry, an inarticulate response to social injustice that was a forerunner of unionism and the emergence of an anti-authoritarian Australian identity. According to the theories, as disenchantment grew, all it took was enough young men with poor impulse control to lead to an outbreak of bushranging. On the other hand, it may simply have been the fault of just one man: Frank Gardiner.

Frank was born Francis Christie in Ross-shire, Scotland, in 1829, but his parents took the family to Australia in 1834 when he was five. They lived at Boro Creek, south of Goulburn, until his mother ran off with a squatter. The children subsequently ran wild, especially Frank. He was soon supplementing the family's fortunes with the odd bit of stock duffing and eventually moved on to more ambitious thefts. He was caught in Victoria in 1850, along with two other men, with twenty-four stolen horses and sent to the newly built Pentridge Prison for five years. He stayed five months, escaping in March 1851.

He was arrested again at Yass in New South Wales in March 1854, this time while trying to sell sixteen stolen horses. He was then sent to the prison on Sydney's Cockatoo Island for seven years.

On Cockatoo Island, Frank either renewed his acquaintance with or met another horse thief, John Piesley (five years Frank's junior), who was doing a seven-year stretch. Both men were eventually released on tickets-of-leave: Frank in December 1859; John in November 1860. Both men went their separate ways. Frank may have gone to the goldfields of Kiandra, in the Snowy Mountains. John's conditions of release restricted him to the Upper Hunter Valley. However, gold strikes in the Bathurst area saw both men drawn there in 1860 and 1861.

Frank went into the butchering business with a man named William Fogg, supplying meat to the miners at the new strike at Lambing Flat (now the town of Young). With more than a thousand men at the diggings it was hard to keep up with demand. It wasn't long before Gardiner was arrested on suspicion of cattle-stealing.

As it turned out, he didn't draw the line at knocking off stock; he was also having an affair with Kate Walsh, wife of the manager of Wheogo station, and sister-in-law of one of the lessees of the adjoining station, Ben Hall. When Gardiner was released on bail, he bolted for the arms of his true love and holed up in the nearby Weddin Mountains, long the rugged, sparsely inhabited haunt of bushrangers, such as Scotchie and Whitton some thirty years before.

Piesley, meanwhile, had already succumbed to the temptation of pockets lined with gold. On 23 March 1861 he bailed up a man named Richard Cox on the road to the diggings at Hill End. Cox was carrying the extraordinary sum of £565. He was also carrying a pistol. Piesley got both.

Gardiner was facing another long stretch at Cockatoo – the conduct of the local magistrates made him sure of that. He decided to throw in his lot with the now-rich Piesley and together they formed the nucleus of a gang that committed a number of robberies in April and May 1861, including bailing up the Cowra mail.

The police pursuit of them proved ineffectual. Both bushrangers could ride as well or better than any of the men who hunted them. They knew the country they were moving through intimately. And with their own pockets now bulging with cash, they were harboured and aided nearly everywhere they went. The good times had begun to roll.

At the end of June 1861 a riot occurred at Lambing Flat that proved to be of immense benefit to the nascent bushrangers. More than 1000 men attacked the Chinese who were working on the diggings. They made a banner out of a tent fly that incorporated an image of the Southern Cross and bore the slogan: 'Roll Up, No Chinese'. Fearing a second Eureka Stockade, the government responded by significantly increasing the police presence in the Bathurst district. The immediate effect was to put further pressure on the native-born community as the extra police were kept busy running down stock duffers. The further effect was to give sufficient impetus to a renewed attempt to reorganise the still-fragmented New South Wales police force. This time the attempt was to prove successful, with a new centralised force established a year after the Lambing Flat riots.

Gardiner and Piesley, meanwhile, continued their depredations, which almost came to an end in July 1861. Acting on information received, Sergeant John Middleton and Constable William Hosie from Bigga police station went to the home of William Fogg, where they found Gardiner. When they attempted to arrest him, he fired at them. Both the police and Gardiner suffered gunshot wounds, but Gardiner was captured. Middleton didn't think Gardiner was going to live and left him, handcuffed on the floor, while he went for help.

What happened next depends on which version one tends to believe. Hosie gave evidence at the trial of Fogg (for harbouring Gardiner) that he despaired of Middleton returning and set out on the road to Bigga with Gardiner in custody. Not far from Fogg's house he was shot at by two bushrangers – Piesley and another man – and was forced to release Gardiner. Fogg had intervened in the affray to stop the bushrangers from shooting Hosie.

Piesley not only denied having done any such thing, a letter supposedly written by him was sent to the *Bathurst Free Press* on 4 September 1861. Piesley wrote: 'I will never be tried for the rescue of Gardiner, in the light in which it is represented; nor did I ever fire at Trooper Hosie. And such I wish to be known, that it is in my power to prove what I here assert, and that beyond a doubt.' He denied his involvement to his dying day.

Piesley's version of what happened is that Fogg bribed Hosie with £50 to let Gardiner go, and Hosie took the money.

In either case, based on Middleton and Hosie's evidence, Gardiner and Piesley were now facing the death sentence if captured. They had nothing to lose.

The identity of the third bushranger was not ascertained at the time. He was described as about twenty-six, 5 feet 6 inches [168 centimetres] in height, with light hair and whiskers, a small light moustache and a sallow complexion. It may have been Johnny Gilbert, who was described in 1863 as 'between 22 and 24 years of age, boyish appearance, 5 feet 7 or 8 inches [170 or 172 centimetres] high, between 9 and 10 stone [57 or 64 kilograms] weight, slight, light brown straight hair'.

Gilbert wasn't one of the native-born. He was born to English parents in Canada in 1842 who were lured to the goldfields in Victoria in 1852, when he was ten. An account of his early years has him bolting from his family not long after arriving in Melbourne. A writer to the *Sydney Mail* some years later described meeting him at a pub near the gold rush at the Ovens River:

He was then only a growing boy; but had even thus early apparently commenced his career on the road, for he was betting notes on every stroke of the billiard-table, and seemed to be possessed of any amount of money.

He was eventually arrested in Goulburn, for horse-stealing, and sent to what was to become something of a finishing school for bushrangers, Cockatoo Island, where he became acquainted (if he wasn't already) with Piesley and Gardiner.

Towards the end of 1861 reports of three bushrangers holding up travellers all around Bathurst proliferated. The *Bathurst Free Press* noted: 'Robberies have now become of such every day occurrence that we are surprised when a day passes without hearing that something fresh has occurred.' In fact, there was every suggestion there may have been more than one gang committing the crimes.

The bushrangers didn't have it all their own way. A writer to the *Bathurst Free Press* described one encounter:

> A few days afterwards a hut near Bland (between Cowra and Young) was attempted. One or two men were in this hut, when the door was burst open, and the usual salutation took place – 'Stand! Or your brains,' &c., &c.
>
> One of the men in hut sang out, 'Take care, Gardiner, what you about, for I am armed!'
>
> 'So am I,' was the reply, a shot being fired on the instant.
>
> The fire was returned, and the assailant was observed to reel back with a stagger as if shot, and shortly after made his escape without further molestation to the brave inmates of the hut; so you see . . . the folks out that way (Bland) are not to be trifled with.

Piesley also robbed on his own or with just one accomplice, as Gardiner may still have been recovering from the encounter at Bland. In September Piesley robbed a traveller on the road from Cowra to Marengo (now Murringo) and a hut at Marengo Gap. Late in October he robbed three more travellers while in company with an unidentified bushranger.

On 25 December 1861 John Piesley celebrated Christmas in true bushranger style. He went to the pub of Thomas McGuinness and began drinking. Three days later, he was still at it. By then, he and another man, James Wilson, had gone to the farm of childhood friends, William and Stephen Benyon, where the drinking continued. Piesley challenged Stephen Benyon to a fight, by any means he cared, but Benyon would have none of it. Eventually he relented, fought Piesley hand to hand, and flattened him.

When Piesley got up, his demons rose with him. He accused William Benyon of cheating him in a horse deal when they were kids. The Benyons tried to reason with Piesley, who then pulled a gun and threatened to 'settle' them. He fired at Stephen, hitting him in the arm. Stephen ran. The *Sydney Mail* of 1 March 1862 detailed the ensuing melee:

> Piesley then met a son of William Benyon's, and threatened to shoot him if he did not show him the way that Stephen ran, but the boy pointed in the wrong direction; Piesley then returned to the barn, and struck a man named George Hammond on the arm and side with the butt end of the gun, which went off while he was striking at him. William Benyon, Wilson and the servant girl then came up, when they were all bailed up in a corner of the barn yard. Piesley told William Benyon that he had got a ball in his revolver for him; that Benyon had had his game with him, and now he intended to have his game with Benyon. The servant girl got before her master, and entreated of Piesley not to shoot him. Benyon then sprang towards Piesley, it being his only chance to save his life, when Piesley shot him in the neck, and he fell on some straw; the bullet passed through the windpipe and lodged in the spine, and paralysed the whole of the limbs downwards. Benyon survived seven days.

When Piesley became a murderer, support for him rapidly disappeared. He certainly ceased to be a bushranger with Gardiner, although that relationship may already have been at an end before the incident at Benyon's.

Gardiner, on the other hand, was gathering recruits. On 13 January he, Johnny Gilbert, John O'Meally, John Davis and John McGuinness 'stuck up every person on the road to Lambing Flat'. On 14 January they stuck up the Bogolong Pub.

On 15 January 1862, a party of police caught up with Piesley. It was not to be their finest hour. According to the *Sydney Mail*:

Three of the police who are now scouring the Abercrombie country in search of Piesley, were returning from one of his hiding places towards Bigga, when the outlaw met them, mounted on a well-bred black horse. The three officers to whom he thus suddenly presented himself were Murphy and Sampson of the Western, and Morris, of the Goulburn police, the latter stationed along with district constable Pagett, at Binda.

On coming up, Piesley told them at once that he was the man they were looking for and, addressing himself further to Morris, said he should like to have 'a turn over with him', requesting him at the same time to dismount, and lay down his gun. To this, it would appear, Morris assented, having, however, a revolver concealed beneath his coat, and available in case of necessity. In thus acting there can be no doubt that Morris fully expected the challenger would follow his example, and calculated under such circumstances he would be more easily mastered.

Piesley, however, had no intention of dismounting, and after some further parleying with Morris and his companion, he turned his horse's head, put spurs to him and galloped away. Morris, immediately he noticed Piesley's purpose, fired at him with his revolver, but without effect, although the third bullet passed between the reins and the horse's neck, and Piesley called out 'that was a good one.'

We cannot help joining with the Bathurst journals and crying

> 'Shame' on the Western Patrol, whose business it specially has been to capture this robber and murderer.

A fortnight later Piesley narrowly escaped being captured by Constable Carroll at Tarcutta, near Wagga Wagga. He then travelled north to Mundarlo station. The manager of nearby Wantabadgery station, Mr Beveridge, rode to Tarcutta to inform the police that Piesley was there, then went back to Mundarlo, where the bushranger was now at the inn. When the police didn't show up, the locals took matters into their own hands. Innkeeper McKenzie, Beveridge and a man staying at the inn, James Campbell, decided to attempt a capture. They found Piesley in the kitchen, arguing with a drunk. The drunk was offering to fight him for a pound. James Campbell later wrote about the ensuing events:

> I began to get tired while they were wrangling, and sat down on the form beside Piesley, thinking about the safest way to catch him. He had his left hand on the table, and was lifting the cup of tea to his mouth, when I put my two arms under his arms, and getting my hands together, at the back of his, bent his head downwards and cocked his arms out. Mr McKenzie and Mr Beveridge then rushed on him. I told them to take the revolver from him, and Mr McKenzie put the handcuffs on him, and he was thus secured.

He was handed over to the police and transported back to the Bathurst district. He managed to escape from the Marengo police station, but was quickly recaptured and tried for the murder of William Benyon. On 13 March 1862 he was sentenced to death.

On 10 April 1862 police had another success with Gardiner's gang. Near Lambing Flat they came upon John Davis, John McGuinness, and a third man, John Connors. A ferocious gunfight ensued during which John Davis was shot down. He'd been shot twice in the head, in the thigh and wrist. Connors and McGuinness escaped, but Davis survived to stand trial. He was found guilty and sentenced to death but it was later commuted to fifteen years' imprisonment.

Davis appears to have been a particularly close friend of Gardiner. On 14 April 1862 Gardiner stopped a coach on the road to Lambing Flat, but didn't rob it. Instead, as the *Sydney Mail* reported, he was 'in search of someone, probably one or other of the police who shot and captured Davis at Brewer's . . . In all probability Gardner [sic] will stop Greig's coach with a strong armed party every time it passes along the road till he avenge the fall of his mate'.

Not long after, the body of John McGuinness was found in the bush. Again the *Sydney Mail* reported:

> There are strong reasons for believing that McGuinness was shot at the instance of Gardner himself, for deserting Davis during the late fight. McGuinness was standing in the bush . . . when a ball from a distant piece treacherously killed him on the spot . . . McGuinness lay unburied where he fell by the hands of his mates for three whole days.

At around the same time, four men stopped and robbed a dray 20 kilometres from Forbes. Three of the men were identified as John Youngman, Frank Gardiner and Ben Hall. Hall was a 25-year-old native-born who was leasing a 6500-hectare station, Sandy Creek, in the Lachlan Valley in partnership with a man named John Maguire. The two were related by marriage to two sisters, Ellen (married to Maguire) and Bridget Walsh. Hall had been born and raised in the Hunter Valley and was a highly skilled stockman. However, his family were not rich and where he obtained the capital to both lease and stock his station is a matter of surmise. Nevertheless, Hall had the looks and manner of a confident and capable young man on the rise.

It appears that at the time of his first robbery, his marriage to Bridget had already broken down and it's thought he was living with a woman called Betsy. He may have no longer been at Sandy Creek, although he remained on good terms with his partner, Maguire.

John Maguire, who paid his bail, also paid John Youngman's bail, after which Youngman bolted to parts unknown, never to be seen again. Hall managed to get off his charges when the dray driver, William Ferguson, became unsure of his identification of him. He is believed to have been bribed, by John Maguire.

At the time, so many robberies were being attributed to Gardiner that he ended up writing to the newspapers to set the record straight, as best he could, at the same time detailing his confidence and sense of honour. The *Lachlan Miner* of 19 April 1862 published one of them:

Sir,
Having seen a paragraph in one of the papers, wherein it is said that I took the boots off a man's feet, and that I also took the last few shillings that another man had, I wish it to be made known that I did not do anything of the kind. The man who took the boots was in my company, and for so doing I discharged him the following day. Silver I never took from a man yet, and the shot that was fired at the sticking up of Messrs Horsington and Hewitt was by accident, and the man who did it I also discharged. As for a mean, low, or petty action, I never committed it in my life . . . In all that has been said there was never any mention made of my taking the sergeant's horse and trying him, and that when I found he was no good I went back and got my own . . . A word to Sir W.F. Pottinger. He wanted to know how it was the man who led my horse up to me at the Pinnacle, did not cut my horses reins, as he gave me the horse. I should like to know if Mr Pottinger would do so? I shall answer by saying no. It has been said that it would be advisable to place a trap at each shanty on the road, to put a stop to

the depredations done on the road. I certainly think it would be a great acquisition to me, for I should then have increase of revolvers and carbines . . . Three of your troopers were at a house the other night and got drinking and gambling till all hours. I came there towards morning when all was silent. The first room that I went into I found revolvers and carbines to any amount, but seeing none as good as my own, I left them . . .

Fearing nothing, I remain, Prince of Tobymen, Frances Gardner [sic] the Highwayman.

Sir W.F. Pottinger was Frederick William Pottinger, newly appointed inspector of police in the western district of the newly organised force under the 1862 *Police Regulation Act*.

If there's any truth in the adage 'set a thief to catch a thief', Pottinger would have been the perfect appointment. The son of Lieutenant-General Sir Henry Pottinger had been forced to flee his debts in England after gambling away his inheritance. After equally poor luck on the Australian goldfields, he eventually joined the New South Wales police force. He kept his knighthood secret (perhaps to avoid revealing how far he'd fallen), but when it was discovered, he was rapidly promoted. He continued to rise through the ranks despite his involvement in a drunken brawl at Lambing Flat at Christmas 1861 that earned him a public rebuke from the premier of New South Wales, Charles Cowper.

It is perhaps significant that Gardiner and his men were at pains to make it clear that they were honourable in their robberies, particularly in their dealings with women. To some extent this may have been dictated by their reliance on the support of family and friends that would evaporate if they transgressed an unwritten 'Bushranger's Code'. Certainly, support for Piesley disappeared after the murder of William Benyon.

Of course, Gardiner's protest that he 'never stole a shilling' was as pragmatic as it was honourable. Robbing poor people of small change wasn't worth the trouble. And one woman who wasn't robbed while her husband was relieved of nearly £200 told the bushrangers, 'Thanks for nothing.' She wasn't robbed directly, but she'd still suffered a major loss.

From the outset there was much criticism of the newly organised New South Wales police force. The reorganisation saw much of the force's experience lost as preference was given to migrant officers over the native-born. The promotion of Sir Frederick Pottinger on the basis of a title, rather than merit, was just one example. A writer to *Empire Magazine* less than a year after the organisation was completed noted the differences between the old and new:

> The system had grown out of the penal times, and it embraced the matured art of thief catching in the bush of Australia, as practiced by experienced officers who, in their respective districts, were like spiders in the centre of their webs, cognisant not only of every illicit movement, but of every flutter of their lawful prey. But all this having been swept away, bushranging became rampant at once.

In 1862 only thirteen out of thirty-five senior officers in the force were former officers. Those former chief constables who were accepted into the new force were transferred to new districts in the hope that it would sever them from any corrupting influences. Matters were not helped by the lack of adequate facilities. Many police stations didn't have cells. Others were far from escape-proof, as has been seen in previous chapters. In one case, there was nowhere to hold three bushrangers arrested at Bourke in 1862, so they were kept in a kitchen for six weeks until they could be taken to a proper gaol. In other cases they were handcuffed to bullock chains.

Frank Gardiner's letter to the *Lachlan Miner* identified other matters that hampered police. He refers to 'trying' the horse of a sergeant of police and returning it because it wasn't up to the standard required by a bushranger. In 1862, and for some years after, police couldn't legally commandeer a fresh horse when in pursuit of a bushranger. Gardiner also mentioned finding a cache of police weapons, none of which were as good as the weapons he had.

The consequence was that when police pursued a well-mounted second-generation bushranger, the chances of getting close enough to make an arrest were low. In the lucky event that it happened, the bushranger was better armed for the encounter. So, as the fledgling New South Wales police force was settling into its new configuration and ironing out the teething problems inevitable with any new organisation, it was woefully unprepared for what was to be one of the greatest challenges in its entire history.

8

Eugowra

1862

At noon on Sunday, 15 June 1862, the regular gold escort from Forbes, in western New South Wales, departed for Orange carrying 2067 ounces of gold and £700 from the Oriental Bank; 521 ounces of gold from the bank of New South Wales; and 129 ounces of gold and £3000 owned by the Commercial Banking Company – a total value in today's figures of around $10 million. The escort was under the command of Sergeant Condell with John Fagan driving and troopers Henry Moran, William Havilland and possibly a third, unnamed officer also on board.

Near the present-day town of Eugowra the road passed a rocky outcrop before fording Mandagery Creek. At four or five o'clock in the afternoon, as the escort approached the rocks, the road was partially blocked by two bullock teams that had apparently chosen such an inconvenient place to stop. The bullocks had settled down and were quietly chewing their cud. The drivers were nowhere to be seen.

To pass the bullocks the escort had to pass close to the rocks. It was just level with them when a volley of shots rang out. Seven bushrangers sprang from ambush behind the rocks.

Constable Moran fell in the first round of firing, shot through the groin; Sergeant Condell was hit in the side. The escort horses attempted to bolt, startled by the noise, and the coach lurched forward, struck the edge of the rocks, and overturned. Constables Fagan and Havilland were thrown to the ground, disoriented. The bushrangers, all dressed in red shirts and with their faces blackened, closed in, still firing.

'Shoot the bloody wretches,' one of them reportedly cried.

Fagan and Havilland, their clothing pierced by bullets but themselves unharmed, managed to fire one shot each before they surrendered. The bushrangers, now numbering as many as a dozen, swooped in. They had, in fact, been coordinating their gunfire, with one squad of six or seven firing while the second squad reloaded.

Now they commenced looting the escort, and managed to make off with most of the gold and money. The haul rivalled the robbery at the Ballarat branch of the Bank of Victoria in 1854 and was more than double the amount stolen from the McIvor Gold Escort in 1853 (although almost a carbon copy in its execution). It was the biggest haul in bushranging history. More than that, in a matter of a few minutes it had dealt a near-fatal blow to the prestige of the New South Wales police force.

Initially, none of the bushrangers could be identified, except Frank Gardiner. Sergeant Condell wrote in his official report, 'The bushrangers were commanded by one man, who gave them orders to fire and load. I believe it to have been the voice of Gardiner, as I know his voice well. I cannot identify any of them with the exception of the voice I heard.'

When the news reached Forbes, later that night, Sir Frederick Pottinger immediately set out with eleven troopers and two trackers, as well as a number of civilian volunteers. He also sent Sergeant

Sanderson, superintendent of the Bathurst police force, with four men and a black tracker, to follow the Lachlan River down in case the bushrangers made for their usual haunts in the Weddin Mountains.

Sir Frederick reached the crime scene at 2 a.m. on Monday, where the tracks of the bushrangers were easily found and followed. They led through rough country to a lofty ridge 5 kilometres from the Eugowra Rocks, where the bushrangers had camped. The embers of a fire were still burning, consuming the shirts and scarves the bushrangers had used to hide their identities. The mailbags had been searched for valuables and then discarded. Many of the registered letters, potentially containing significant sums of money, were ignored.

The police paused only briefly before continuing their pursuit, only to have men drop out as their horses 'knocked up' (became exhausted) in the rugged terrain. The bushrangers were headed towards the vicinity of Forbes. When the pursuers were 20 kilometres from the town, heavy rain set in, making the tracks difficult to follow. By then the trackers thought the bushrangers had split up, as there now seemed to be fewer horses in the group they were following.

Sergeant Sanderson, an experienced local, was having better luck. He headed for the Weddin Mountains and the then home of Ben Hall. They were nearly there when Sanderson's tracker saw a horseman riding down the ridge of a nearby mountain. The horseman also saw the police and immediately turned and rode away at speed. The pursuit was on. The police galloped to where the horseman was seen.

His tracks were then followed several kilometres over the mountain. They were lost for a moment in a creek bed then found on the other side where the rider had jumped his mount clear across. The tracks led straight to a bush camp. A billy of tea was still on the fire, bread and beef were left as if dropped in a hurry. A discarded set of scales suggested that the camp had been the site where the gold had been divided.

The fresh tracks of five horses led away from the camp, heading further into the Weddin Mountains. The police rode hard, following the trail through dense bush and rugged terrain, and were rewarded when the tracker called out that he'd caught sight of the bushrangers. Sanderson and his men broke into a gallop, but their tiring mounts were no match for those of the bushrangers. The bushrangers, who were four in number, spurred their horses to get away, and turned loose their fifth horse, a riderless packhorse. It was found to be carrying about half of the gold taken from the escort.

The bushrangers still couldn't shake the trackers. All they could do was outdistance them as they led them on a tour of the Weddin Mountains. Only at nightfall did the bushrangers make good their escape.

Sir Frederick was now heading south, following the trail of five bushrangers and two packhorses apparently making their way to Victoria. He was a day's travel behind them. By then, his team was reduced to himself, a former police officer named Mitchell, and a detective named Lyons. They met a coach travelling north and were informed that one of the men in the group was almost certainly Gardiner. They continued on until they reached Hay, whereupon the trail apparently went cold.

They turned back and on 30 June, near Merool station, came upon three men, mounted, each with a packhorse. Noting the quality of their mounts, Sir Frederick asked one of the men if he had a receipt for the horse. While the man searched for his papers, he edged his horse away and when he had a clear path, he drove in his spurs and galloped off. Rather than pursue, Sir Frederick and Mitchell covered the other two men with their revolvers.

They gave their names as Charles Darcey and Henry Turner. The names meant nothing to the police, but the contents of their saddle-bags, £150 in notes from the Commercial Banking Company and 213 ounces of gold, told them a great deal. The two men were handcuffed for the journey back to Forbes, 250 kilometres away. Two days later, in the early afternoon, the prisoners were being escorted with Detective Lyons in the lead and Sir Frederick and Mr Mitchell behind them. Suddenly, three men emerged from the bush, their faces blackened and wearing red caps.

'Bail up, you bastard!' they reportedly shouted, and immediately fired at Lyons. His horse was shot in the neck, reared and threw him before he could fire a shot. He lost his revolver in the fall and bolted into the bush.

Four more men emerged from the bush and started firing at Sir Frederick and Mitchell, while the other three reloaded. The pair returned their fire, galloped away to reload, then came back to continue the fight. Only when they ran low on ammunition did they retreat to a nearby station. They had lost their two prisoners, but they still had the gold. Lyons had managed to lose the £150 when he was thrown from his horse.

Sir Frederick returned to Forbes with the gold under guard. The men named Darcey and Turner were re-arrested not long after – Darcey at Murrumburrah and Turner at Yass. In Forbes, Sergeant Sanderson arrested Patrick O'Meally, John O'Meally and a man named Trotter, all on suspicion of involvement in the robbery. Sir Frederick and Sergeant Sanderson then got a tip that Frank Gardiner was at Wheogo.

Sir Frederick reported what took place:

Being aware that Frank Gardiner, the bushranger, was enamoured of Mrs Brown, and believing that he would take advantage of her husband's absence to tender his addresses, I proceeded on Saturday with eight men to the premises; I arrived at 12 PM, and leaving four of the men in charge I went with Senior-Sergeant Sanderson and Trooper Holster to watch the place; I subsequently sent Sub-Inspector Norton and Trooper Holster to guard the front while Senior-Sergeant Sanderson and I hid ourselves in the bush; we discovered the house dark and silent as though everybody was asleep; after about half an hour we saw a light struck and in a few minutes a woman made her appearance and commenced to collect wood for the purpose of making a fire, but neither Sergeant Sanderson nor I could identify the woman, as we were concealed at a distance of 150 yards [137 metres] from where she was standing, in a thick pine-tree scrub; it might be 20 or 25 minutes after my seeing the woman that I observed a man mounted on a white horse approaching Brown's house at a quiet pace, upon which I called upon Sanderson to fall back, and we did so to our original position; suddenly the noise of horses hoofs sounded nearer and nearer, when I saw Gardiner cantering leisurely along; I waited until he came within five yards [4.5 metres] of me, and levelling my carbine at him across his horse's shoulder (the weapon, I swear, being about three yards [2.7 metres] from his body) I called upon him to stand; I cannot be mistaken, and on my oath I declare that the man was Frank Gardiner; deeming it not advisable to lose a chance I prepared to shoot him, but the cap of my piece missed fire; Gardiner's horse then began to rear and plunge, and before I had time to adjust my gun, he had bolted into the bush; as Gardiner was riding away on the back of the frightened animal, Sergeant Sanderson fired at him, as also did Holster; I called out to those who could hear me to 'shoot the wretch'. Gardiner, however, made his escape; we then proceeded to Mrs Brown's house, and having seen her she frankly admitted that Gardiner had been at her place; I saw a bed made upon the sofa, and a four-post bedstead with a bed upon it in which two persons had been reposing.

Even by Sir Frederick's admission it was a grossly bungled operation. With him in command, nine men couldn't catch one man.

Once again the capable Sergeant Sanderson was able to get results on his own. On 27 July 1862 he went back to Wheogo and arrested John Maguire, Ben Hall, John Brown, Dan Charters and William Hall on suspicion of cattle-stealing. One of the men was found to have notes thought to be stolen in the Eugowra escort robbery. All the men were subsequently charged with their involvement in robbing the escort. The legality of the arrests was questionable, even if the involvement of some of the men was probable. While their lawyers argued for their release, the police put pressure on the imprisoned men.

They finally got a breakthrough after Dan Charters was released on bail. He went to see Sergeant Sanderson and confessed his involvement. He also named Alexander Fordyce, John Bow, Henry Manns, John O'Meally, John Maguire, Johnny Gilbert, Frank Gardiner and several other men as being involved.

His confession resulted in some of the men already in gaol being released, a month after their arrest. Fordyce and Bow were taken into custody. Henry Manns turned out to be under arrest already. He was the man who called himself Turner. Hall and O'Meally were eventually released due to lack of evidence.

Fordyce, Bow, Maguire and Manns were subsequently tried for their involvement in the escort robbery. Maguire was acquitted of being an accessory. The other three were found guilty and sentenced to death. The sentences of Fordyce and Bow were commuted to life imprisonment.

The state government executive decided not to commute Manns' sentence, as an example to others – despite the fact that on Charters' evidence, Manns' involvement in the escort robbery may have been slight. Charters' evidence could only establish his presence at Eugowra, as Charters had minimised his own involvement to that of watching the horses of the other men.

There were numerous petitions sent to the government pleading for leniency in the treatment of Manns. One, quoted in Charles White's *History of Australian Bushranging*, noted that 'the prisoner is a young man who has passed his life in the interior away from all moral and religious training'. In fact while the government was reaping a bonanza from the gold being taken from the western districts, it was penny-pinching when it came to providing any services for the rural poor in the same areas.

In the end, Manns' death proved to be yet another acutely low point in the administration of New South Wales. As the *Sydney Mail* reported on 28 March 1863:

> When . . . the bolt was drawn, there ensued one of the most appalling spectacles ever witnessed at an execution. The noose of the rope, instead of passing tightly round the neck, slipped completely away, the knot coming round in front of the face, while the whole weight of the criminal's body was sustained by the thick muscles of the poll [head and neck] . . .
>
> The sufferings and struggles of the wretched being were heartrending to behold. His body swayed about, and writhed, evidently in the most intense agony. The arms repeatedly rose and fell, and finally with one of his hands the unfortunate man gripped the rope as if to tear the pressure from his head – a loud guttural noise the meanwhile proceeding from his throat and lungs, while blood gushed from his nostrils and stained the cap with which his face was covered. This awful scene lasted for more than ten minutes, when stillness ensued, and it was hoped that death had terminated the culprit's sufferings. Shocking to relate, however, the vital spark was not yet extinguished, and to the horror of all present, the convulsive writhings were renewed . . . and a repetition of the sickening scene was only at last terminated at the instance of Dr. West, with the aid of four confines, who were made to hold the dying malefactor up in their arms while the executioner readjusted the rope, when the body was let fall with a jerk, and another minute sufficed to end the agonies of death.

As at least some of the culprits in the Eugowra escort robbery were brought to justice, Sergeant Sanderson was promoted to sub-inspector, having all but done his boss's job for him. Despite demonstrating that he had been promoted beyond his level of competence, Sir Frederick kept his rank.

Frank Gardiner, having introduced perhaps a dozen men to a life of crime, eluded the police and completely disappeared. He took with him Kitty Brown. Some accounts suggest that all the money and gold from the escort robbery was recovered. However, as much as 1000 ounces of gold and several thousand pounds remained in the hands of the bushrangers. When the proceeds of countless other highway robberies are considered, Gardiner may have collected quite a large nest egg.

Johnny Gilbert also fled the vicinity of the New South Wales diggings. 'Happy Jack', as he was called, was probably the horseman who galloped away from Sir Frederick Pottinger. He and his brothers (Charles and James) went first to Victoria, then on to New Zealand, prospecting for gold.

For those who remained, the police turned up the heat. When Sir Frederick had failed to catch Frank Gardiner, he'd arrested a fifteen-year-old boy, a brother of Kate Brown he'd found in her house at the time. 'Warrigal Walsh' was held in the cells in Forbes for six months while Pottinger tried to convict him of any charge that would stick. The boy was still there, uncharged, when he died of 'gaol fever' (probably pneumonia).

While Ben Hall and John O'Meally were in prison, in August 1862, Sir Fred had their homes burned to the ground, probably illegally. His actions achieved nothing. The reality was that a few bit players were convicted while the ringleaders escaped. For the downtrodden rural workers, the underclass and underdogs, from whose ranks the robbers came, it was a huge win. Their heroes had outgunned and outridden the police. They had shown themselves to be men of action. In a fair fight between the anti-authoritarian native-born and the English migrants determined to impose their system of policing and feudal employment and land allocation on the Australian bush, there was no question who had triumphed.

From the perspective of social banditry, if bushranging was a forerunner of Australian nationalism and workers' unity and unionism, it may not have been able to articulate its goals, but it had certainly achieved them. While Eugowra may not have marked the beginning of bushranging in the 1860s, it was certainly a high point. And it turned out to be a long way from the end.

9

Bushranging triumphant

1862–1864

By the end of 1862 Johnny Gilbert had tired of gold prospecting in the land of the Long White Cloud and returned to the Lachlan River district. There John O'Meally and Ben Hall may have endured the harassment of Sir Frederick Pottinger until they were provoked to turn to bushranging. Either that or, as criminals who get away with one crime tend to be, they were confident that they were smarter than the law and could get away with it again. And for the likes of Gilbert, O'Meally and Hall, the glamour and excitement of bushranging was a stark contrast to the usual routine of rural life. When they could take the toffs down a peg or two at the same time, how could they resist?

On Gilbert's return, the boyish 22-year-old, who was so perennially cheerful that he was also known as Happy Jack, became the leader of what had been the Gardiner Gang, but would soon become the Gilbert-Hall Gang.

Fred Lowry had a long association with Frank Gardiner, having served a sentence on Cockatoo Island for horse-stealing. However, he was operating on his own on 1 January 1863 when he and a friend, John Foley, attempted to hold up more than a hundred punters at a race meeting at Brisbane Valley, on Fish River Creek, in the Lachlan district.

Lowry was marching a crowd of hostages towards McQuirk's Pub, a revolver in each hand, when he noticed a man standing outside. He ordered the man to go with the others, but the man refused, saying he was 'not afraid of his revolvers'.

Lowry reportedly hit the man across the face, causing the revolver in his hand to go off. The bullet hit and wounded a tethered horse.

The gunshot and ensuing commotion brought another young man, named Foran, out of the pub. It may have been his horse that was shot. In any case, he went for Lowry without a moment's hesitation.

'Stand back!' Lowry shouted, but Foran ignored him. Lowry fired, the bullet hitting Foran in the chest and passing through his right lung. Despite his wound, Foran grappled with Lowry, while Foley took to his horse and escaped. Several men came to Foran's assistance and Lowry was captured. He was charged with shooting with intent to kill. It may have been Lowry's first attempt at bushranging, and it appeared that, like many would-be bushrangers, it would also be his last.

However, on 13 February 1863, he was awaiting trial in Bathurst Gaol when someone from a road party working outside the gaol passed a pickaxe to him and four other prisoners through a drain that ran under the prison wall. The men congregated in a corner of the yard, screening the view of the one warder who was in a watch-house at the far end of the yard. They began removing bricks from the wall until there was a hole 45–60 centimetres square.

According to the *Bathurst Free Press* of 14 February 1863:

> The alarm was first given by Mr. H. Blunden, who was crossing the square, and observed a hole in the gaol wall. He saw two men get

> through the hole; but seeing that the bricklayers were at work upon the wall, he did not take much notice of the matter until one of the men passed him, saying, 'Don't say anything about it, old fellow' or something like it. His suspicions were then aroused, and he ran to the gate of the gaol and gave the alarm. In the mean time, before he could return to the hole in the wall, three other prisoners made their escape . . .

All five, including Lowry, fled before they could be captured.

In early March a tracker arrived at Forbes with an extraordinary story to tell. He said that 'a desperate conflict had taken place between sixteen bushrangers and a body of mounted troopers' and that 'Inspector Norton', a new appointment in the western district, had been captured. He said the bushrangers claimed they would hang Norton if the escort robbers – Fordyce, Bow and Manns – were executed.

When Sub-Inspector Norton (his actual rank) was released, only a few hours later, he told a quite different story. According to him, the force he was commanding hadn't met him at a rendezvous in the Weddin Mountains, leaving him and the Aboriginal tracker dangerously exposed. Three bushrangers confronted him when he and the Aboriginal tracker stumbled on their camp. When he'd used all his ammunition against them they took him prisoner. He was released three hours later, having done nothing to offend the bushrangers because he was a 'new chum' in the district, plus he had a wife and family in Sydney. Norton (as reported in the *Maitland Mercury* of 14 March 1863) identified his attackers as O'Meally, Patsy Daley and Ben Hall. He regarded them as cowardly and said that if he'd managed to shoot one, the others would have fled.

The fact remains that Norton's story and that of the tracker bear little relation to each other. As with many bushranging stories, the various versions tend to cast the teller in the most heroic light, or least criminal light. In this case, Norton's version may have saved the police from the embarrassment of humiliating defeat at the hands of the bushrangers.

Throughout the rest of March there were robberies and police pursuits, but in most cases the police were outdistanced by their quarry, who were mounted on the best horses a bushranger could steal. From the Goulburn district north to the Hunter Valley, the number of incidents steadily increased.

In early April a bushranger was shot dead near Mudgee, during a robbery he was committing in company with another man. He was a local in the district, who'd worked as a timber cutter and bullocky. Mudgee's *Western Post* noted that at the inquest into the bushranger's death, 'Several members of the "Bush Telegraph" were present during the investigation, evidently deeply interested in the proceedings.'

The bushranger's colleague was subsequently captured in western New South Wales after a police pursuit reputed to have covered 300 kilometres.

April also saw other bushrangers captured. Daley, one of the bushrangers Sub-Inspector Norton said had captured him, was himself apprehended by Sir Fred Pottinger. While Norton couldn't confirm his identity, his tracker and other people he'd robbed could. Another associate of Gardiner's gang, John Connors, was captured by constables Wright and Cleary after Daley had robbed the Sydney to Mudgee mail. After his capture he boasted that 'he knew Gardiner, Gilbert and all the gang who were creating such a sensation in the country'.

By the end of April, it appears that the Gilbert-Hall Gang, as it became known after Gardiner's disappearance, had recruited more members. The escaped Fred Lowry had joined Gilbert, Hall and O'Meally. While police and military patrols scoured the Goulburn and Forbes districts, the gang struck at widely dispersed locations, drawing police resources first in one direction, then another. At all times, they were provided with high-quality intelligence regarding police movements by their sympathisers and bush telegraphs.

To counter the support base of the bushrangers, during April police in the region were provided with details of property ownership and commenced checking the occupancy of runs of 'cockatoo squatters' who were thought to be helping the gang. It was hoped that by cutting off their sources of information, apprehending the bushrangers would be made easier.

Of course, increasing the workload for the police didn't help. Businessman John Barnes wrote to the *Yass Courier* on 29 April 1863:

> Sir.- . . . On Tuesday morning last [21 April], at sunrise, my son's store at Cootamundry [sic] was stuck up by four armed and mounted men [Gilbert, Lowry, O'Meally and Hall], and property &c. valued at about £100 stolen and taken away on pack-horses. There must be something wrong in our police arrangements, as up to Thursday morning, none of the police made their appearance – and I think did not till Saturday, although information was sent on Tuesday. I believe the same four men were on the road between Wallendbeen and Cootamundry on Saturday last, apparently courting the appearance of the police, who of course could be seen going the other way, the usual course being to put in an appearance about a week after the commission of the robbery.

With each success, the gang grew in confidence. On 7 June they began a spree of robberies from Opossum Flat, where they robbed the stores, all the way along the road to Lambing Flat. They robbed O'Brien's, McCarthy's, McConnell's, Hooley's, Heffernan's and Regan's pubs.

A week later, on 14 June, Gilbert and Lowry bailed up a number of drays near Marengo, but their robbery was more like shopping. They took tea, sugar and bottles of gin from their victims. One of the victims, a German saddler, was interviewed by a local newspaper:

> In answer to a question from our reporter, he said he gave no information to the police, nor did he intend to do so, as he, in common with everybody else, considered it useless. How long is society to continue thus disorganised, and its present state of insecurity to life and property to exist, and how long will the country bear with the reign of terror before it hurls the present imbecile police before the winds?

The Gilbert-Hall Gang's continued success encouraged others, and on 17 June 1863 Daniel Morgan stepped onto the bushranging stage. Dan was thirty-three, of average height, and distinguished by a long beard that surrounded his face. A *New South Wales Police Gazette* article from 29 March 1865 described him as 'loose jointed' and that he 'seems to have weak knees [and] speaks slowly and quietly'. His 'loose joints' may actually have been the result of a life spent in the saddle.

Dan undertook his first robbery in Victoria in 1854 and was sentenced to twelve years' imprisonment by Redmond Barry, of which he served six before gaining a ticket-of-leave in 1860.

He'd stopped reporting to police a month later, and moved to north-east Victoria where he worked as a horse breaker – supplementing his income with the occasional horse theft. In August 1861 a stolen horse was tracked to a cave where Dan was sleeping. The men tracking the horse, Evan Evans and Edmund Bond, fired at Dan and hit him. Despite having twenty-seven pieces of shot in his right arm and shoulder, Dan managed to escape. He went to the New South Wales Riverina, where he made a living catching brumbies in the high country then breaking and selling them.

He must have decided there was easier money in bushranging. On 17 June 1863 he robbed John Manson and two other men at Walla Walla, 50 kilometres north of Albury. Flushed with success, the following day he robbed seven more men. He had become just one more of the growing number of bushrangers west of the Great Divide.

On 21 June 1863 gold prospector John McBride was on his way to church when he passed by Duffer Gully, near Lambing Flat. A woman who kept a shanty there, Margaret Sinnet, had been entertaining a two men who she suspected were bushrangers. One was probably the distinctively tall Fred Lowry, who had a belt lined with revolvers.

When Lowry and the other man saw McBride, they approached him and bailed him up. McBride only had a few shillings, but he was also armed. He drew his revolver and attempted to open fire. His first two shots missed fire, and the bushrangers retreated. He then drew a Colt Navy revolver, of the type issued to New South Wales police, and fired three more shots.

Seeing the weapon, the bushrangers assumed he was an off-duty policeman and decided to attack him. McBride had only two shots left, so moved to cover behind a tree. Unfortunately, the two bushrangers separated and approached him from two sides. One fired at him and shot him in the thigh. McBride fell, hit in a major artery. The bushrangers robbed him of his meagre amount of cash.

The two then set about robbing nearly everyone who passed along the road. According to the *Sydney Mail* of 4 July 1863:

> To give a detailed account of the daring proceedings of these desperadoes on this eventful day would fill a volume, and therefore I must content myself by briefly stating that men and women, singly or in company with their friends or families, whether walking or riding, were indiscriminately stopped, ordered to stand, and plundered of what they possessed . . . Another precaution taken by the desperadoes on Sunday morning was that of cutting the telegraph wires which communicate with this district and the metropolis by way of Forbes.

McBride died on the journey to Lambing Flat, despite being attended by a doctor. His murder sparked further outrage among law-abiding citizens, but once again, to no avail.

On 13 July 1863 Fred Lowry had the best day of his career. He was joined by his former partner in crime, John Foley, the man who'd fled after Lowry had attempted to stick up the Brisbane Valley racegoers at the beginning of the year. They lay in wait for the Mudgee mail, bound for Sydney, at the top of the steep climb it had to negotiate at Ben Bullen. The coach had two passengers – Henry Kater, from the Joint Stock Bank, and Mrs Smith, who ran an inn with her husband.

Henry Kater had alighted from the coach to lighten it on the climb. Mrs Smith may have done so as well, while the driver, William Tinker, urged his horses up the climb. They all saw two men casually riding down the slope towards them. When they reached the coach, one of the men grabbed the horses' harnesses; the other drew a revolver and bailed up Henry Kater. Kater pulled a gun, but John Foley prevented him from using it. The revolver was taken from him and one of the bushrangers added it to the arsenal of revolvers stuck in his belt.

'Now I have eight,' the bushranger, probably Fred Lowry, reportedly said.

The coach was then turned off the road and taken into the bush, where it couldn't be seen by passers-by. Kater was searched and relieved of a gold watch and chain. Mrs Smith, who was carrying £200 in takings from her inn, wasn't searched. The bushrangers said they never molested women.

Lowry then turned to William Tinker. 'Now I'll see, driver,' he said, 'what you have got aboard.'

He searched the coach and the mailbags, opening every letter. He then searched Henry Kater's carpet bag. Inside he found a huge bundle of banknotes.

Lowry exclaimed, 'We've just copped you right, today, mate.'

Kater was carrying £5700 from his bank, the amount representing the fourth biggest haul in bushranging history to that date, after the robberies of the Eugowra and McIvor gold escorts and the Ballarat branch of the Bank of Victoria. Kater told Lowry the banknotes were useless, as they were being taken to Sydney to be destroyed.

'Never mind,' one of the bushrangers reputedly replied. 'We can make a bonfire of them.'

The bushrangers then turned the coach horses loose and rode off. Kater rode to the police station at Hartley. Sub-Inspector Norton and four troopers set off in pursuit, to no avail. That afternoon, Mrs Smith again met Lowry, Foley and a third man, Larry Cummins, bushranging on the road to Hartley.

Notes from the robbery were soon circulating south of the robbery – at Goulburn and Braidwood. When police searched the home of the mother of John Foley, they found one of the notes from the robbery, but not the thousands that had disappeared almost without trace.

After a robbery of such magnitude, it hardly seemed necessary for the bushrangers to do any more. However, only a fortnight later, on 26 July, Larry Cummins with his younger brother John, robbed two men at Richlands.

Dan Morgan was also active towards the end of July. On 29 July he bailed up Wallandool station. He tied the owner, the manager and their friend to trees.

On 2 August Michael Burke and John Vane, new members of the Gilbert-Hall Gang, robbed Coombing station, near Carcoar. Vane came from a well-to-do family that lived in the area. The two young men, who with Burke's cousin James had been stealing horses and cattle since their youth, attempted to steal two fine horses from the station. One belonged to Police Inspector Davidson, who was enjoying the hospitality of the station's owner, Mr Icely, after a day spent tracking bushrangers; the other belonged to Icely, and was one of his best mounts. As they were stealing the horses, Burke and Vane were confronted by a station worker, German Charley. Burke responded by shooting at the man, hitting him in the mouth. The pair then rode off, leaving in their wake a hornet's nest of futile activity.

The police had a better day on 6 August when Senior Constable Murphy and Constable Molloy managed to arrest John Cummins, who had been involved in the robbery at Richlands eleven days before. He didn't remain in custody for long. While he was being escorted to the lockup a shot was fired at the police from an ambush. It hit Cummins instead, killing him.

At the same time, police also arrested three men who they suspected of being sympathisers and bush telegraphs for the Gilbert-Hall Gang. They attempted to transport them from the town of Carcoar to Bathurst in the mail coach, with a police escort that consisted of Superintendent Morrissett, Sergeant Grainger and Senior Constable Merrin in the coach, and Trooper Sutton riding behind the coach on the superintendent's horse.

Five kilometres from Carcoar, three bushrangers burst from cover and called on the coach to stop. The police piled out and exchanged fire with the bushrangers. Sutton, the only mounted policeman, charged the bushrangers, one of whom was riding Mr Icely's horse, another of whom was riding Inspector Davidson's mount.

Trooper Sutton fired two shots, but was hit in the arm and chest by shots from the bushrangers and was forced to retreat. The gunfire continued for some time before the bushrangers eventually gave up the attempt to free their friends and galloped away. They were later identified as Gilbert, O'Meally and Vane.

The temptation to join the bushranging gang was explained in a letter written by a Carcoar resident on 9 August 1863:

I believe there is scarcely a house between Mount Macquarie and the Abercrombie River that will not afford any criminal shelter when required, and I am satisfied that there are hundreds of lads in that neighbourhood under twenty that would give one of their eyes to have the same notoriety as Gilbert and Gardiner. They never work, never have worked, and are without exception the flashest lot I ever did see.

Something must be done by the Government or things will become worse and worse, and what will be the end of it no one can tell.

On 23 August Dan Morgan and an accomplice, German Bill, were standing on the Wagga Wagga–Urana Road when they saw Wagga Wagga police magistrate Henry Baylis riding towards them. The magistrate feared the worst when he saw the men and galloped away. Four kilometres down the road, thinking himself safe, he stopped to talk to a man driving a dray. Shortly after, two horsemen galloped towards him.

Morgan and German Bill were now mounted. Baylis tried to escape into the scrub, but was soon bailed up. The magistrate wasn't carrying anything of value and Morgan returned what little there was. Nevertheless, Baylis sent word to the Wagga Wagga police to meet him when he finished holding the business of his court at Urana. When they arrived, he set out in pursuit of the bushrangers.

While he was following that trail, on 24 August, the Gilbert-Hall gang was busy on the Lambing Flat Road, robbing four stores.

Back in the Wagga Wagga district, Baylis caught up with Morgan and German Bill on 26 August. In an exchange of gunfire Baylis was able to shoot German Bill, but was himself shot. Morgan and German Bill managed to escape. It wasn't realised at the time, but German Bill was fatally wounded. His remains weren't found until two years later. Baylis survived his wounds. The following night a shepherd was shot dead in a nearby hut at Urangeline Creek. His killer was never identified, but it was strongly suspected that Morgan had executed the man in revenge for passing information to the police.

In late August 1863, Lowry and Larry Cummins were in the environs of Crookwell. Cummins' family lived in the area and Cummins had many friends there that he'd known since childhood. He went to see one of them, Michael Hogan, after which he and Fred Lowry moved on to Cummins' local watering hole at Cooks Vale Creek. The Limerick Races Inn was owned by Tom Vardy, who'd known Cummins since he was a boy. Cummins and Lowry spent the evening of 28 August there, ate dinner, had a few drinks then went to bed at around nine or ten o'clock. They both slept in a small room off the parlour.

They were still there at 7 a.m. when detectives Camphin and Saunderson, Senior Sergeant James Stephenson and Constable Herbert arrived at the inn, having received information that Lowry might be there. All was quiet except for a girl on the verandah who seemed frightened by the arrival of the police and was 'half-crying'. Constable Herbert was sent to cover the rear of the building. Camphin stayed at the front while Stephenson and Saunderson rode up to the inn and dismounted.

They went inside and called for Vardy, then asked if he had any strangers in the house. He nodded to the door leading off the parlour. According to Stephenson (as reported in the *Argus*, 9 September 1863):

> I asked if he knew who they were. He said, 'No,' and to look out. I went to the parlour-door adjoining the room he mentioned and leading to it. It was locked inside; I knocked and asked for admittance; I got no answer; I then said if the door was not opened at once I would break it open; I then knocked my shoulder against the door for the purpose of breaking it open; I failed in the first attempt, and I no sooner took my shoulder away than a shot was fired from inside, and a voice exclaimed 'I'll fight you b-----s'; the shot came through the door and wounded the horse I had been riding; I removed the horse from that place and gave him to Vardy, and told him I should hold him responsible for him; I then went back to the bar-door, and then the parlour door was opened and a man came out with a revolver in each hand, crying out 'I'm Lowry;

> come on ye b-----s and I'll fight ye fair'; at the same time he presented one of the revolvers at me; I covered him directly; I think we both fired together; at that time we were four or five yards [3.5 to 4.5 metres] apart; he then advanced upon me within three feet [1 metre]; I then covered him again and we both fired in each other's faces; the second shot I fired he dropped his revolvers and staggered; I jumped forward and seized him by the neck, struck him with my revolver on the head, and told him he was my prisoner.

Despite being shot, Lowry continued to struggle. With the help of Saunderson, Stephenson dragged him into the yard, rolled him onto his back, got his knee onto his chest and handcuffed him. According to Stephenson, 'He then said he was Lowry and was done.' He'd been shot in the throat.

Stephenson left Lowry with Saunderson and went back into the inn. When he entered Lowry's room, Cummins was only just getting out of bed. He was captured without a shot being fired. Stephenson also arrested Vardy and five of his male relatives and employees for harbouring bushrangers or being accessories after the fact.

Stephenson attempted to take Lowry to Goulburn with a horse and cart. He reached Woodhouseleigh around nightfall where he was forced to put up for the night. He later testified that Lowry 'suffered very much on the way, choking in the throat, and seemed to be like suffocated; the place I shot him was near the wind-pipe.' Stephenson sent for a doctor and more police. Dr Waugh arrived at 3 a.m., but there was nothing he could do for Lowry.

Detective Camphin was with Lowry in his last moments. Lowry asked for a priest, but there was none available. Camphin later testified (as reported in the *Sydney Mail* on 15 September 1863):

> He then asked if I would do him a favour; I said that if it did not interfere with my duty I would; he then told me that he had a brother-in-law

Martin Cash in later life. Cash survived bushranging (in Tasmania in the 1840s) and a subsequent prison sentence to become an officer of the law.
He was also one of the few bushrangers to see old age.

(State Library of Tasmania PH30-1-672)

Matthew Brady was good-looking, audacious and courteous to his victims. In the 1820s in Tasmania he became one of the first bushrangers to be accorded hero status.

(State Library of Tasmania PH3014134W150)

'Skirmish Between Bushrangers and Constables, Illawarra', by Augustus Earle, 1827. Convicts escaping the brutalities of penal settlements found shelter in heavily wooded terrain and when confronted, many fought to the death rather than be captured. (National Library of Australia an2818470)

'Convicts Plundering Settlers' Homesteads', wood engraving by Frank Mahony. Early bushrangers were motivated both to rob and exact revenge on harsh masters by burning their property and driving off their stock.
(State Library of Tasmania AUTAS001124869306)

'Woman Pleading with Bushrangers', Patrick Marony, painted in 1894. While some bushrangers behaved in a 'gentlemanly' manner towards women, and didn't rob them, many women found themselves suffering nevertheless when their husbands were robbed or their loved ones' lives were threatened. (National Library of Australia an2292621)

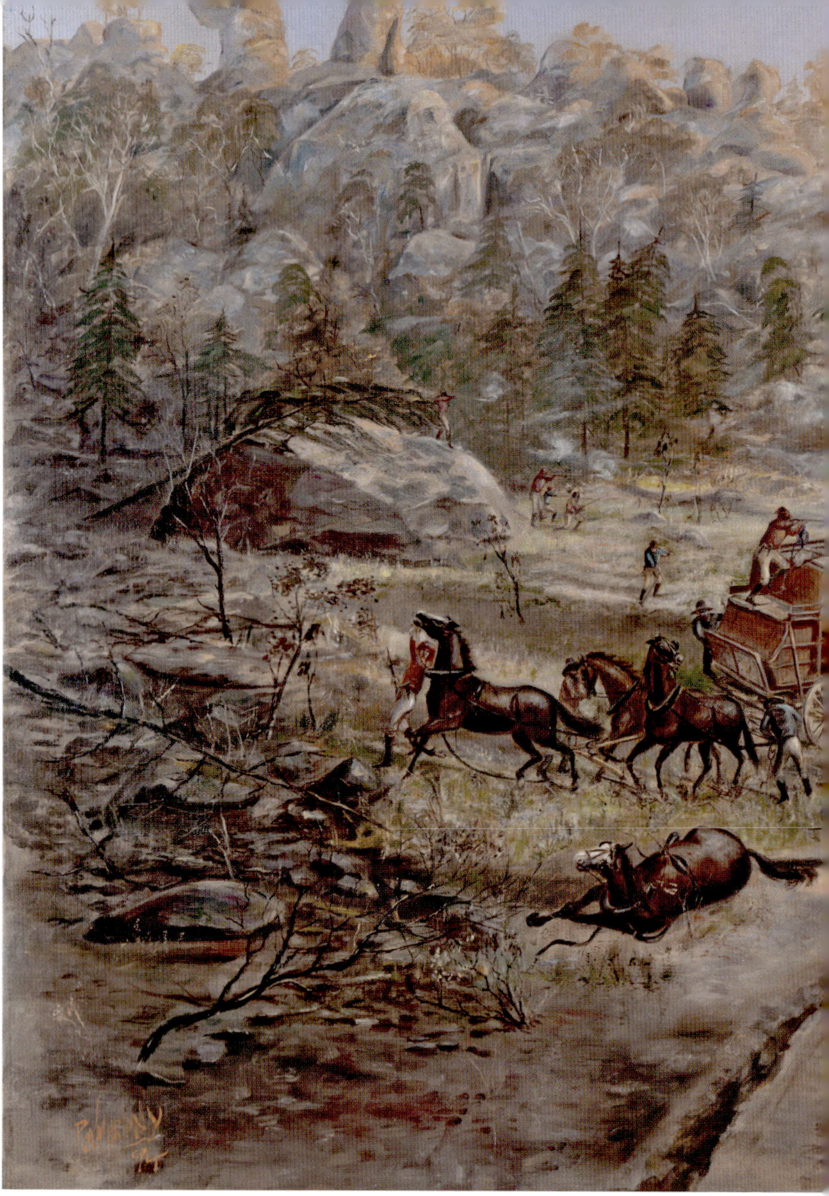

'Stage Coach Hold-up, Eugowra Rocks, NSW', painted by Patrick Marony in 1894. The ambush (in 1862) by up to 10 bushrangers, led by Frank Gardiner, was the largest highway robbery in Australia's history, netting gold and cash worth an estimated £14 000, close to $10 million in modern values. (National Library of Australia an2292684)

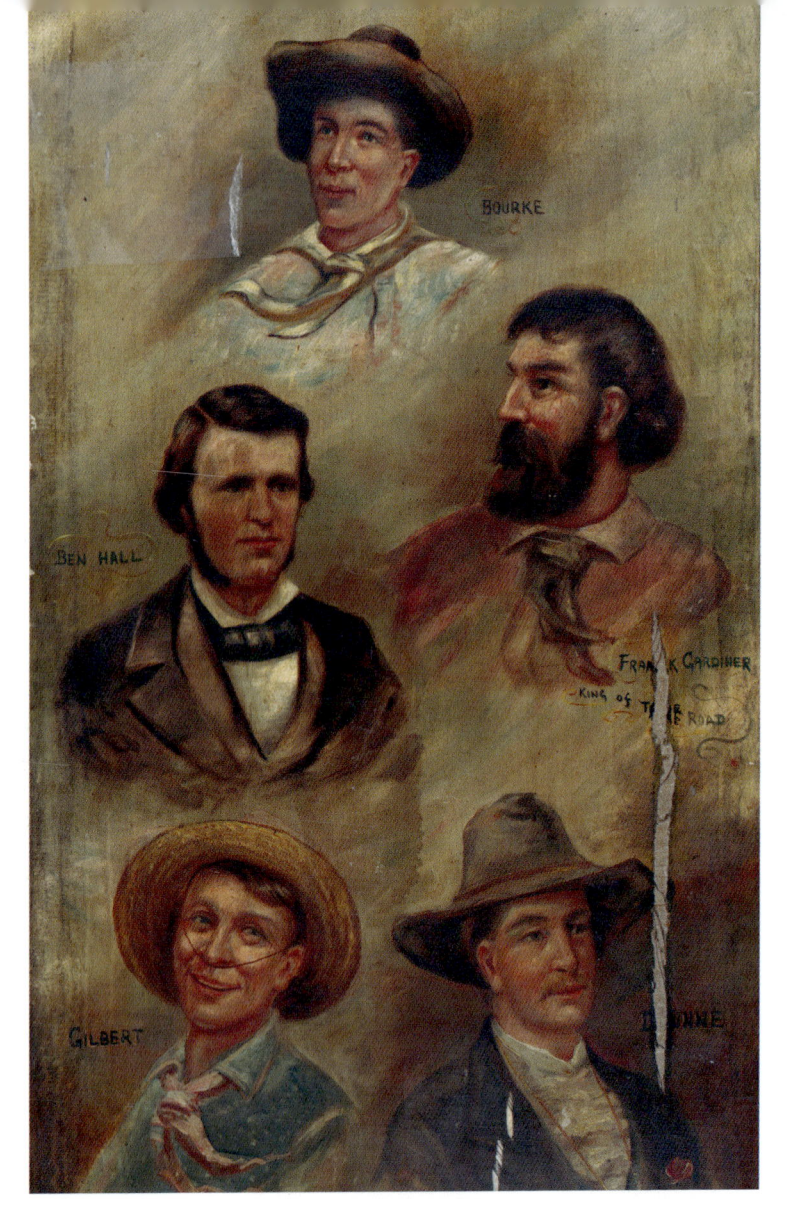

'Members of the Gardiner-Gilbert-Hall Gang', Patrick Marony, 1894. Clockwise from top: Michael Burke (shot dead 1863, aged 18), Frank Gardiner (served 10 years of a 32-year sentence then exiled), John Dunn (executed 1866, aged 20), John Gilbert (shot dead 1865, aged 23), Ben Hall (shot dead 1865, aged 28).

(National Library of Australia an2263680)

'Flight of a Bushranger', S.T. Gill, from a collection dated 1853–74. The brand on the animal suggests it was a stolen racehorse, giving the rider (thought to be Frank Gardiner) a distinct advantage over the inferior mounts of the police. (Mitchell Library, State Library of NSW a1833002h)

'Bushrangers Attacking Goimbla Station', Patrick Marony, 1894. The November 1863 attack by the Gilbert-Hall gang was provoked by the station's owner, David Campbell, voicing opposition to the bushrangers. Campbell made good on his word, shooting John O'Meally (the bullet nearly decapitating him) even as part of his property was razed by fire.

(National Library of Australia an2259818)

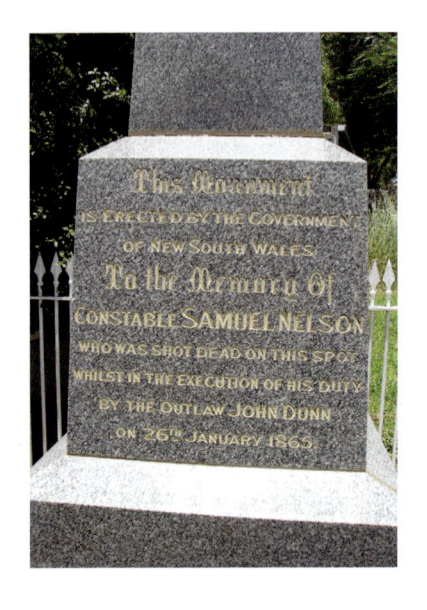

Inscription on the Nelson Memorial, Collector. While many police were heroes according to the definition of the word (risking their lives to protect others), in their encounters with bushrangers they were often portrayed as incompetent or antagonistic. (Photo: Michelle Havenstein)

The Bushranger Hotel, formerly Kimberley's Inn, in the town of Collector, near Goulburn, NSW. The Gilbert-Hall gang stuck up the Inn in early 1865, and during the attack John Dunn shot dead Constable Samuel Nelson. A memorial (centre-right of picture) has been erected in the approximate location that Nelson fell. (Photo: Michelle Havenstein)

Two views of the death of Ben Hall, near Forbes in May 1865.
A contemporary newspaper illustration, based on the accounts given by
police, shows him being shot while attempting to flee. (State Library of Victoria mp000877).

The scene painted by Patrick Marony in 1894 reflects the account attributed
to tracker Billy Dargin, suggesting Hall was shot while lying on the ground,
possibly while asleep. (National Library of Australia an2263709)

'Morgan the bushranger, sticking up Round Hill Station', wood engraving by Frederick Grosse, 1865. Events at Round Hill in 1864 typified Morgan's erratic behaviour: one moment chivalrous, the next murderous.

(National Library of Australia, an10322891)

Daniel Morgan, shortly after he died of a gunshot wound at Peechelba Station, Victoria, in April 1865. Morgan had ranged over southern NSW for several years but lasted a matter of days once he crossed the Victorian border into unfamiliar territory.

(Photo Henry Pohl, State Library of NSW a928608r)

Thomas and John Clarke in Braidwood prison, 1867. John Clarke's left arm appears to have been strapped, due to a bullet that passed through his body during his capture. Both men are wearing their hair long, in the style favoured by young 'native-born' Australians.

(Dixon Library, State Library of NSW a128082h)

'Capture of Thunderbolt, near Uralla', by Constable Walker, an illustration by Alexander Binning for the *Illustrated Sydney News* in 1870. In fact Captain Thunderbolt (Fred Ward) was shot dead in the encounter, effectively bringing bushranging in NSW to an end. (National Library of Australia an8420644-v)

'Bushrangers Holding Up Coach Passengers', Patrick Marony, 1894. Such scenes, where every traveller on remote country roads was robbed at gunpoint, were almost commonplace at the height of the bushranging era in the 1860s. (National Library of Australia an2292687-v)

'Bailed Up', by Tom Roberts in 1895, 15 years after the last high-profile bushranger, Ned Kelly, was apprehended. Arguably the most famous image of bushranging, the painting mythologises the crime, giving it the appearance of a social exchange rather than an armed confrontation.

Tom Roberts 'Bailed Up', 1895, 1927 oil on canvas, 134.5 x 182.8 cm Purchased 1933
Collection: Art Gallery of New South Wales Photograph: Ray Woodbury (Art Gallery of NSW 833)

Kelly at Glenrowan, June 1880. This contemporary
newspaper illustration presented the towering helmeted
figure that would come to symbolise bushranging and
ensure its and Ned Kelly's enduring fame.

(National Archive A1200, L38707)

'The Capture of Ned Kelly', Patrick Marony, 1894. Kelly was the only member
of his gang to be taken alive at Glenrowan, despite his and his gang's
attempts to take his life. He was executed in November 1880, effectively
bringing the bushranging era to an end. (National Library of Australia an2263702-v)

Wanted poster (with photographic images added some time later), offering a reward for information leading to the capture of the Kelly gang. The two images of Kelly show him in his teens, when he first started getting into trouble with the law, and in his mid-twenties, just prior to his execution.

(National Library of Australia an8391421-v)

The scene at Glenrowan Railway Station shortly after the capture of Ned Kelly. The besieged Glenrowan Inn is in the background. It was burned to the ground later that day, incinerating the bushrangers Dan Kelly and Steve Hart.

(Photo: William Howship, University of Melbourne UMA I 4643)

'Native Police', by Samuel Gill, 1864. Throughout the history of bushranging Aboriginal people played a significant role as trackers and in apprehending offenders, their efforts often underrated and underpaid.

(National Library of Australia an7149195-v)

named Elliott in the employ of a person named Cummins living on the
Lachlan, and he wished me to let him know that he had died game; he
said that he had always said that he would not be taken alive but would
fight for it; he said that the reason why he fought so was that he knew
he should be hung if taken.

Camphin read the Catholic litany for departing souls. Lowry could only repeat some of the responses. He died at 6.30 a.m.

Lowry's accomplice in his New Year's exploit and the robbery of the Mudgee mail, John Foley, was also arrested in August. A tracker led constables Donald, Lee and Nicholls to McKay's Pub, where the publican was harbouring him. Foley was charged with robbing the Mudgee mail and sentenced to fifteen years' hard labour. He revealed where his share of the robbery was hidden and £2000 was recovered. Lowry's share was not found.

Larry Cummins was charged with the robbery of a man named McKinnon and sentenced to fifteen years' hard labour on the roads. He was to escape from Berrima Goal on 2 November 1866 and briefly resume his bushranging career.

Despite these police victories, the other heirs to the Gardiner legacy, the Gilbert-Hall Gang, continued to rob the countryside at will. They bailed up a house at Demondrille on 29 August. They then moved on to Boorowa.

According to the *Sydney Mail*'s local correspondent:

About eight o'clock in the evening of yesterday, the residents here were
greatly terrified and disturbed by a report which turned out to be too
true, that the premises of Mr. Webb, a storekeeper, had been entered
by four armed men who, after helping themselves to all they could lay
their hands on in the way of notes and cash, carried off property to
the value of £250 . . . It is said by a female who was present when the
party entered the premises, that Jamison [sic] was one of them. She

recognised him immediately, having lived on his father's station. The others were supposed to be Gilbert, O'Meally and Ben Hall.

John Jamieson was a prime example of the lure of bushranging for rural youth. His father was Sir John Jamieson and John Jnr was a cattle owner in his own right. When he committed the robbery in August, he was on bail for a robbery under arms committed in June. He had also robbed a man named William White at Lambing Flat in February. He was eventually captured and tried for the latter crime. He was sentenced to fifteen years on the road, the first year in irons. In 1863 he was eighteen years old.

Two young women in the Marengo district also caught the bushranging bug. Kate Meally and Elizabeth Mayhew had dressed in their brothers' clothes and 'gone out on a spree' when they encountered Senior Constable Clark, Constable Moore and two trackers who were patrolling for bushrangers. When they saw the police the girls turned their horses and galloped away. The police gave chase. The women were captured and faced the Police Court in Young on 23 August. According to the *Burrangong Courier*, they were discharged on the recommendation of Senior Sergeant Musgrove and 'the frolicsome pair left the Court attired in riding habits and hunting hats, apparently highly amused by the fun they had occasioned'.

On 6 September, Gilbert and O'Meally were surprised by four police at a shanty near Demondrille. As they attempted to escape from the rear of the shanty they encountered Constable Houghey. They fired at him and hit him in the leg. The shot travelled down his leg, from his knee to his ankle, the pain so intense that the officer immediately passed out. The bushrangers then escaped on foot.

Hearing the bushrangers were in the vicinity, John Barnes (quoted earlier in this chapter) attempted to reach his son's business at Cootamundra, to help him defend the place from being robbed yet again. Instead, he and a companion encountered the two bushrangers on the road who had already got hold of one horse but wanted another. The man with Barnes put spurs to his horse and escaped, leaving Barnes with the bushrangers. Exactly what happened isn't clear, but Barnes's body was found not long after, riddled with eighteen bullet wounds. The fatal shot was in the centre of his forehead.

On 13 September 1863 Marengo shoemaker Mr Yuill was stuck up by John O'Meally, whom he'd known for years. He was robbed of several pairs of boots he was carrying, but begged to keep one pair of highly polished Napoleon-style boots. Instead, O'Meally tried them on and found they were a perfect fit. By way of compensation he didn't take Yuill's money.

Yuill (and the Marengo correspondent for the *Yass Courier*) made some remarkable observations about the gang's methods:

> Mr Yuill states that about 10 minutes before he was stuck up he met striding along the road a tall ungainly looking woman, and from what afterwards occurred firmly believes it to have been no woman at all, but Gilbert disguised as one; if so it is not the first time Gilbert has adopted female apparel, for I am credibly informed that when he stuck up Hammond's Station at Junee, one of the servant girls there was making some remarks about his long and well oiled hair, and he laughingly observed, 'I'm obliged to wear it long, for I've sometimes to dress in women's clothes, and I intend to escape out of the country in petticoats'. It is well-known that he attended the last Young races, mounted on horseback, disguised in a lady's riding habit, hat, and feather. His smooth good-looking face much assists him in this respect.

The gang next stuck up the Cowra–Bathurst mail on 19 September, the store at Caloola on 24 September and Grubbenbong station on the same day. There Johnny Vane reputedly displayed his musical prowess on the homestead's piano – playing a 'farewell tune' before the bushrangers departed.

Meanwhile, the prison on Cockatoo Island continued to operate as a finishing school for bushrangers. Fred Britten, who had robbed the Bathurst mail in November 1862, was sent there after being convicted in February 1863. There he met Fred Ward, a former drover and horse breaker. Ward, who'd been born at Windsor, was then twenty-seven. He'd been a level-headed stockman in the Hunter Valley, much liked by those who knew him, but in 1856 was sentenced to ten years in prison for receiving seventy-five stolen horses. He was released on a ticket-of-leave in 1860, but it was cancelled in 1861 after he went absent. He was again convicted of horse-stealing shortly after and returned to Cockatoo to finish his sentence, with an additional three years.

Ward and Britten had tried to escape from the supposedly escape-proof Cockatoo Island in July 1863. In September they made another attempt. On this occasion they may have been assisted by Ward's female companion, a part-Aboriginal woman named Mary Ann Bugg. One story has it that she swam to the island (a distance of about 500 metres from the nearest, northern shore) with a file and clothes to help him escape, then helped him swim back to the mainland, braving the aggressively territorial bull sharks that inhabit the inner-harbour waters.

Ward, Mary Ann and Britten headed north towards the country familiar to Ward and his female companion. However, Ward and Mary Ann soon separated from Britten, possibly after a brush with a police patrol.

Bushrangers had engaged in many daring exploits during their long history, but in October 1863 the Gilbert-Hall Gang took bushranging to an entirely new level. On Saturday 3 October 1863 they visited Bathurst. They rode in during the evening, when much of the town was doing its weekly shopping and the streets were thronged with people. They first went to a gun shop in William Street, where the selection was limited due to a rush on revolvers because of the bushranging menace. At McMinn's Hotel they went in and found the family eating dinner. One of the McMinn women recognised the men at the door and screamed. When they told her to be quiet, she screamed even louder.

Word that the bushrangers were in town spread like wildfire. The police rapidly mounted and galloped off in what they thought was pursuit – except the bushrangers hadn't left town. The *Bathurst Times* of 5 October could hardly believe the audacity of the men, but was close to the mark in understanding the criminal mind:

> The street chosen in which to commence operations was by many odds the throngest part of town; and that section of the street in which is situated the largest number of well-lighted establishments was certainly the spot where everyone would suppose such a band of marauders would be least likely to come; yet come they did, and business they essayed to do, at three immediate adjoining places of business. But all this was exceeded by the cool effrontery and dreadless impudence which they turned into Mr. De Clouett's yard and robbed the inmates of the house, at the very time when the whole town was in a state of alarm; and the police galloping in their supposed track. Bushranging by the gang is evidently not followed as a mere means of subsistence; this could be obtained in the usual way, with little trouble and less risk; but it is their life. Every new success is a source of pleasure, and they are stimulated to a novelty of action from a desire to create a history. This has become their great ambition; and the spirit of adventure is fed in them by the popularity that attends almost every incident of their career. Every word they say, and everything they do, is recorded, and they aspire to a name. Individual travellers carry less cash on their persons than once was customary; mails are less profitable and better guarded than they were formerly; and bushranging proper is partially stale.

This analysis held true for their activities just over a week later. On the morning of Monday, 12 October 1863 O'Meally, Gilbert, Hall, Vane, Burke and several other bushrangers rode into the town of Canowindra, between Bathurst and Forbes. They went to Mr Robinson's hotel, bailed it up and took the modest sum of £3. However, that was just the beginning.

Several gang members were posted at the approaches to the town to keep watch. As travellers appeared, they were taken into custody and escorted to the pub. They were kept there, but were allowed to refresh themselves – at the bushrangers' expense. They were allowed to move about freely, but weren't permitted to leave town.

According to a report in the *Bathurst Times* of 17 October, the bushrangers then amused themselves in a variety of ways by 'holding a robbers' jubilee'.

Johnny Gilbert acted as master of ceremonies. He was described as 'a jolly fellow, of slight build and thin – always laughing' and as 'the life of the party'. Even a subsequent police description referred to him as having 'light grey laughing eyes'.

The gang held the town all that day and night. They were still there at ten o'clock on Tuesday morning when three men – Hibberson, Twadell and Kirkpatrick – drove up. According to the *Bathurst Times*:

> Ben Hall informed them that he was sorry to inconvenience them, but they really could not be permitted to proceed on their journey, and he must therefore trouble them to leave their vehicle and put up for a while. On getting out, O'Meally, who was present, saw a revolver in Mr. Kirkpatrick's possession, and presenting one of his own weapons at that gentleman's head, he compelled him to give it up, remarking that he did not require it, but as it might be used against them it was as well to take the precaution of keeping it out of harm's way. He promised, however, to leave it at Mr. Loudon's residence at Grubbenbong, as they intended to pay him another visit before long.

Apart from the £3 taken from the publican, the revolver was the only other item the bushrangers took. Eventually, more than a dozen drays were lined up outside the pub. None of them were robbed. Instead, the gang ordered food for the people taken hostage and paid for everything. Johnny Gilbert bought cigars and passed them around.

While their hostages were allowed to drink whatever they wanted, it was noticed that the bushrangers were restrained. They only drank 'bottled ale and porter, the corks of which they insisted upon having drawn in their presence'.

> [Throughout Tuesday] great festivities were kept up, and, from the description given of the gang, they entertained not the slightest apprehension of being disturbed, and did not seem to think they were incurring any risk. Amongst a variety of amusements, shooting at a target seemed to be the favorite, and nothing occurred to mar the revels, except the accidental dropping of a carbine, which went off, and sent its contents flying past O'Meally's legs.

When some of the town's residents needed to go home (by this stage some forty people were being held hostage) they were given 'passes' and were allowed to be away for an hour. A couple of people took longer, and Ben Hall went to check on them, but did nothing but chide them for their tardiness. At one point he went and took the local policeman, who was housed in a nearby barracks, prisoner as well. Back at the hotel, disarmed, he was allowed to mingle with the other prisoners.

In their conversations with the good people of Canowindra, the bushrangers detailed their many crimes. They were said to have expressed 'a lively contempt for policemen generally, and their officers in particular – saying that when the police came all they had to do was to ride away'. The reason they gave for bailing up the town was that they were scouting the area and didn't want anyone to leave before their scouts returned.

It seemed an unlikely reason for exposing themselves to danger. From a criminal perspective, the incident at Canowindra is almost unique in bushranging. The prolonged detention of hostages, without the actual crime of robbery, suggests that for successful bushrangers, the attraction of bailing people up was as much about wielding power over the victim as achieving actual gain. Victimless crimes may be common, but this was a case of crimeless victims.

That night, the bushrangers also bailed up a man named Grant, at his home near town. They burnt the place to the ground in retaliation for his giving information to the police. They told him they'd been watching when he pointed out their tracks.

In all the bushrangers were reported to have occupied the town for nearly three days and nights – from late Sunday night or early Monday morning until noon on Wednesday. When the news of the extraordinary affair reached the police, the day after the bushrangers left, it seemed so incredible it wasn't believed. Nor was the information the bushrangers gave that they intended to visit Bathurst again.

The *Bathurst Times* described the bailing up of Canowindra as 'being characterised by a cool audacity which has hitherto been unequalled'.

The gang certainly seemed to be trying to raise the stakes with every new venture. It seemed inevitable that they would eventually go too far, but the thought clearly hadn't occurred to them.

On the evening of Saturday, 24 October 1863, Gilbert, O'Meally, Hall, Vane and Burke went to the home of Assistant Gold Commissioner Harry Keightley at Dunn's Plains, near Rockley, south of Bathurst. Keightley was on his front verandah when the bushrangers rode up. He ran inside when they ordered him to stand, succeeding in doing so uninjured despite half a dozen shots being fired at him.

Keightley had a double-barrelled gun by the door. He poked the barrel outside and fired at Mick Burke, hitting him in the abdomen.

'I am done for,' Burke was reported to have said as he staggered to the side of the house. In intense pain he attempted to take his own life by shooting himself in the head. The bullet entered under his chin and exited through the top of his head, but failed to kill him. He managed to fire again, the bullet entering above his right ear, passing through his brain and exiting at his left ear. But that shot didn't do him in either.

His companions, meanwhile, were pouring gunfire into Keightley's house. The commissioner, his wife and a doctor named Peechey were inside, attempting to return the fire with the one weapon and small amount of ammunition at their disposal. When it was expended they had no choice but to surrender.

When Keightley emerged from the house, the enraged bushrangers were determined to shoot him, especially Burke's close mate Johnny Vane. He was only saved when one of his servant women, Mrs Baldock, threw herself in front of them and refused to get out of the way. She pointed out that Mrs Keightley would be widowed, with a newborn baby.

The Keightleys stood to gain the £500 reward for shooting Mick Burke and in a neat twist the bushrangers decided they would let Keightley go for a ransom of £500. If it wasn't paid by two o'clock the following day they would shoot or hang Keightley and Dr Peechey. Mrs Keightley and Dr Peechey's son were allowed to ride into Bathurst to obtain the money from her father, Mr Rotton, a member of the New South Wales Legislative Assembly. The bushrangers posted sentries and told Mrs Keightley that if she brought the police they would shoot her husband.

While she was gone, Dr Peechey attended to Mick Burke. By some accounts he had only lived for half an hour. By others he was unconscious, but in a terrible state.

Despite arriving in Bathurst on a Sunday, Mrs Keightley was able to raise the required sum and return. The bushrangers then left, taking Mick Burke with them in a cart. If he wasn't already dead, he didn't last long. His death put a dent in the gang's ambitions from which they never fully recovered.

After the affair at Dunn's Plains, the reward for the capture of John Gilbert, John Vane, John O'Meally and Ben Hall was increased to £1000 each.

Not long after, a cousin of Johnny Vane, Donald Cheshire, was arrested in Bathurst trying to spend notes that were included in the ransom paid for Keightley. Despite the hurry of getting the ransom together, Mr Rotton had taken a moment to copy the serial number of each banknote. The numbers had been circulated throughout the town. Cheshire had purchased a revolver, black crepe used in disguises and seven gold rings. The rings were thought to be intended to symbolise the fraternity of the Gilbert-Hall Gang. The sympathiser ended up being sentenced to five years' hard labour on the roads.

October 1863 also saw the fall of Charles Cowper's New South Wales government. The principle reason for the fall of 'Slippery Charley', as Sir Henry Parkes referred to him, was a bit of creative accounting that drew a veil over the government's financial woes. The furore over the increasingly out-of-control bushrangers didn't inspire confidence either. It may not have brought about Cowper's fall, but it didn't help.

By then, Cowper was losing faith in his Inspector-General of Police, Captain McLerie, and the centrally administered police force he had created in 1861. At one point he threatened to create a new force. At another he wrote: 'The Colonial Secretary is unwilling suddenly to withdraw [sack] the Inspector-General, but intimates his intention of doing so, if within one month, Gilbert and party are not apprehended. It will then become a question for immediate determination what modification of the police system shall be made to remedy the defects so loudly complained of.'

It made no difference to the bushrangers. In the southern districts of New South Wales, Dan Morgan continued his depredations, despite the loss of his mate, German Charley. He robbed Walla Walla station early in November and while there, asked the station hands how they were treated. He told the owner, Mr Stitt, that if their conditions didn't improve, he would return and punish him for it.

He also went to Burrumbuttock station, where he stole a horse known to be of good quality. At Walbundrie station he demanded another racehorse, which he was given. At Bulgandry station, he made the owner, Mr Gibson, write cheques for £30 for all of his employees and shearers. It's not known whether any of his men tried to cash them. However, after Morgan left, Gibson sent a messenger to the bank in Albury to stop payment.

For Johnny Vane, the death of his mate, Mick Burke, at Dunn's Plains was a wake-up call. The young tearaway may have realised that, for all its glamour, most bushrangers shared the same violent fate. He may have had a fight with his colleagues, as he was seen sporting a black eye not long after the shooting. In mid-November he went to see a priest, Father Tim McCarthy. The following day, they rode into Bathurst and Vane turned himself in. He was put on trial charged with robbery under arms, found guilty and sentenced to fifteen years' imprisonment. He had more minor brushes with the law after his release, but ended up living a full life, dying at Cowra, in the heart of bushranging country, in 1906.

Unfortunately, the gaps in the ranks left by Burke and Vane were all too quickly filled. There were many young men for whom the bushranging life was never more alluring.

However, the gang comprised only Gilbert, O'Meally and Ben Hall when they decided to attack Goimbla station, a property near Eugowra owned by a man named David Campbell, a squatter and magistrate, who had vowed that he would face the bushrangers if he ever met them. He had also organised search parties to go after them.

Campbell was sitting in his drawing room on the evening of Thursday 19 November 1863 when he heard footsteps on his verandah. Suspecting trouble, he picked up his double-barrelled gun and went through his bedroom to the back door of his dressing room. There he was met by a bushranger who fired both barrels of his gun at him. Campbell must have been quite thin, as one shot passed on his right side, the other on his left.

Campbell fired back, forcing the man to retreat. He followed the man to the corner of his verandah where he saw him join two other well-armed bushrangers at the front door. He went back into his bedroom, only to realise that his ammunition and other weapons were still in the drawing room. It was lit by a kerosene lantern and the blinds were open, exposing the room and anyone in it to the fire of the bushrangers.

Mrs Campbell decided to take the risk. Seeing her enter the room, the men who had made much of their refusal to injure women started shooting at her. She managed to dash out with the ammunition without being injured.

Now able to reload, Campbell and his wife retreated to the slab walls separating the house and the kitchen, from where they could cover both corners of the house. For a quarter of an hour shots were fired at them, then a voice called: 'If you don't surrender, we'll burn the place down.'

The loss of property could destroy even a wealthy landowner and was a threat that made many squatters quietly compliant with the demands of bushrangers. Not Campbell.

'Come on!' he shouted back. 'I am ready for you!'

'Oh, that is it!' the bushrangers reportedly replied. They set fire to his barn, which was stacked with hay. A valuable horse was trapped inside and its frantic efforts to escape could be heard by everyone present. O'Meally, Hall and Gilbert allowed the poor creature to be burned alive.

The heat from the barn grew so intense that the bushrangers were forced to retreat 40 metres to a fence beyond the house. Mrs Campbell risked going to reconnoitre and said she could see a man standing by the fence watching the flames. Campbell rushed to the corner of the house, took careful aim and fired. He then retreated to reload, not knowing that he had hit O'Meally in the throat.

There had been sporadic gunfire up to that point, but it now ceased. At 11.30 the Campbells ventured out. At the spot where they'd seen the man standing, they found his cabbage tree hat.

The following morning a constable arrived and an investigation soon revealed a large pool of blood where O'Meally had fallen. His companions had evidently dragged him from the scene, either dead or dying. His body was found not far away, in a stand of oaks. Campbell's shot had torn through his throat to his neck vertebrae, partially severing his spinal cord.

Campbell's barn was a smoking ruin. The body of the horse was hideously bloated. Campbell estimated his losses at around £1000. As it happened, the reward for O'Meally, dead or alive, was the same amount.

A significant element in this and the encounter at Keightley's was that in all the bushrangers' activities, and the community's response to them, the police were never involved. The forces of law and order had become virtually redundant. Citizens were being forced to take whatever steps they felt were appropriate for their own protection.

Also in November 1863, there was more incendiarism at Mittagong station, near Hanging Rock in southern New South Wales. The station manager, Isaac Vincent, had made the same kind of challenging remarks about Dan Morgan that David Campbell had made about the Gilbert-Hall Gang, though the outcome was much different. Morgan visited the station and bailed up Vincent. He tied him to a fence and made him watch while he burned down the woolshed, where shearing had been in progress and thirteen bales of wool were destroyed. He compounded the loss by herding the shearers into the homestead and insisting they be well fed before he left.

Gilbert and Hall remained active after the death of O'Meally. On 1 December they bailed up about forty people 5 kilometres from Boorowa. On 5 December they bailed up the Boorowa mail and four travellers. They opened letters to find that any banknotes they contained had been torn in half with only one half sent at a time to make the money useless to bushrangers. Other letters contained non-negotiable cheques or money orders.

Hall was disgusted at the pile of wealth that was worthless to him. He asked if anyone would cash the cheques, but no one volunteered. The mailman talked him out of burning all the money. Hall then said, 'If I thought it would do the —— injury I would burn the lot.'

On 9 December 1863 the gang stuck up the mail from Forbes and Young. Gilbert read the newspapers regarding Vane and said he was 'a bloody liar'. Once again, they found the mail held little cash.

Gilbert and Hall were joined by two other men when they robbed up to fifty people on the road between Bowning and Binalong on 16–17 December. They may have been James Gordon, known as the Old Man, and John Dunleavy.

Gordon was fifty-eight. He was an ex-convict, having done time from 1857 to 1861 for a minor offence. He'd served his sentence where else but Cockatoo Island.

Dunleavy was around twenty-one, a young local boy, drawn to the excitement of bushranging despite the gang's recent setbacks.

On 16 December 1863 the tollkeeper on the road between Maitland and nearby Rutherford (now a suburb of Maitland) was bailed up. Tollkeeper Delaney said there was no money; it had just been taken to Maitland. Despite this the bushranger pushed into the house, still demanding money.

'No nonsense,' the bushranger reportedly cried, 'I'm Captain Thunderbolt.'

He then took the nearly empty cash box. It was the first known robbery committed by the Cockatoo Island escapee Fred Ward in his new guise as Captain Thunderbolt.

When the lessee of the tollbar returned, Delaney headed for the Spread Eagle Inn. On his way he met the bushranger a second time. The bushranger had found only four shillings in the cash box, and returned it to the tollkeeper.

Thunderbolt then went to the Spread Eagle and ordered lunch. The innkeeper's wife gave him some bread and meat and said there was no charge.

'Well,' said Thunderbolt, 'I came here to stick you up, but as you're so —— hospitable, I won't.'

He then bought a bottle of rum and left.

Shortly after, he stopped Godfrey Parsons and his wife. 'Bail up and hand out,' Thunderbolt told them.

Mrs Parsons burst into tears. Parsons explained to the bushranger that his wife was sick and he was taking her to the doctor. The only money they had was £2 for the doctor's fee.

'Well,' said Thunderbolt, 'I'm a bushranger, but I don't rob sick women. Pass on.'

It was revealed later that Mrs Parsons was actually crying because she had £30 in her pocket and thought she was about to lose it.

Thunderbolt spent the rest of the day robbing some and letting others go. After dinner at the Spread Eagle, he was confronted by four Maitland troopers who covered him with their pistols and told him he was their prisoner.

Thunderbolt simply laughed, spurred his horse and galloped away. The police pursued him for some distance but he gradually drew away from them, thanks to the superior animal he was riding. When the police finally gave up the pursuit, their horses were so exhausted they struggled to make it back to Maitland.

As 1863 drew to a close, bushranging had gone from a rarity to a rampant scourge in the rural districts of New South Wales, and only in New South Wales. Communities had become divided into victims and sympathisers, rich and poor. For many, any connection with a bushranger was a story for life. The *Sydney Morning Herald* had said at the beginning of the year: 'To have seen or spoken to one of them is hailed as an epoch in after existence.'

It was all that Isabella Baldock, Harry Keightley's servant woman, would have to show for her role in saving Harry Keightley's life at Dunn's Plains. She didn't want any of the reward money associated with Burke's death, but had hoped for a gold medal commemorating her role in the affair. However, Keightley promptly downplayed her part in the events, ensuring she received nothing. It was one of several instances where servants received less recognition than masters, who nevertheless expected them to risk their lives when bushrangers threatened.

In the increasing atmosphere of crisis, some police also became victims. Superintendent Chatfield encountered members of the Gilbert-Hall Gang but failed to capture them, in large part because he and his men had been out on patrol for six weeks, in often appalling weather conditions, and they and their horses were exhausted. One of his men had been at the point of shooting Ben Hall at close range when his gun hung fire, only going off after it had been lowered, allowing Ben Hall to escape. Chatfield was dismissed from the service, losing all rights to a pension despite thirteen years in the force. If his men had been issued with better weapons, he'd have been hailed as a hero instead.

Meanwhile, the government did little to tackle the root causes of bushranging. The New South Wales economy was still in recession, unemployment was high and social welfare nonexistent. When two men, Frank Stanley and Charles Jones, were arrested after attempting to become bushrangers, they reported that their gang had been formed 'first to work, but finding they could not make a living, they took to the roads'. Another would-be bushranger said he took to crime 'to give me a start as a poor man'. Even the best bushrangers were finding it hard to make a living. They usually didn't bother with small change, but in one robbery a mailman had sixpence taken from him and not returned.

For Gilbert and Hall, bushranging may have lost much of its glamour. They may have learned that over-confidence led to disaster, and the curbing of their enthusiasm reduced their activities to a dull, if dangerous routine. It appears that Gilbert may have dropped out of bushranging for several months at the beginning of 1864. There are many stories regarding his activities at the time, but the most colourful, and, based on earlier reports, believable, was related some time later by the Forbes correspondent of the *Sydney Morning Herald*:

> A story is told upon the Lachlan, in connection with Gilbert's late dissociation from his mates, which obtains credence in many quarters, and from which we learn that during the period of his disappearance he was sojourning about Canowindra and its vicinity, attired as a female. Now, considering that this worthy is small of stature, beardless, and destitute of whiskers, besides presenting in other respects an effeminate appearance, this is by no means impossible. Further than this, however, by way of conjecture, I will not go. I tell the story as it was told to me.

Hall may also have tired of the bushranging life, although with £1000 on his head, retirement wasn't an option. He may also have found that the loyalty of his sympathisers was purchased by his largesse, rather than freely given, and he needed to keep up his activities to counter the financial incentive to turn him in.

If any of the Gilbert-Hall Gang considered surrender, the stumbling block was the harsh sentences being handed down by the courts. A year later, the Reverend McGuinn, who had been involved in the surrenders of Vane and later James Dunleavy, wrote to the colonial secretary:

> I believe Ben Hall was at one time really determined on giving himself up only the idea of getting 15 or 20 years – and I am certain every one of them would prefer being shot to 15 years imprisonment – I impressed on the two that I surrendered that the government would deal leniently with them – and hence their surrendering.

It was up to other bushrangers to keep the districts of New South Wales in a state of alert.

In January Dan Morgan and two other men robbed a store in Corowa, 50 kilometres west of Albury. A few days later, on 22 January, Morgan stole a horse from Round Hill station. Other minor incidents occurred throughout the state.

Hall was active again with the Old Man (James Gordon) on 1 March, robbing the Wellington–Orange mail. Hall was also nearly captured at the same time. A stake-out at Sandy Creek, the station he'd once leased near the Weddin Mountains, nearly intercepted him. He was forced to gallop past a constable who fired at him and missed.

The police had better luck two days later, far from the Weddin Mountains, in Queensland. They found Frank Gardiner. Information received from a source that has never been disclosed led a detective named McGlone to make his way to Appis Creek with two police officers. Disguised as diggers, they found Mr and Mrs Frank Christie (Gardiner's real name) openly running a pub. Once McGlone had assured himself that he'd found the right man he obtained the help of Queensland police. On the morning of 3 March 1864, Gardiner was taken by surprise and captured after a brief struggle. He was taken under heavy guard back to Sydney.

Even as the police were celebrating, other graduates from Cockatoo Island were keeping busy. Captain Thunderbolt had been seen in the New England area over the previous months, sometimes with Mary Ann Bugg and two children. However, in April 1864 he was with sixteen-year-old John Thompson when he stuck up the Warialda mail, three stations, and Munro's Inn at Boggy Creek, in northern New South Wales, before moving on to another inn at Millie. As the *Tamworth Examiner* reported on 29 April 1864:

> They went on to Walford's Inn at Millie, sticking up Mr Baldwin on the road. Mr Walford, having been informed of their approach, had hidden away everything of value, so that they got very little, except more grog. The police also had been informed, and three troopers, with a black tracker, soon arrived on the scene. As they approached, the bushranger on guard outside whistled, and the other man came out and mounted, Thunderbolt waving a revolver and pointing to a field behind the house as a challenge. He led his men [there were only two] to the clearing and made a stand. The police followed, and a number of shots were fired on both sides. The police closed up, and Constable Dalton shot one of the bushrangers, a mere lad, and he fell. Dalton shouted to Constable Morris to 'look after him', and turned towards Thunderbolt, when the boy raised himself on his elbow and fired. Constable Lynch shot the boy in the neck, probably in time to save Dalton's life. Ward made a dash forward, perhaps with a view to driving the police away from the boy and carrying him off, but the police fire was too brisk, and after a few more rounds the robber turned and rode into the bush. The police followed, but as their horses had travelled 50 miles [80 kilometres] that morning, they were obliged to give up the chase.

Frank Gardiner wasn't so lucky. The gaols of New South Wales may have been wanting in many respects, but when he arrived in Sydney in April, to a celebrity's welcome, every precaution was taken to ensure he was securely held.

When it came to prosecuting him, the problem for the authorities was that the evidence of Gardiner's involvement in the Eugowra escort robbery was based on an informer motivated by self-interest rather than honesty. A similar situation unfolded when it came to charges that carried the death penalty.

In May 1864, when he defended charges of wounding Sergeant Middleton with intent to murder at William Fogg's house in July 1861, he was found not guilty. When the verdict was announced there was pandemonium in the courtroom, with the gathered throng cheering, shouting, whistling, stamping their feet and applauding. The outraged judge fixed on a young boy who was clapping excitedly, and tried to have him remanded to Darlinghurst Gaol for contempt of court. Only then was order restored. The *Sydney Morning Herald* of 23 May noted:

> His Honor with great warmth remarked that it was astonishing that there should be such an utter want of common decency among such a number of people in New South Wales; it was a disgrace, an utter disgrace to the colony.

The verdict didn't make Gardiner a free man. At the time, it was general practice to charge a bushranger with their latest crime, rather than all their crimes, particularly if a guilty verdict for their latest crime was likely to lead to the death penalty. It was a waste of time and effort to secure multiple death penalties when the culprit could only be hanged once. In Gardiner's case, once one charge failed, the next charge was brought up. The wheels of the law would eventually get him on something.

Johnny Gilbert returned to the bushranging business with Ben Hall on 20 May 1864. With the Old Man, they went to McGregor's Inn at Bong Bong, near Bowral. They bailed up twenty patrons, then Gilbert and the Old Man went down to the stables where constables Scott and Macnamara were guarding several valuable horses being taken to Young for the Queen's Birthday Races.

When the bushrangers attempted to bail them up, the police started shooting. They managed to hold the bushrangers off until they gave up and rode away. As they did, Hall's hat fell off, creating the incorrect belief that he'd been shot. The two constables feared the bushrangers' return in greater numbers and rather than give chase, they barricaded themselves in the stable. They were still there when Sir Frederick Pottinger arrived with four troopers, at midnight, by which time the trail of the bushrangers was cold.

During his lifetime, Daniel Morgan does not appear to have been referred to as Mad Dan or Mad Dog Morgan. The earliest published references may be as recent as 1936. However, his activities on 19 June 1864 at Round Hill station near Albury made a significant contribution to his subsequent reputation.

He bailed up the station late in the morning or early in the afternoon. He took hostage the manager (named Watson) and his wife; overseer McNeil; cattle overseer McLean; and the visiting son of a neighbour, John Heriot, at gunpoint while he enquired if they had any grog.

He was told there were six bottles of gin, one of which was open. Watson poured the bushranger a glass, but he refused to take the first nip, saying, 'You must drink that yourself as you may have had it ready for me.'

He then had his horse stabled while he invited himself to lunch with the station's management. As with other bushrangers who had enjoyed a career of more than one robbery, for Morgan the thrill of the crime may have been fading, leading to an escalation in the audacity of the crimes committed and the confidence in his ability to escape any consequences. While he ate, Morgan kept two cocked revolvers at hand, with four more tucked conspicuously in his belt. Throughout the meal he continued drinking.

After lunch, Morgan mustered the station workers and marched them and the managers (his hostages now numbering eleven) into a cattle shed. He then had gin served all around, until the dozen men had consumed four bottles. Morgan had his horse brought down and was about to mount it when he turned and fired two shots indiscriminately into the crowd, one shot grazing a carpenter's hand.

He then took another bottle of gin, mounted and started riding away. As he did, Watson commented, 'Those are the irons [stirrup irons] you stole from so and so.'

From 15 metres away Morgan turned, aimed at Watson's head and fired. As he did Watson threw up his hand, through which the bullet passed before grazing his scalp. Chaos ensued, as described in the *Argus* of 25 June 1864:

> The wounded man ran behind the shed and hid himself, but Morgan returned to the door of the shed, fired right and left amongst the inmates. The first shot went through young Mr. Heriot's leg, between the knee and ankle, shattering the bone in pieces, and then hit another man's leg behind, but not, luckily, breaking the skin as its force had been spent. The second ball hit no one. The men then all ran away in different directions, the poor wounded young man among them dragging his broken leg after him for about thirty yards [27 metres], when he fell from pain and exhaustion. In the meantime, Morgan galloped after another man across the yard, with pistol cocked; but the fugitive escaped through the kitchen . . . Morgan then galloped back to young Heriot, dismounted, and put the revolver to his head. Mrs. Watson, in

the meantime, was running screaming and terrified about the yard.

Young Heriot said, 'Don't kill me, Morgan, you have broken my leg'; and Mr. Watson, who had also, seeing Morgan with the pistol to the boy's head, come out of his hiding-place, cried out, 'For God's sake, Morgan, don't kill anyone!' The villain, who seemed to act with the inconsistency of drunkenness, or of a murderer gone mad, then cried out, 'Where are all the d------ wretches gone to?' and swore a fearful oath that he would blow the brains out of every man on the station if they did not come to Heriot's assistance.

Morgan then helped cut the boot from the lad's leg. Two men came out from hiding and Morgan threatened to kill them if they didn't help carry the boy inside. At that point, two more bushrangers appeared. 'Morgan's men' kept watch (as they may have been doing since Morgan's arrival at the station) while their leader was occupied with young Heriot. After he'd been attended to, Morgan then cared for Mr Watson's wounds.

As the bushranger seemed to have recovered some semblance of reason, McLean asked if he could fetch a doctor for Heriot. Morgan agreed to the request, but may have admonished McLean to go for Dr Stitt at Walla Walla, not the doctor at Germanton, where there was a police station. McLean either deviated to Germanton within sight of the station or did as he was told. In any case, Morgan went after him. When he caught up with him, apparently without any form of challenge or warning, he shot him in the back. The bullet entered above the hip and exited near his navel. The 'gut shot' man fell from the saddle.

Morgan then lifted the wounded man onto his horse, carried him back to the station and saw that he had the best possible attention. He and his men then remained at the station, drinking and 'socialising' until 2 a.m. Five minutes after they left, the police arrived. According to the *Argus,* 'A great many reports are circulated as to their conduct when they did come, but until we can vouch for the truth, we decline to publish them.'

What is clear is that the police declined the opportunity to pursue three heavily armed men who had the advantage of darkness to cover their movements. They were well aware that their quarry had already shot and wounded four people on the station. McLean eventually died of his wound. Morgan and his colleagues escaped. The reward for Morgan's capture was increased to £1000.

Also in June 1864, Hall and two other bushrangers, most likely the Old Man and James Dunleavy, visited Canowindra again and bailed up the store of a man named Pearce. They demanded money. Pearce said he had none. They then took him hostage and marched him several kilometres into the bush. They told him they wanted a £300 ransom, but Pearce said such a sum was beyond him. Hall and his men fixed bayonets on their carbines and threatened to pin him to a tree. Still Pearce was not forthcoming and eventually they were forced to set him free.

It was possible that their predations on the district and the continuing economic hard times had reduced the money that remained in the community. After letting Pearce go, the bushrangers went on to the estate of a man named Rothery, near Carcoar. Rothery had seen them coming and was barricaded inside his homestead. He 'ordered them off, threatening to shoot the first man of them that crossed his threshold'. The bushrangers set fire to 20 tonnes of his hay, but otherwise left empty-handed.

On 24 June Morgan continued what was becoming a reign of terror in the southern districts. On the Tumbarumba Road, on the western slopes of the Snowy Mountains, he encountered Sergeant David McGinnity and Constable Churchley. The police may not have recognised the bushranger as they engaged him in conversation.

Then Morgan said, 'You are one of the bloodthirsty wretches looking for bushrangers.'

With no further warning he pulled out a revolver and fired at McGinnity, at near point-blank range. McGinnity immediately fell dead. Churchley was able to return Morgan's fire, shooting at him twice without effect, before galloping off.

Morgan stripped McGinnity's body of valuables, revolver and rifle. He also took his horse. He then left McGinnity's cap in the middle of the road, marking the spot where the body could be found.

Churchley was later charged with cowardice in not capturing the bushranger. On the other hand, he'd escaped with his life.

In Sydney, the trials of Frank Gardiner continued. On 7 July 1864 Gardiner went before the court charged with robbery under arms of the carriers Horsington and Hewitt. He pleaded guilty to both charges. He was then charged with feloniously wounding Constable Hosie with intent to kill him and with feloniously wounding Hosie with intent to do grievous bodily harm (these charges relating to the affray at Fogg's in 1861, for which he'd already faced charges two months earlier). The former charge carried the death penalty, the latter a sentence of up to fifteen years. The jury found him guilty of the lesser charge.

When it came to sentencing, Chief Justice Sir Alfred Stephen didn't miss his opportunity. He sentenced Gardiner to 15 years for wounding Hosie, 10 for robbing Horsington and 7 years for robbing Hewitt, the sentences to be cumulative for a total of 32 years' imprisonment. It was harsh by any standard for the charges proven, but clearly showed Gardiner was being sentenced for what he was believed to have done rather than the case at hand.

Gardiner may have counted himself fortunate he wasn't facing the death sentence, especially given his involvement in more serious crimes if not the precipitation of a new reign of bushranging. Nevertheless, the sentences sent a clear message to bushrangers that they could expect no mercy from the justice system. Under the circumstances, they might as well die on the road than rot in a prison. There were still plenty of escapes at this time, but not for the likes of Gardiner.

Morgan managed to add yet another outrage to his increasingly violent attacks. On 3 September a party of police who were hunting him were camped near Kiamba for the night when shots were fired into their tent. One hit a senior sergeant named Smyth in the chest, just above his heart. The shooter then escaped. Smyth was in a perilous state when he was transported to Albury to receive medical attention. He lingered until 29 September, when he became the fourth person to die at the hands of Dan Morgan.

On 25 September 1864 Hall and the Old Man bailed up the Gundagai–Yass mail near Jugiong. The Old Man and James Dunleavy were both wounded in robberies committed early in October. At that point the Old Man decided he'd had enough and quit the gang, only to find police patrols hot on his heels soon after. He was captured within three days. Within a month, the Old Man was charged with six offences, to all of which he pleaded guilty. He was given a 25-year sentence, the first year in irons.

Dunleavy's wounds meant he was unable to carry a firearm, let alone use it. The injury forced him to contemplate a future where liberty was all too frequently terminated by an untimely and violent death.

Early in November, James Dunleavy went to see Father McCarthy, the priest who had persuaded Johnny Vane to surrender. Not long after, James Dunleavy became the second member of the mercurial gang to surrender. He was charged with six counts of highway robbery, to which he pleaded guilty. At his trial the *Sydney Mail* reported:

> The prisoner was not twenty-one years old, and bore an excellent character up to the time of his entering upon the foolish career of crime

which had brought him to the felon's dock. He . . . was led away by the evil persuasion of others, and when at last he awoke to a sense of his degradation, he voluntarily relinquished the life he had adopted, and surrendered himself to justice.

Dunleavy was sentenced to fifteen years, the first year in irons. Once again, it gave little incentive to other bushrangers to surrender. Within three years of going to prison he was dead, having contracted tuberculosis. He passed away in October 1868.

The places of the Old Man and James Dunleavy were taken by a knockabout young Yass lad named Johnny Dunn. The teenager was small enough to be a jockey, and had won the main race at Yass that year. He was a good mate of Johnny Gilbert, who may have convinced him to join the adventure of bushranging, such as it was for the hunted Gilbert-Hall Gang. He was soon cast in the role of messenger, his ability to ride long and fast of great value for the gang's operations.

No sooner had Dunleavy left and Dunn joined the Gilbert-Hall Gang than the *Yass Courier* reported, 'Messrs Hall, Gilbert and Dunn seem to have obtained a lease of the Main Southern Road.' They robbed the Gundagai mail two weeks in a row. Expecting it would be robbed again, police organised an escort.

Four officers were detailed: Trooper McLaughlin rode ahead of the coach; Constable Roche was seated next to the driver, despite the driver's objections that having a policeman beside him would make him a target; and Sub-Inspector William O'Neill and Sergeant Edmund Parry rode behind the coach. Inside the coach, A. C. S. Rose, a local magistrate, was a passenger.

Despite the escort, on 16 November the coach was bailed up by two bushrangers, Johnny Gilbert and Ben Hall. They first forced McLaughlin, riding ahead, to surrender. O'Neill and Parry then rode forward to attack the bushrangers, two against two. As the first shots were fired, Constable Roche disembarked from the coach and ran into the bush. Rose remained inside the coach, firmly of the view that everyone should oppose bushranging but not to the extent of risking their lives. The gun battle continued until Sergeant Parry was hit, and fell from his horse, dead. O'Neill had no choice but to surrender.

Ben Hall reportedly looked at the body of the policeman and said, 'Well fought, very well, very well indeed. You're a couple of game men.'

Hall's view wasn't shared by the top brass of the New South Wales police force. O'Neill was later sacked by Inspector-General McLerie for sending a man ahead on his own, not telling Roche what to do if the coach was attacked and surrendering even though he still had a gun. McLerie's view seemed to differ from Rose's on the matter of self-preservation – he believed all police should fight to the death, no matter what the odds against them might be.

It was a similar story on 21 December 1864 when the bushrangers went to the town of Binda, 20 kilometres north of Crookwell. Gilbert, Hall and Dunn first robbed the store of an ex-policeman named Morris. Afterwards, they remained in town, unmolested, and went to a dance. The bushrangers danced freely until they received word that Morris was attempting to organise their capture. With guns drawn, they began searching for Morris. He escaped out of a window, tried to steal one of their horses in order to ride for the police, but was sighted and shot at. He fled for cover.

The bushrangers then set about burning down Morris's store. There were a hundred or so people at the dance. Nobody tried to stop them. Subsequently, three women – Christina McKinnon, Ellen and Margaret Monks – were charged with being 'bush telegraphs'. There was insufficient evidence to convict Margaret Monks, but the other two had been seen helping the bushrangers pile fuel onto the store verandah.

During the attack at Binda, Johnny Gilbert was asked why he didn't give up bushranging. He answered, 'Because Government won't let me; if they will grant me a free pardon, I will not only do no harm, but all the good I can, both for the country and the people in it.' He went on to explain that he felt the government only increased crime, instead of putting an end to it, by the severity of its law; that it had no consideration for 'youth, folly, ignorance or misfortune' and that if persons committed one act through any of those frailties, the police 'chase them about until they were compelled to do worse'. He said he was persuaded to take to the bush more out of pity for the person being alone that he went with, than 'any inclination to rob'.

While Christina McKinnon and the Monks girls were willing helpers in the Gilbert-Hall Gang's burning of Morris's store, many rural women had little choice when it came to aiding bushrangers. When armed men arrived at their door demanding food and/or shelter, they were often in no position to argue. Many were left alone in huts far from help. Even if they were armed, retaliation could be disastrous.

With so many active bushrangers, police were hard-pressed to apprehend them all, particularly when they enjoyed the support of many in the communities in which they operated. Since 1861 the police had actually enjoyed a great deal of success in apprehending many bushrangers, while others had been shot dead or had surrendered voluntarily. Yet the reality of 1864 was clear to all: in the never-ending battle between good and evil, the bushrangers were triumphant.

10

The scum of the earth

1865–1869

The year 1865 was a year of blood. There were more bushrangers, more robberies and more violence than in any previous year in Australia. And it was all concentrated in New South Wales.

The justice system, obsessed with punishment, provided no incentives to turn away from crime. In 1865 seventeen-year-old James Burke and an older man, John Mitchell, committed two stick-ups in two days. Burke then gave himself up, while Mitchell was captured. They both got the same sentence: fifteen years.

For bushrangers who had longer careers, the increasing rewards offered for them tested the loyalty of their supporters. It was inevitable that among people with a criminal disposition everything had a price. In some cases, of course, support could be gained through intimidation, rather than loyalty. Bushrangers like Dan Morgan and the Gilbert-Hall Gang had demonstrated that arson was a potent weapon. When it came to prominent landholders, the threat of burning hay, grain, or even pastures, was sometimes sufficient to obtain compliance. The *Deniliquin Chronicle* of 18 December 1864 noted that an unnamed landholder had 'given orders that whenever Morgan calls at his station he is to be given everything he wants, and when he does not call food is to be taken into the bush and left for him'.

Morgan also went to another station to shoot an overseer who he thought was too friendly with the police. He found only his wife, whom he harassed for a sum of money he thought the man had been paid. When she was not forthcoming, he pushed her into a fireplace and held her in the flames. She was badly burned before he pulled her out and doused her with a bucket of water.

At the beginning of 1865, New South Wales police were still hampered in many ways. When it came to waging guerrilla warfare against bushrangers who used terrain, speed of manoeuvre and local support, their training was hopelessly inadequate. They were more adept at marching in straight lines, like soldiers. The recruitment age for the force was thirty, and the uniform was bulky – thus older men in heavy boots struggled to pursue barefoot youths who easily outran them. When it came to pursuing bushrangers on horseback, police mounts were still inferior to the stolen racehorses of many of the bushrangers. Bushrangers could steal fresh horses as they needed them, while police were stuck with horses that were often exhausted after being ridden for days.

One writer, responding to a letter in the *Sydney Morning Herald* criticising police methods, cited first-hand experience of the problems for police in 'Morgan country':

> I met two men riding in the bush, who, at first sight, I took to be bushmen in search of employment, but, upon closer observation, I found they were police officers with an ordinary swag, which was merely composed of one pair of blankets and holsters for pistols, and not loaded like elephants and with turbans, as your contemporary's informant describes, and their horses appear to have been ridden for a long

period. Upon the 17th of this month I had occasion to pull up at a hut in the bush, which to me appeared to be a deserted one, at about eight o'clock in the evening, and where I was surprised to find a sergeant and three or four blacks who had just taken shelter for the night, and were as ragged as gipsies ... The men appeared – like the horses – literally and thoroughly knocked up, and the horses nearly starved, in consequence of the want of sustenance in the grass, and being upon duty since November last. Instead of stowing themselves away comfortably in bed at night, they just unrolled their pair of blankets, and went off to sleep in five minutes.

Next morning I said to the sergeant, 'If Morgan were to gallop across the plain now in your sight, what could you do?'

He answered, 'Nothing, for we have not got one horse that could stand an hour's chase.'

The writer went on to detail a key reason for the success of Morgan in his district, while Victoria was without bushranging in any form.

It is not generally known that this south-western district, under Superintendent Carne, is nearly as large as the whole of Victoria, and the number of constables under his command only thirty-five, while they have 900 men in Victoria, and stations every fifteen miles [24 kilometres] or so.

In total, New South Wales actually had more police than Victoria (1250 in 1865), but the state had an area of 800 000 square kilometres, while Victoria covered only 227 600 square kilometres. This meant that in New South Wales there was one policeman to 666 square kilometres, while in Victoria there was one policeman to every 225 square kilometres.

Pursuing men like Fred Ward, an excellent horseman, only made the job of policing more difficult. In January 1865 Thunderbolt robbed a hawker on the Culgoa River, near Bourke in the north-west of New South Wales, and was pursued by police to Queensland. It was then learned that he had a bush camp some 40 kilometres from the police station at Biliandoon.

The Queensland police joined the hunt and at dawn they rushed the camp. However, they only found Mary Ann 'Ward' and two children, the men being absent. They also found the proceeds of the robbery and a horse. It appeared that Thunderbolt had been using the camp for eight months.

The capture of Mary Ann was no simple matter either, as a letter to the *Maitland Mercury* explained:

> [She was] a perfect amazon, who sprang like a tigress upon one of the police, ribboning his uniform, and taunting him with cowardice for seeking her apprehension instead of Thunderbolt's, finally challenging them to single combat, and resisting her apprehension with such desperation that forcible means had to be adopted to secure her. Whatever motives led to the arrest of this auxiliary of Thunderbolt's, she was almost as speedily released, and she remained at Forrester's Willbie Willbie Station, upon the Narren Creek, until the 4th instant, when, at about five in the evening, four genteelly equipped horsemen rode up to the station, alighted, and after a few commonplace observations placed a pistol at the head of each inmate, and searched them. They then asked for powder and being furnished with what was obtainable, they replied 'It was of more value to them than gold.'
>
> After again searching the residents (four in number) but obtaining no money, they left, the Captain taking with him the half-caste woman.

At the beginning of January 1865, there were a number of sightings of Dan Morgan, but not while committing crime. He was reputed to be living on a tributary of the Murray, and was seen bathing in the river near Howlong, west of Albury. A New South Wales detective believed he'd gone to the races at Howlong where he was recognised by racegoers, none of whom tried to capture him.

By mid-January, he needed money. He stuck up a group of road contractors, but finding they had little cash, he burned their tents. He robbed five Chinese labourers, with similar results, and in his frustration shot one in the arm. He then moved on to the Albury road and robbed the mail, travellers and hawkers. For good measure, he then cut the telegraph line to Sydney.

In mid-January the Gilbert-Hall Gang held the roads between Goulburn and Braidwood for days at a time. Numerous travellers were bailed up. Then, on 20 January 1865, they stuck up a group of people near the hamlet of Collector and marched them to Kimberley's Inn (now the Bushranger Hotel) in the town. While Gilbert and Hall robbed the customers, Dunn kept watch outside. He told a boy to mind the horses and that if he let them go he'd blow his brains out.

Inside the pub the bushrangers engaged in sufficient merriment to arouse the interest of the town's only police officer, Constable Samuel Nelson. He left the police station to investigate and seeing what turned out to be his son tending some horses, he asked him what was going on. His young son told him the bushrangers were in Kimberley's. Constable Nelson went to get his gun then returned.

He approached the inn on foot, not seeing Dunn concealed behind a wall on the southern side of the building.

Nelson had almost reached the inn when Dunn suddenly stood up and without warning, fired a shot at him. Nelson was hit, almost at point-blank range, and fell. Dunn then approached the fallen officer, put a revolver to his head and fired another shot, killing him. The sound of the shot brought Gilbert to the door.

'I've shot the bloody trap,' Dunn reportedly said.

Gilbert went to the body and turned it over. He removed the dead policeman's belt and said, 'This is just what I wanted. I've lost mine.'

The murder was probably committed in front of the constable's son.

Nelson, however, wasn't the only policeman shot in January 1865. On the Talbragar gold diggings, a Chinese miner named Sarm Poo (some accounts identify him as Sam Poo) had taken to bushranging when his luck as a prospector ran out. He bailed up several people in the area and shot at one of his victims. Local policeman Senior-Constable Ward went after him and soon tracked the bushranger down.

When Ward confronted Sarm Poo, the bushranger reputedly called out, 'You bloody policeman. Me shoot you.'

He then fired at Ward, several shots hitting their target and killing him. Sarm Poo was captured soon after. He was convicted of the attempted murder of Henry Hughes and the murder of Senior-Constable Ward. He was hanged at Bathurst Gaol at the end of 1865.

The bloody start to the year fuelled an atmosphere of crisis that spurred the New South Wales government to take drastic action. Early in the year it introduced the *Felons Apprehension Act*. It was only to be in effect for a year, but it echoed the draconian bushranging legislation of years gone by. For example, it contained provisions for declaring specified bushrangers as outlaws. If they didn't turn themselves in by an advertised date, anyone encountering them would be legally empowered to shoot them on sight. However, the legislation also took account of some of the difficulties police faced in pursuing bushrangers. In particular, the act allowed police to appropriate horses when the need arose, meaning they could commandeer any fresh horse that was available when they were pursuing a bushranger. No longer would they be left behind on exhausted, inferior mounts while bushrangers galloped away on freshly stolen racehorses.

Sir Frederick Pottinger was to become another casualty in February. Early in January 1865 he'd attended a race meeting at Wowingragong and actually ridden in one of the races, against police regulations, when he should have been hunting bushrangers. He maintained that he was trying to draw the bushrangers out and that his action 'fully warranted the discretionary departure in point from the letter (tho' not the spirit) of the rules'. It was yet another misjudged action from the knight of the realm. He was dismissed from the force on 16 February 1865.

His sacking caused an uproar in the media and among the law-abiding, and led to moves to reinstate him. He was on his way to Sydney on 5 March 1865 to plead his case when a gun in his pocket went off as he was mounting a coach. The wound was serious, but not life-threatening. However, an infection set in and he died a month later.

On 13 March 1865, at about eight o'clock in the morning, the gold escort from Araluen (near the New South Wales south coast) to Braidwood left Redbank on its regularly scheduled journey. The gold was held in an iron safe enclosed in a wooden box and placed in a cart drawn by two horses, driven by local gold dealer and storekeeper J. H. Blatchford. Four constables were detailed to escort duty.

The escort had climbed most of the steep winding track up Majors Creek Mountain, with Constable Burns ahead of it, Kelly alongside it and Stapleton and another constable bringing up the rear. It was a kilometre from the top of the climb, near the place where an attempt to rob it had been made two years earlier, when Constable Kelly suddenly threw up his arms, then fell from his horse. A split-second later the sound of a gunshot was heard. In the bush to the right, there was a puff of smoke.

Four bushrangers then emerged from cover. Three were identified as Hall, Gilbert and Dunn. The fourth had his face covered, however the *Braidwood News* of 15 March reported that he was 'supposed to be a well-known character of this district, for whose apprehension there are now several warrants out'. The most likely candidate was a member of an extended family of local 'notorious horsestealers',

Thomas Clarke. He'd been on the run since the previous November, when he'd shot at three police constables who'd attempted to arrest him on charges relating to stock theft.

Clarke reputedly shouted to the other bushrangers, 'Shoot that —— on the cart!' Shots were then fired at Blatchford. One hit the wheel, then the side of the cart, then Blatchford's calf. Blatchford stopped the cart and jumped off, just as another bullet whizzed over his head.

Constable Burns reacted quickly and with good sense. He returned to the cart, dismounted, blocked the wheel of the cart and threw a quantity of cartridges onto the ground in front of him, where he could use them to quickly reload if necessary.

'Come on you wretches!' he cried. 'I'll lose my last breath before you touch this gold!'

Burns was unable to see the bushrangers due to the number of trees in the area, but they could see him and they proceeded to fire a dozen shots at the cart.

Blatchford initially tried to help Kelly, who was badly wounded but still alive. He then fled down the mountain. Stapleton and the other constable's movements were less clear. By some reports they attempted to circle around the bushrangers and cut off their retreat.

The bushrangers weren't prepared to risk attacking the stubborn Burns, who was using the cart for cover. They were falling back when they encountered Stapleton and the other constable, who had reached the heights above them. As the bushrangers mounted their horses, Stapleton fired at Gilbert, narrowly missing his head.

'You're a —— good shot,' Gilbert said, as he turned to see who was shooting at him. 'Take that!'

His shot hit Stapleton's horse.

Meanwhile, Blatchford reached a pub on the mountain where he was able to get a horse and ride to Redbank, where he sent a telegram to Braidwood. When the news reached Araluen, 200 miners downed tools, armed themselves and headed up the mountain after the bushrangers. However, they were already long gone. At seven o'clock, three of the bushrangers stuck up a homestead, fed their horses, took what they wanted and headed towards Long Swamp.

A search of the area where the escort stopped revealed that the bushrangers had come prepared. They left behind a sledgehammer, chisel, axe and other safe-cracking tools.

Constable Kelly survived his wounding.

For some time the Victorian police force had been crowing about the fact that bushranging in their state was virtually nonexistent. As already mentioned, they enjoyed certain advantages over their hard-pressed New South Wales counterparts. However, their taunts prompted Dan Morgan to cross the Murray on 2 April with the intention of 'taking the flashness out of the Victorian police'. Another reason may have been that the New South Wales police were becoming increasingly active in hunting him and he had little choice but to abandon familiar territory to escape them.

Without his established network of sympathisers, Morgan resorted to intimidation. He stole a racehorse at Tallangatta, robbed a station at Tarwonga and on 6 April 1865 he set fire to the haystacks on another station before heading west to Winton, where he dined. The next day he bailed up travellers on the road between Benalla and Wangaratta. On Saturday, 8 April 1865, he bailed up the homestead of a man named Warby, 5 kilometres from the town of Glenrowan, mainly for the purpose of having breakfast.

He then proceeded to McPherson and Rutherford's Peechelba station, 30 kilometres from Wangaratta. He bailed up the residents of McPherson's house at around six in the evening, holding the family and servants in one room while covering them with two revolvers that he placed on the table. He ordered a meal to be served, and by some accounts had Mrs McPherson play the piano for him. He told the family that he didn't intend to rob them, but that he needed a horse. He had also heard that, while many stations were turning away itinerants seeking tucker, Peechelba still had a reputation for showing some generosity to travellers down on their luck.

He mentioned that he had taken to bushranging due to a heavy sentence imposed on him in 1854, while he was known as Bill the Native. He had vowed revenge on society ever since. While he was talking, one of the servants, Alice Keenan, managed to slip away from the homestead and ran down to the house of McPherson's partner, Rutherford, to tell him that Morgan was on the property.

Rutherford sent word to Wangaratta, while organising his own men to stake out the McPherson homestead. When word reached Wangaratta, at 9.30 p.m., Police Magistrate Shadforth organised a party of volunteers under the town's Senior Constable Evans, armed them and set out for Peechelba. Police reinforcements were also sent for.

By 1 a.m. on Sunday morning, a dozen men had surrounded the McPherson homestead. Given the ferocious reputation Morgan had acquired, and the presence of a number of unarmed people in the building, it was decided to wait until Morgan left the homestead before making any attempt to capture or shoot him. The plucky Alice Keenan then went back into the homestead to tell Mr McPherson what was going on.

It appears that Morgan never slept during the night he was at Peechelba. If he did, he never afforded anyone in the building an opportunity to disarm or apprehend him. At the first light of dawn he shared a whisky with Mr McPherson then went out onto the verandah. He stood there for about five minutes, during which time Constable Evans considered attempting a shot. However, fearing the consequences if he missed, he refrained.

At 7 a.m. more police arrived in the form of Detective Mainwaring and three troopers. Evans managed to intercept them before they attacked the house and before Morgan was alerted to their presence.

Morgan, meanwhile, was taking some time over washing his face and combing his hair and beard. After wolfing down breakfast he asked McPherson what horse he was going to be given. McPherson said he'd send a boy for it, but Morgan said he'd go himself. According to the *Ovens Advertiser* of 11 April 1865 (reprinted in the *Argus* on 13 April):

> In going to look at the horse Mr McPherson had promised him, he said he would require the others who were bailed up (not including the females) to accompany him. Mr McPherson, his son, a youth of 16, Mr Telford, the overseer on the station, and the other two men he originally brought to the house, were ordered to accompany him. Mr McPherson walked next to Morgan. When they had got about 200 yards [183 metres] from the house, and had crossed over to a paddock where several horses were feeding, Mr McPherson said, 'This is the horse I intend lending you', at the same time stepping two or 3 yards [1.8 to 2.7 metres] aside so as to give those in ambush, who were closing upon him fast behind, a fair chance for a good shot. James Quinlan [his name was actually Wendlan], a young man engaged on the station, took aim at Morgan at a distance of about 60 or 70 yards [55 to 64 metres] behind him, fired, and brought Morgan to earth – the ruffian falling forward on his face heavily. Constables Percy and Evans (who were immediately behind [Wendlan], and who were prepared to face Morgan in case of a miss) instantly rushed on the now helpless scoundrel, seized his revolver – his other revolver being left in the house, unloaded – and threw it away from him.
>
> On the constables taking him up, he said 'Why did you not give me a chance? Why did you not challenge me first?'
>
> On his removal to the wool shed, he was placed on a mattress. Someone suggesting sending for a doctor; [Wendlan] said it was no use, he

would die. The now helpless bushranger turned up his eyes and said audibly, 'You will die some day, too.'

The ball had penetrated through the shoulder bone, and had come out by the throat.

Morgan died at 1.45 p.m., by which time a crowd of about fifty people had assembled. As soon as he was dead, several of them swooped on the body to cut locks from his hair and beard. It was said that if not for the intervention of Detective Mainwaring, he would have lost all his hair. Photographs of Morgan in death, however, show no signs of extensive interference.

In April, as soon as the *Felons Apprehension Act* passed into law, a proclamation was issued that would make Gilbert, Hall and Dunn outlaws if they did not surrender themselves to the police by 10 May. Even before then, the gang was already being hunted. The deadline of 10 May passed, whereupon it became legal for anyone to shoot them on sight.

As the Gilbert-Hall Gang were more pressed by increasing numbers of police, they began to be less discriminating in the targets for their crime. They stole from the poor as well as the rich, losing sympathy among a group who had been their supporters.

The *Felons Apprehension Act* also provided for sentences of up to fifteen years for harbouring bushrangers. As the risks for harbouring increased, the rewards for turning in the bushrangers beckoned. Some of their supporters may have realised that it was only a matter of time before someone decided to cash in. As it turned out, they had to be quick.

Ben Hall was betrayed even before he officially became an outlaw. According to the police account, published in the *Sydney Morning Herald* of 20 May 1865, Sub-Inspector Davidson, Sergeant Condell, four constables and a tracker located his camp at Billabong Creek, near Forbes, in thick scrub, some time after nightfall on 4 May 1865. They kept watch until the morning when he rose to fetch his horses, then sprang from cover and ordered him to stand. Hall ran instead only to be followed by shots from his pursuers and to face more gunfire from four police who emerged from cover in front of him. He was hit by at least sixteen shots and killed. Said the *Herald*: 'The brain was penetrated at two points through the forehead, the left arm lacerated with slugs or large shot, and the body perforated in sundry places by bullets and rifle balls. In short, the body was literally riddled.'

The tracker involved in Hall's capture was Billy Dargin. He reputedly had encountered Ben Hall once before, back in 1863. Hall had turned on him and had him at gunpoint when he decided to spare his life. Hall commented, 'By God old man you are a plucked one. We will let you go.'

Dargin contradicted the police account given above. His version of the story, which he told for years after, was that Ben Hall received his wounds while lying on the ground, possibly while asleep.

Ben Hall's betrayer, Mick Connelly, who had revealed the location of his camp, was a 'close friend'. He received £500 of the £1000 reward, and may have also kept some of the proceeds of the robberies Hall had given him to bank.

After Hall's death, the people who had harboured bushrangers in New South Wales since the outbreak began in 1861 practically fell over themselves in the rush to betray them once their race appeared to be run.

On 12 May Gilbert and Dunn went to Dunn's grandfather's smallholding near Binalong.

As Charles White put it in his *History of Australian Bushranging*, 'That [Grandpa Kelly] received them only to betray them does not admit of any question.'

Shortly after they arrived, Binalong police surrounded the place. They remained in position all night, keeping hidden the whole time. As nothing appeared to be happening they returned to the police station. Then fresh information arrived and they went back to Kelly's. They watched the Kelly family going about their daily business for about an hour before deciding to approach the place.

Grandpa Kelly saw them first. 'Look out!' he cried. 'The house is surrounded by troopers.'

The police then rushed the house, firing wildly. Gilbert and Dunn escaped from the rear of the house, crossed a paddock and reached a creek. There Gilbert got behind a tree while Dunn kept running. Gilbert attempted to fire his revolving rifle at the constables, but it misfired. He then turned and fled, the police close behind. He got down the bank of the creek and was running along its dry bed when two police, constables Hales and Bright, fired at him. He was hit and fell.

While Gilbert, who had been mortally wounded, was secured, other police went after Dunn. They were hot on his heels, but young Dunn was fast on his feet and although he may have been wounded, he nevertheless managed to escape.

After betraying his grandson Johnny Dunn, and Johnny Gilbert, Grandpa Kelly maintained a façade of innocence. Superintendent Zouch described his performance as 'a palpable piece of acting, quite natural to, and in keeping with his class, sympathies and characteristics; performed doubtless for the purpose of imposing upon, and deluding the Public, so as to cloak his conduct as an Informer.'

In June 1865 Johnny Dunn and an unidentified companion went to a house near Cowra. They asked for some things that had been left there by the Gilbert-Hall Gang. They got what they were after, then left.

For some months after, Dunn disappeared. It was thought by some that he might have died in the bush. In any event the Gilbert-Hall Gang was effectively finished.

However, there still remained at large some of those schooled by the gang, including Thomas Clarke. He had been arrested in relation to a series of robberies dating back to the previous year, but was released on bail on each charge. Police also suspected him of involvement in the attempt to rob the Araluen Gold Escort, but didn't bring a charge until August 1865. On that occasion bail was refused and he was held in custody at Braidwood, awaiting trial.

The wheels of the law may grind slowly, but in Clarke's case you'd be hard-pressed to detect any motion at all. He was still languishing in Braidwood's lockup on 3 October when, according to the *Sydney Morning Herald*:

> At 6 o'clock, Thomas Clarke got over the gaol wall, and ran about one hundred yards [91 metres] to where a horse had been left in readiness for him. The warder outside and two constables followed, and caught hold of the horse, but were ridden down. Clarke had neither hat, boots, nor coat on, and mounted the horse without saddle or bridle. Two mounted police followed immediately after him, and after two hours' absence returned reporting they had lost him in the bush. Tomorrow Clarke was to have been taken to Goulburn, for trial.

Clarke's escape warranted only a brief mention at the time. However, it was an event police would regret for a long time after.

Braidwood, a gold-digging district in New South Wales, was another area where the divide between settler and rural worker, gold prospector and rural poor, was pronounced.

The mountainous area south of Braidwood, extending from the Jingera and Tinderry ranges in the west down to the diggings at Araluen in the east, was ideal bushranging country, especially for capable young horsemen with a good network of sympathisers. Such were the Clarke boys, Thomas and his brother John (their brother James was already doing a three-year stretch for horse-stealing).

Their relatives in crime included their uncle Patrick Connell, and other Connells, plus an assortment of relatives, friends and itinerant villains including the Berrimans, James Dornan (an old Port Arthur hand who was convicted in November 1864 for a robbery in Braidwood and got eighteen months), William Bruce, William Scott (known as the Long Tailor), James Griffin and others.

In November and December 1865 Captain Thunderbolt hooked up with 36-year-old Irishman Patrick Kelly and Jemmy the Whisperer (who with Patrick McManus had been involved in a police shooting back in 1862) to commit a number of robberies around Tamworth, culminating in the bailing up of an inn at the town of Carroll on 10 December 1865. While the customers were being robbed, Senior Constable Lang and constables Aggett and Shaw arrived just on nightfall.

One of the customers reportedly managed to approach them and say, 'We are all bailed up here.'

Lang replied, 'We are the police. Where are the bushrangers?'

The customer pointed out Thunderbolt, whereupon Lang levelled his carbine and fired. He missed, despite being only metres from his target. The bushrangers fired back and Lang was shot in the arm. The shooting continued for the next fifteen minutes, with no further casualties. Eventually Thunderbolt and company escaped into the night.

New South Wales police wrapped up 1865 with the capture of Johnny Dunn. He'd been working on a station in the state's northwest when police, acting on information received, attempted to arrest him. He escaped but was forced to keep moving. On 24 December he was accidentally found by police near Coonamble. They were actually hunting another man when Dunn fell into their hands. When he ran, he was wounded in the back, but as he lay on the ground he managed to shoot Constable McHale in the thigh. He held the police at bay until he ran out of bullets.

One of the bullets that hit Dunn damaged the sciatic nerve, leaving him in constant pain. After his capture he was transferred to Coonamble, then on to Dubbo. He was more dead than alive, but his race was not yet run.

At Dubbo Gaol, Johnny Dunn's physical condition appeared to take a turn for the worse. Despite the best efforts of the prison doctor, on 14 January he seemed to have sunk so low that he was at death's door. Thinking the end was near, the doctor attending him asked for his irons to be taken off.

Not long after, when an officer went to check on him, it turned out Dunn wasn't as sick as he appeared. He had managed to make his way out through a window and was gone.

A large search of the immediate area found no sign of him. As it turned out, Dunn's determination to escape wasn't matched by his ability to get far. The following evening, only 2 kilometres from the gaol, he emerged from the bush to ask a wood carter for some water, having had nothing to eat or drink since his escape thirty-six hours earlier. The carter instead went for the police.

When he was back in custody, Dunn told the officers that if he'd been able to get hold of a revolver, he'd have shot everyone who came near him, saving the last bullet for himself.

In February 1866 the Clarke Gang committed the first robberies that would earn them widespread notoriety. They literally robbed their way down the Araluen Valley, supposedly with the police in pursuit. Exactly what happened varies depending on the source. The *Queanbeyan Age* of 8 March canvassed several accounts that cast the four police in varying lights ranging from courage to cowardice.

What is not in dispute is that at 8 p.m. on 23 February, four bushrangers in disguise bailed up Hoskins' public house at Crown Flat. One of the customers, the owner of the store opposite, Mr Eaton, was robbed of between £20 and £30, after which the bushrangers crossed the street to ransack his premises. Eaton's brother-in-law, Mr Duggan, then managed to escape and ran for the police. Here the accounts diverge.

In version one, at the police station he found Constable Dasey (or Lacy), who was reluctant to face four bushrangers on his own. Dasey eventually went with Eaton, leaving a message for his colleagues to follow when they turned up. By the time he arrived at Eaton's store, the bushrangers had moved down the valley to Morris's pub at Mudmelong. Back at the station constables Curran and Richardson got Dasey's message and somehow managed to overtake him on the way to Mudmelong. The pair found no bushrangers at the pub and lay in wait, apprehending one (either Tom Connell or Joseph Berriman) when he came in. The other bushrangers then realised their mate was being held and after an exchange of gunfire threatened to burn the place down. Curran and Richardson surrendered. Constable Dasey was then taken prisoner when he arrived. Constable Stapylton having heard what was going on, then proceeded to the pub on his own and was similarly bailed up when he arrived.

In version two, Duggan found all four police at the station. They went with him to Crown Flat, then on to Mudmelong where they found one bushranger in the bar, guarding several prisoners. They arrested him and were still at the pub when the other three bushrangers arrived. In this version, the three bushrangers simply entered the pub, got the drop on the constables and forced them all to surrender at once. They then forced the police to go behind the bar and serve drinks all round.

Other versions of the story vary slightly from these two. However, what is beyond doubt is that one bushranger was taken prisoner by the police but freed after a gunfight with the other three. The bushrangers were identified as Thomas Clarke, Pat Connell (Clarke's uncle), Thomas Connell (Clarke's cousin), and either Berriman or William Bruce.

Constable Richardson was made the scapegoat and was subsequently dismissed for his part in the affair. William Bruce faced trial for his involvement, at which Constable Dasey gave a garbled account of what occurred, and Bruce was found not guilty.

On 19 March 1866 what should have been the final act in the long career of the Gardiner-O'Meally-Gilbert-Hall Gang took place in Sydney. The *Sydney Morning Herald* of 28 March reported:

> A sadder scene was never enacted in that arena of sorrow, suffering, and sin comprised within the walls of Darlinghurst Gaol, than when John Dunn – the last of the notorious trio who, setting religion and law at defiance, excited feelings of indignation, insecurity, and terror throughout the colony – died an ignominious death upon the scaffold.

Dunn had actually been convicted for the particularly ruthless murder of Constable Nelson at Collector. The *Herald* summarised the fate of the other members of the gang. Gardiner, Vane, Bow, Fordyce, the ill-fated Dunleavy (who died of tuberculosis before any hope of release) and the Old Man were serving long prison sentences. Piesley and Manns had been hanged. Lowry, Burke, O'Meally, Hall and Gilbert had been shot dead.

The gang's history should have ended there, yet within a decade, New South Wales would be plunged into political turmoil as the leader of the gang, Frank Gardiner, engineered an escape from prison that saw most of the surviving bushrangers legally walk free. Until that time, the death of Dunn marked the end of an era – except, of course, for the numerous bushrangers the gang had inspired who were still at large.

In March 1866 an extraordinary story circulated when a woman emerged from the bush near Stroud to say she'd been held prisoner by Captain Thunderbolt.

She had attended to 'Mrs Thunderbolt' when she was giving birth, and afterwards he had held her captive for ten months, presumably in the role of hostage-cum-nanny. According to the Stroud correspondent of the *Maitland Mercury*:

> She states that Thunderbolt is hurt in the back from a fall off his horse, also suffering from a bad knee, preventing his getting about without assistance, that his wife had herself had to put him up on horseback, his wife always accompanies him (dressed in men's attire) out to plunder, that she has a large butcher's knife fastened on the end of a stick, rides up alongside the cattle and with this instrument she hamstrings the beast, and then kills it. They principally live on beef (very seldom they have flour), wild yams, and wattle gum. The last place they stayed at they remained from June to January, near to a station of a Mr Parnell, and were never molested. The informant made her escape while Thunderbolt's wife was out after beef; she wandered six days through the bush before she came to an inhabited place, and three days from there to Stroud, living on yams and wattle gum during that time. She asserts that there is no one else with Thunderbolt except his wife and three children. He has in his possession ten head of horses, and all are in low condition.

On or about 28 March 1866 Stroud police just missed Thunderbolt, but managed to capture Mary Ann and her growing family. The *Sydney Morning Herald* reported on 6 April 1866:

Mrs Thunderbolt was taken at Pignaum Barney, with three children, but got away at Mr Hooke's station, where she was left while the police went out again in search of Thunderbolt; she was retaken by Sergeant Kerrigan, and brought on here [Stroud]. This morning she was tried under the Vagrant Act, and sentenced to six months' imprisonment in Maitland gaol. The other two children, with the informer, arrived today in [the] charge of troopers Cleary and Underwood.

The report clarified some of the points made by the woman who had escaped Thunderbolt a few weeks before. She may also have been the informer the report referred to. It turned out Thunderbolt wasn't as crippled as was thought and was able to mount his horse and 'ride like the wind'. He did appear to have a bad back and leg, but wasn't incapacitated.

At her trial, Mary Ann acknowledged that she killed cattle as the woman had described, but denied going about in men's costume. However, another report, published in the same paper, stated that when she was captured: 'The girl [Mary Ann] was clothed completely in men's apparel, and rode as men usually do. One of her children about six years of age, is also described as a good rider.'

Emboldened by their victory over the police at Araluen, the Clarke Gang, now numbering six or seven adventure-seeking young men, moved on to the diggings at Nerrigundah. From 3 p.m. on Monday, 9 April 1866 they robbed travellers at the intersection of three roads near Gulph Creek. After each traveller was bailed up they were marched into the bush and guarded to prevent them raising the alarm.

The gang met little resistance until John Emmott, who was carrying a large quantity of gold, was bailed up. He attempted to escape, but was followed by a volley of shots, one of which killed his horse. He was trying to throw his gold into the bush when he was hit by another shot from the bushrangers. The bullet hit him in the back of the thigh, travelled 30 centimetres down his leg and exited out of the front of his leg.

Crippled and faint from loss of blood, Emmott was ordered to join the other victims in the bush. When he didn't move, the bushrangers pistol-whipped him and threatened to kill him. One of the bushrangers eventually gave him some water and the injured man struggled to join the other prisoners.

Everyone was then moved to a nearby pub where two bushrangers guarded them and the remaining four or five went into Nerrigundah. They bailed up Wallis's pub, the first they came to, and robbed the customers. They, too, were guarded while two bushrangers went to Pollock's store. Pollock was a gold dealer and had several hundred ounces of gold in his safe. However, the bushrangers didn't find the gold as they ransacked the place. While marching the Pollocks back to Wallis's they noticed Mrs Pollock trying to hide a key. It was taken from her, but just as they reached the pub she gamely snatched it back and threw it over the bushrangers' heads into the street. The bushrangers were searching for it when the police arrived.

According to the *Moruya Examiner* of 13 April 1866:

> Constable O'Grady had risen from a sick bed, and in company with Constable Smith had proceeded to the scene. Fletcher [one of the bushrangers] was in the doorway of the public house when O'Grady fired, the bullet glanced on Fletcher's arm which it struck and afterwards entered his body at the armpits. The bushrangers immediately returned the fire and poor O'Grady was shot in the hip, the ball entering in an oblique direction at the side, and coming out at the lower part of the belly. Fletcher died about an hour afterwards. Poor O'Grady lingered for about three hours.

The bushrangers, later identified as Thomas Clarke, William Berriman, William Fletcher, Thomas Connell and Pat Connell, then fled the town. They proceeded to Deep Creek where they bailed up more people. They threatened to kill a Chinese miner, who eventually was found to be carrying only five shillings. Another Chinese miner managed to escape and alert his camp. Night had fallen and the Chinese turned out en masse with lanterns to hunt the bushrangers. Seeing a mass of lights approaching, one of the bushrangers reportedly cried out, 'Make haste, the Gulph people [the whole miners' camp] are on us.' They at last fled.

At Nerrigundah, Sergeant Hitch arrived from Moruya and quickly organised a volunteer party to pursue the bushrangers. Locals decided there was only one route the bushrangers could take and one of them believed he knew a short cut that would allow them to be intercepted and ambushed. According to the *Moruya Examiner*:

> The guide well fulfilled his promise, but just as they reached the desired point on the Belimbla Creek, before the party had time to hide, the five robbers appeared with a sixth horse. The one believed to be Tommy Clark [sic], leading the horse, was in advance of the rest, and entered the creek; the others stopped on the opposite bank to that where were Sergeant Hitch and his party, who fired on the ruffians when they were so situated, at about sixty or seventy yards [55 or 64 metres] distance. It is said that Clark reeled in his saddle after the discharge of firearms. However, he instantly turned and joined the rest, when Sergeant Hitch fired again, the bullet striking a tree between him and the robbers. They immediately galloped off.

The volunteers were unable to pursue the bushrangers because, in their haste to go after them, they hadn't brought enough ammunition. The only one with any bullets left was Sergeant Hitch.

It was noted that when Fletcher was buried, a large crowd gathered, suggestive that the Clarke Gang, in effect an extended clan, had numerous sympathisers.

Subsequently, Thomas Clarke and Pat Connell were outlawed under the *Felons Apprehension Act*. The proclamation was issued on 19 April 1866 and the deadline for their surrender was 4 May 1866.

On 1 June Tommy Clarke, the two Connells and another bushranger (possibly Thomas Clarke's younger brother John or a man named Hyland) bailed up the town of Micalago (now Michelago) between Queanbeyan and Cooma.

Their intentions were hinted at by William Bruce who had appeared in town earlier that day. When the bushrangers arrived that afternoon, riding in from the Tinderry and Jingera ranges, just east of the town, they stuck up a number of homes, taking prisoners as they went and leaving them under guard at the pub.

They then found a man named Fowler, an employee at Levy's store, and demanded he open the store for them, on threat of death. He refused, reached into his pocket and reputedly said, 'Here's the key, and now you may go and look for it' as he threw the key over the roof of the store. Instead, the bushrangers broke down the front door. They then ransacked the place. When the bushrangers demanded money, Fowler told them it was in a box in another room. When they went to look, he took the opportunity to throw five pounds in coins that were in his pockets into the fire.

The bushrangers returned to the pub and eventually got drunk, after which they took to brawling and firing their weapons in the streets and the local area until midnight.

In July 1866 members of the Clarke Gang again visited Mudmelong in the Araluen valley, bailing up several people in the neighbourhood. However, news of the attack soon spread and police from Ballalaba were despatched to intercept them on their way back to their hideouts in the Jingera Range.

Sergeant Creagh, Senior Constable Byrne and constables Kelly and Gracy set out on 17 July in company with a tracker. They hid themselves on a mountainside and were soon rewarded when they spotted Pat Connell and another member of the gang driving a mob of horses along a bush track. They managed to follow them without being seen for some 25 kilometres, when the pair reached a bush camp and joined two other bushrangers. The other bushrangers were later identified as Thomas Connell, John Clarke and Thomas Lawler. The police closed to within 60 metres of the camp.

On Sergeant Creagh's command, the police fired a volley at the camp then rushed the bushrangers. Three fled across the creek into thick scrub, from where they held Creagh and Byrne at bay. Pat Connell was on horseback and made off up the creek with Kelly and Gracy in pursuit. According to the *Braidwood Dispatch*:

> Kelly says that when he got within sixty yards [55 metres] of him he fired upon him. Just before doing so Connell all intent, apparently, upon urging his horse over the hill, looked round and said, 'Stand back you ——.'
>
> These were the last words the robber uttered for immediately the words were out of his mouth Kelly's bullet had accomplished its fatal mission, and passed through his back between the left shoulder-blade at the bottom of the shoulder and the spine. The outlaw threw up his arms, groaned, and fell backwards from his horse, with his head foremost to the ground.

When Kelly realised Connell was dying or dead, he went back to help his senior officers in their fire-fight with the other bushrangers. The shooting continued for an hour and a half. As darkness began to fall, the police retreated from the stalemate, took possession of everything in the camp and took Connell's body back to Braidwood.

West Australia had been largely spared the predations of bushrangers, in part due to its being settled later than the other colonies, and due to the fact that, like South Australia, most of the state is so dry and barren that there's not much bush to be ranged. However, that changed in August 1866 with the escape of a former convict who went by the name Moondyne Joe.

Joseph Johns (Moondyne's real name) was originally from Wales, where in 1849 he was sentenced to ten years' transportation. He arrived in Fremantle, to which prisoners were still being transported, in 1853. Johns was conditionally pardoned in March 1855 and soon found work in the Avon Valley and Darling Range as a stockman. He was arrested in August 1861 on a technicality that amounted to horse-stealing. The horse in question was a cleanskin (unbranded) and he'd branded it without first advertising his intention to do so, as required by law.

Moondyne promptly escaped from Toodyay Gaol, stole another horse and fled. When he was captured, shortly afterwards, he faced additional charges including escaping and stealing a police horse. He got three years and was released in 1864. In July 1865 he was charged with killing an ox with felonious intent, again on a technicality (i.e. either an unbranded animal or in a way that hid its brand), and given ten years. He escaped, was recaptured, and was given an extra twelve months in irons. He escaped yet again, was captured and was given another six months in irons.

On 8 August 1866 he escaped again. This time he did so with Thomas Bugg, John Bassett and John James. Shortly after, they robbed a farm in the Avon Valley, stealing a double-barrelled gun, revolver, ammunition and food. They then took to the roads, robbing travellers and stations throughout August. Bassett was captured at the end of the month.

Moondyne, Bugg and James decided to attempt to leave Western Australia by crossing overland to South Australia, a feat only achieved by explorer Edward Eyre up to that time. In September they robbed a store at Toodyay and stole food and kangaroo dogs from several farms and huts. They headed east, passing Youndegin (100 kilometres from Perth) before reaching Boondalin Soak. There, on 29 September 1866, the police caught up with them. In the armed confrontation that followed, Bugg was shot before the bushrangers surrendered.

The prison authorities were clearly fed up with Moondyne's persistent escape attempts. When he was returned to Fremantle Prison (with another five years added to his sentence for his most recent exploits), he was chained by the neck to the bars of his cell while an 'escape-proof' cell was specially constructed to hold him. When it was completed, Moondyne was moved in.

The gaol's controller, Mr Hampton, reputedly told him that if he managed to escape from this cell, he'd deserve his freedom. However, it was soon clear that close confinement, chained to a ring in the floor and only able to move a metre in any direction, was destroying Moondyne's health. The prison authorities eventually relented and allowed him to do some prison work outdoors. Closely watched, he was given the task of breaking rocks in the prison yard. Unfortunately, he wasn't watched closely enough.

Back in New South Wales, on 22 September 1866 four 'special constables' – Darlinghurst Gaol warders John Carroll, Patrick Kennagh, Eneas McDonnell and former Clarke associate John Phegan – were sent to Braidwood by then-premier Henry Parkes on 'a secret expedition for the capture of the bushranger Thomas Clarke and his associates'.

On 23 September 1866, before the special constables arrived, Braidwood police actually had some success in their pursuit of the Clarke Gang. Constables Woodlands, Hughes and Egan sighted Thomas Connell in company with William Bruce and Lucy Hurley (Connell's girlfriend) and gave chase. According to one report,

Hurley tried to assist her boyfriend's escape by 'rush[ing] in front of one of the constables, shaking her dress about and screaming, so that his horse swerved, and he lost sight of the fugitive'.

In evidence given at the trial of William Bruce for harbouring Connell, Constable Woodlands, stationed in the lion's den at Jingera, gave more detail:

> The constables were about 150 yards [137 metres] from the party when they first saw Tom; Bruce called out 'Look out Tom, here are the police'; Tom Connell sprang behind a tree and presented his rifle; constables Hughes and Egan dismounted and as soon as they got off, Connell sprang upon the horse that was tied up and galloped away; [Woodlands] pursued Connell, who had been previously called upon to surrender; Connell went through a scrub into which [Woodlands] was following him when Lucy Hurley sprang out with a butcher's knife in her hand. [Woodlands] passed her and followed Connell up a steep ridge, but had not gone far when the horse stood, being blown [meaning it was exhausted]. He afterwards saw Connell in a creek below, aiming his rifle at him. He fired, and saw Connell fall off his horse. He was going down to where Connell was when he heard Hughes call for help. He went to him and found him struggling with Bruce. [Woodlands] told Bruce to take it easy, and the latter said he would.

The constables handcuffed the prisoner and Woodlands went after Connell, but could find no sign of him. Bruce didn't go quietly. He was put on a horse, and although handcuffed, he spurred the horse to try to escape.

'Go it, you ——, you can't catch me,' Bruce reportedly taunted the officers as he galloped off.

He was intercepted as he tried to cross the creek.

Woodlands explained in the *Sydney Morning Herald* of 16 August 1867:

There Bruce was again arrested. He refused to go with them, and laid down on the ground biting mouthfuls of the earth and spitting it up into the air. After going on in this way for some time he consented to proceed. They took him to the station. When within a mile of the place Constables Egan and Hughes went on, and prisoner then offered witness £5 to let him escape.

Shortly after, the special constables arrived in the district. At first they pretended to be surveyors, but when their real identities were exposed in a night attack on their camp, they openly set about rooting out the gang's harbourers. Several harbourers were brought before magistrates, but the special constables' leader, John Carroll, soon found the local magistrates reluctant to convict, while local police hindered his efforts. Both may have had their motives. The magistrates feared for their own property while the bushrangers were at large. The police resented the activities of special constables whose only job was hunting bushrangers without the restrictions of red tape.

After the attack on their camp, Carroll and his men slept in the open, the better to hear an approaching ambush. They attempted to move rapidly through the district, hoping to outpace the bush telegraphs and surprise their quarry. They also began paying bribes in return for information. Soon they had sufficient information to arrest Michael Connell (cousin of the outlaws, and postmaster and storekeeper at Orenmeir) and another relative named Berry.

Carroll also concluded that some police in the district were corrupt. He openly accused them of receiving proceeds from a robbery at Foxlow station (between Ballalaba and Jingera) and of having had improper relations with women in the bushranging clan.

There was no doubting the energy of the special constables. However, one prosecution of an unlicensed publican proved so unpopular that even Henry Parkes decided they'd gone too far. He intervened and forced John Carroll to abandon the case.

While the special constables scoured the Braidwood district with little to show for their efforts, the regular police continued trying to do their job. On 9 November 1866 Sergeant Daniel Byrne, constables Laughlin and Callahan, and a tracker from the Ballalaba station, south of Braidwood, caught sight of Thomas and John Clarke and Tom Connell near Run of Water Creek. They gave chase to Tom Connell.

Byrne's later testimony was reported in the *Sydney Morning Herald* of 29 November:

> When he got to the creek, [he] jumped off his horse and crossed it on foot, and when he had run about 40 yards [38 metres] on the other side he got behind a tree, and constables Callahan and Laughlin fired at him. Laughlin [and I] then rushed over the creek on foot after [Connell], who ran away from the tree up the hill and over the ridge, they and the tracker following him. When [I] got on the top of the ridge he saw [Connell] standing alongside a tree with his rifle levelled at Laughlin, who was about 60 yards [55 metres] away. [I] immediately covered [Connell] with his revolver, and called upon him to surrender. [Connell] turned round, but still held his rifle in a line with his waist. [I], keeping him covered with his piece, told him if he did not drop his rifle he would shoot him. [Connell] said, 'all right, I'll surrender', but did not immediately drop his rifle till [I] further called upon him to do so, when he let it fall.

The arrest of Tom Connell was a significant success for the police of the Braidwood district, which had become the focus of bushranging activity with the frequent robberies committed by the Clarke Gang. The Ballalaba police were singled out for praise by one local, who remarked that they were familiar with the country, and were 'of more use than three times the number of other men would be'.

By comparison, in Maitland, headquarters of the pursuit of Captain

Thunderbolt, all the police were new to the area.

Despite the successful arrest of Connell, in 1866, the superintendent of the Braidwood district requested more officers in order to deal with the increasingly active Clarke Gang. Not only did he not get what he asked for, but by the end of the year the number of police in the district had actually fallen. However, the events of early 1867 were about to change everything.

Towards evening on 8 January 1867 Special Constable Carroll and his men set out on foot from Jinden, in the midst of the Jingeras, south of Braidwood, intending to visit the house of a man named McGuinness, whom they suspected of harbouring the Clarkes. The property was 6 kilometres from the hamlet, the last kilometre of the road passing through thick scrub.

At about 8.30 p.m. residents in the McGuinness house heard shots coming from the vicinity of the scrub. Some time later, more shots were heard. Nobody thought to leave the house to investigate.

The following morning, stockmen found the bodies of special constables Phegan and McDonnell lying on the road. Both had suffered multiple gunshot wounds. Three revolvers lay near Phegan's body. A kilometre away, the bodies of Carroll and Kennagh were found by a police patrol from Ballalaba. Carroll had been shot in the head and through the heart. He was lying on his back with a neatly folded handkerchief and a pound note pinned to his chest. Kennagh had been shot in the throat. None of the men were robbed of their valuables.

It was thought that all four men were ambushed in the scrub – Phegan and McDonnell being hit and falling immediately. Carroll and Kennagh managed to run but were cornered and forced to surrender. They were then executed. Powder burns on Carroll's face suggest he was shot at close range.

The outrage led to an immediate response from the New South Wales government. A reward of £5000 was offered for the apprehension of all of the murderers. In making the proclamation, Henry Parkes added that, 'All parties are cautioned that by harbouring, assisting, or maintaining the murderers, they will make themselves accessories to the crime of murder, and render themselves liable to prosecution accordingly.'

The reward was backed by action, and a special police contingent was despatched from Sydney to scour the region. Soon forty extra police were operating in the district, ten times the number of special constables. However, rather than retreat, the Clarke Gang grew even bolder in its robberies. They divided into at least two groups and on some days robbed every traveller on two roads simultaneously.

Several known sympathisers and harbourers were rounded up, although there was outrage in Araluen when one of them, Michael Connell, was released on bail despite being charged with being an accessory in the murder of the special constables. A town meeting accused the magistrates of going light on Connell out of fear that their property would be targeted. A commission of enquiry was sent from Sydney to look into the matter.

After the murder of the specials, guidelines for hunting bushrangers were drawn up. A minimum of eight men were required, divided into two parties of at least three troopers, each with a tracker. One party was to remain in reserve, resting their horses, but ready to move at a moment's notice. If both parties were out, they should maintain communication to avoid interfering with each other. They were to have good horses or be given them by locals when necessary. They were to encourage volunteers.

The employment of trackers was a significant step for the relatively recently reorganised New South Wales police force. In its early days, trackers were considered unnecessary. However, as time went on their skills were recognised, in some cases because, in addition to their skills as trackers, they also possessed far more local knowledge than their commanders. However, the trackers weren't treated as equals. They were almost exclusively Aborigines, and when reward money was divided, they were discriminated against on the basis of race and generally received less. They also received lower pay, even though the work they did was often identical to that of other police.

North of the Hunter Valley, Captain Thunderbolt, seeming positively kind compared to the Clarke gang, was sighted again in January 1867. He had been rejoined by Mary Ann Ward, who had served her six months for vagrancy. They were spotted at the Upper Allyn, among the scenic southern foothills of the imposing Barrington Ranges. According to a letter in the *Maitland Mercury* of 15 January 1867:

> Several parties gave chase after him, and after a gallop of a few miles he gave his pursuers the slip, by forcing his horse (a fine chestnut) to leap over some rocks. In his hurry to depart he left his wife and child in the hands of the pursuers. Several shots I am told, were exchanged, the manner of his disappearance astonished the natives. I am informed by parties competent to judge, that if Ward were well mounted he is scarcely to be surpassed in horsemanship.

Mary Ann was arrested by a Constable Johnson and charged with possessing stolen goods: 6½ metres of unbleached calico and 5 metres of derry [Irish linen]. She said she'd bought them from a shop in Maitland, but was unable to produce proof. The local magistrate, E. G. Cory, Esquire, 'considered this not satisfactory' and on 24 January sentenced her to three months in Maitland Gaol. She'd been there just over a month when the government, bowing to 'local discontent', quashed her conviction and ordered her release.

During 1867 it was proposed that Thunderbolt, who may have been tiring of bushranging, be offered a job as a policeman. The proposal came from Barraba local George West. Similar suggestions had been made regarding Piesley and even Frank Gardiner. However, such proposals were stamped on by a government that believed criminals should face severe penalties in all cases. West's suggestion got the same reaction.

On 4 March 1867 fifteen-year-old William Parsons may have had the shortest career of any bushranger. He bailed up three wagon drivers on the Ringwood Road at Lilydale, near Melbourne, getting a pound from the first, nothing from the second and a fight for his pistol from the third. The gun went off, the bullet grazing Parsons' neck. He bolted, but was soon caught by his intended victims. His adventure had lasted less than five minutes. However, it was notable for the sentence handed down by Justice Redmond Barry:

> It is almost incredible that you, with arms in your hands, should have stuck-up three men. You could scarcely know how to use them; indeed, you did wound yourself, and nearly blew your own brains out. It is almost incredible crimes like this should occur in our neighbourhood, and it would be laughable were it not lamentable. I think the proper way to deal with gentlemen of tender years like you is the following:– (His Honor then read the clause giving power to judges to flog criminals under sixteen years of age.) This is an instance in which I think it would be judicious to correct you in this manner; and though I have a great reluctance to flog men, you have not yet got from under the correction of the rod, and it appears to me that it would have done you good if it had been administered earlier . . .

Newspapers reported that 'the prisoner appeared quite crestfallen at the prospect of the flogging ordered for him'. The judge might have been crestfallen when he realised the series of floggings he ordered couldn't be carried out until after the lad's next birthday, when the lad turned sixteen and the floggings became illegal.

In Western Australia, Moondyne Joe had been diligently breaking rocks in the prison yard during the months in which he'd been allowed out of his escape-proof prison cell during the day. As it turned out, he wasn't just breaking the rocks he was given.

On 7 March 1867 he exited from the prison yard via a hole he'd gradually broken in the prison wall. He'd kept the hole hidden behind the large pile of rocks he'd been breaking. Before he left, Moondyne put his cap and jacket on a pick he jammed into the rock pile, and for a time the makeshift dummy had fooled the guards. Given that he was supposed to be closely watched – though clearly not closely enough – his absence was soon noticed, and a cry promptly ensued.

The *Perth Gazette* of 15 March observed: 'When the escape was discovered the consternation amongst the prison officials is said to have been something worth witnessing.'

When the news reached Western Australia's governor, and Prison Controller Hampton, it was said 'to have greatly disturbed His Excellency and Mr. Hampton's digestion of their dinner, and did not greatly contribute to their repose during the night, or the day after, if we are to believe that he [Hampton] then offered a reward of £20 from his private purse (!) if Johns [Moondyne Joe] was brought in that day either DEAD or alive. This kind consideration of Mr. Hampton for Joe's health was not productive of benefit to either, for the latter is still enjoying his liberty, and has completely vanished without making tracks.'

However, it was not to be the end of Moondyne Joe.

In April 1867 the Clarke brothers remained at large and unbowed. A letter written from Goulburn documented the defiance of one of their sisters:

> Annie Clarke is in Goulburn, and it is supposed that her presence here is one of sympathy. I can't say about that. She is, however, here, and would no doubt have passed without notice, had she not apparently coveted distinction. Let me afford her vanity scope. She is really not a bad-looking girl, about twenty years of age, fully the proper height for a woman, with a figure that would pass anywhere. But she strives for observation. I only saw her during one day, and then – mimicking the ladies of the land – she changed her dress four times – possibly more than that, because I did not see her 'full-dressed for the evening'. There was something quiet in the first two costumes, but in the afternoon she came out in a 'blood-red' one, with hat and feather, and nether pendants well ankled; presently, out she appeared in blue silk, with white shawl, ankled as before, but without that finish as to hose that lends its particular charms to criticising eyes. I would not have dwelt on the subject had it not been my impression that the Protean change of costume appeared to be as if in bravado – as if to show the less aspiring of her sex how much value there was in being connected with the most worthless of the 'manly' sex. Such an example does more harm than fifty revolvers. I have nothing to say against the girl herself, except to condemn her want of judgement and womanly taste.

The bravado didn't help Annie's brothers. On 27 April 1867 Senior Constable William Wright, constables Egan, Lenehan, Walsh and Wright (no relation) and highly regarded tracker Sir Watkin were patrolling 30 kilometres from Ballalaba, in the rugged Jingeras, when they (reputedly) picked up the tracks of the bushrangers. The police were all on foot and followed the tracks until failing light and heavy rain forced them to stop. However, the police knew the country well enough to be aware that there was a hut 3 kilometres away and conjectured that it was the intended destination of the bushrangers. They were also helped by information provided by a cousin of the Clarkes, Thomas Berry.

When the police reached the hut they watched it from a distance until they were sure the men they were seeking were inside. A constable was sent back to Ballalaba for reinforcements. In the cold, wet and darkness, the remaining police settled down behind a haystack to keep watch until the moon rose. By its light they saw two horses grazing in the paddock adjacent to the hut. They managed to quietly drive them as far from the hut as possible, without alerting the occupants. The police then waited for dawn.

Just after first light, Thomas and John Clarke emerged from the hut carrying bridles. Intent on catching the horses, they started walking across the paddock. Then one of them cried out, 'Look out! There's someone at the stack.'

They turned and started running back to the hut. The police left their hiding place and called on the Clarkes to stand. The brothers kept running as the police opened fire, then drew their revolvers and fired back. They reached the hut, but John Clarke had been hit, the bullet entering near his right shoulder then passing through his body without hitting any bone or vital organ.

From gaps in the slabs of the hut the bushrangers began firing with their rifles. The more accurate fire told on the police: Constable Walsh was hit in the thigh; Sir Watkin in the arm. The police sought what little shelter there was in the yard. The police held the bushrangers at bay until the looked-for reinforcements arrived in the form of Sergeant Byrne and six troopers. When the bushrangers saw they were surrounded by a force of a dozen police, rather than fight to the death, they called out that they wanted to surrender. They emerged from the hut, unarmed, and were handcuffed and taken to Ballalaba. No attempt was made by sympathisers to free them.

Sir Watkin's arm was so badly damaged that it ultimately had to be amputated. It was said that he underwent the operation without anaesthetic of any kind, and without a murmur. He was given a sham promotion to 'sergeant-major' in recognition of his services. Sham or not, his colleagues reputedly treated him with the true respect due to an officer.

Thomas Berry received £750 out of the £1500 available for the capture of the two bushrangers. It may seem extraordinary that the Clarkes were betrayed by a member of their own family, as was Johnny Dunn by his grandfather. However, it should not be forgotten that crime can put family loyalty under extreme pressure. In addition, the Clarke clan's life of crime had been marked by endless manoeuvrings based on loyalty, treachery and the desire for gain. Betrayal among its members was only one of a range of character flaws.

Just five days after the Clarkes' capture, the bushranging career of Larry Cummins came to an end. He was arrested on 2 May 1867. An accomplice, John Foran was arrested at the Cummins family home at the end of the following month. Cummins ended up with a sentence of thirty years' hard labour. Foran was sentenced to fifteen years of the same.

With the exception of Captain Thunderbolt, who was still at large, it appeared that bushranging in New South Wales was virtually at an end. It was certainly a view that informed the remarks of Chief Justice Sir Alfred Stephen when, on 28 May 1867, he sentenced John and Thomas Clarke to death after they were found guilty of their last crime, wounding Constable William Walsh with intent to murder. The chief justice also passed judgement on the most violent era in Australian bushranging:

> I will read you a list of bushrangers, many of whom have come to the gallows within the last four and a half years. I believe they are all caught but one. Many of these were young men capable of better things; but died

violent deaths: – Piesley, executed; Davis, sentenced to death; Gardiner, sentenced to thirty-two years hard labour; Gilbert, shot dead; Hall, shot dead; Bow and Fordyce, sentenced to death, but sentences commuted to imprisonment for life; Manns, executed; O'Meally, shot dead; Burke, shot dead; Gordon, sentenced to death; Dunleavy, sentenced to death; Dunn, executed; Lowry, shot dead; Vane, a long sentence; Foley, a long sentence; Morgan, shot dead; yourselves, Thomas and John Clarke, about to be sentenced to death; Fletcher, shot dead; Patrick Connell, shot dead; Tom Connell, sentenced to death but sentence commuted to imprisonment for life; Bill Scott, a companion of your own, believed to be murdered by you. There is a list! The murders believed to have been committed by you bushrangers are appalling to think of. How many more wives made widows, and children made orphans! What loss of property, what sorrow have you bushrangers caused! I have a list here of persons killed or wounded in the perpetration of robberies since August 1863 – six killed and ten wounded. Unfortunately, of the police, seven have been killed and sixteen wounded in three years. I say this is horrible. Much as I dread crime, and much as I have had to do with the punishment of criminals, I don't know anything in the world that could furnish such a long list of horrors as that which I have laid before this crowded court tonight. And yet these bushrangers, the scum of the earth, the lowest of the low, the most wicked of the wicked, are occasionally held up for our admiration! But better days are coming. It is the old leaven of convictism not yet worked out, but brighter days are coming.

The Clarkes were executed at Darlinghurst Gaol on 25 June 1867.

Reports of the death of bushranging were premature. Only three days after the Clarkes went to the gallows, a 'young man who used to run the mail down the Murrumbidgee' (probably Jeremiah Duce) and a nineteen-year-old named Robert Cotterall, wearing a blue eyeshade to protect his eyes due to a sensitivity caused by ophthalmitis, robbed the pub and store at Stony Creek in the New South Wales south-west. Cotterall became known as Blue Cap. Duce called himself the White Chief.

On Thursday, 4 July 1867 they bailed up Jerralong station; on Friday the Fowler residence; and on Saturday a party of Chinese on Stony and Spring creeks. They then robbed the Sydney Hotel. Flushed with success, on 15 July 1867, Blue Cap, the White Chief and one of their mates, John Cavan (who called himself Scotch Jock), bailed up Marshall's Inn at Merool Creek (now Mirool), 100 kilometres north-west of Wagga Wagga, taking goods and money to the value of £70, as well as a rifle and revolver. Scotch Jock and the White Chief had once worked for Marshall and knew where everything of value was kept. A correspondent to the *Yass Courier* despairingly wrote: 'A new era of trouble seems at hand.'

It appears that Scotch Jock had a connection with the late John Dunn, according to another *Yass Courier* correspondent who detailed an all-too-familiar encounter between Blue Cap's Gang and the police on 2 August 1867:

> The three worthies of the hemp and the hangman, Blue Cap, Duce, and 'Scotch Jock,' the pilot of Dunn over the Levels, came off the hills to a public-house at the Billabong, on Friday last, while constables Corbett, Dunlop, and M'Gee, from the Weddin Station, were at breakfast there. Corbett happened to go out, and sighting, fired at the bushrangers; they appeared surprised, and dropped the rifle and revolver which they had taken from Marshall's. The police immediately mounted, and gave chase by following the tracks for nearly three miles [4.8 kilometres], but could not get within eye-shot of the fugitives. Their horses became jaded, while the bushrangers were splendidly mounted.

The three bailed up Barellan station, between Griffith and Ardlethan, the next day, taking the racehorses Waratah and Geebung.

Near Bringagee station, they found the station's manager, stripped him naked and threatened to make him walk 30 kilometres to the homestead to get a rifle that could fire sixteen rounds without having to reload. They eventually relented and went to the station to get it themselves.

On 5 August 1867 the gang bailed up Gorton and Waller's station and took a prized revolver. They then went to the pub at Darlington Point (on the Murrumbidgee River between Narrandera and Hay) and got on the grog. When they were drunk, an old shepherd robbed one of them of £100 in cash and cheques. According to the *Queenslander* of 31 August 1867:

> The [gang] conducted [the shepherd] to the verandah, and a stirrup-leather was adjusted round his neck, when he confessed to the robbery, said he had planted it, and for the life of him he could not remember where. In order to effect further confessions, he was hanged by the neck to the verandah until he was black in the face, his eyes apparently starting from their sockets, when he was released from almost death by the bushranger, who could extort no tidings of the booty. They cautioned him not to go away as they meant to shoot him. No sooner, however, did an opportunity occur than the sensible old gentleman, probably pretty well sobered by partial suffocation, made serious and expeditious tracks, much to the dismay of the highwaymen.

On 6 August they robbed Benerembah station, 80 kilometres west of Narrandera. On 7 August they robbed a hawker, then a station at Howlong. The *Wagga Express* of 24 August 1867 reported that they then spent several days at an out-station on Chalk Springs, 'spending quite a jolly time of it, singing, dancing, and practising with their firearms, in the use of which they seemed particularly expert, hitting small marks with the greatest ease'.

By then they had been joined by John Scott, a boy of around

seventeen who called himself Jack the Devil. He had been working on a local property when he succumbed to the temptations of bushranging and robbed the place, taking weapons, food and horses, and then joined the youthful gang. Another bushranger, named King, brought the gang's number to five.

On 20 August 1867, the *Maitland Mercury* ran an opinion piece on Captain Thunderbolt's impact on crime among the young and impressionable, such as the members of Blue Cap's Gang. Thanks to his policy of not harming women (except by robbing their men), Thunderbolt had become known by some as a 'Gentleman Bushranger', although by then he had been involved in several shootouts with police, wounding several. In the *Mercury*'s opinion:

> This man has won notoriety rather by the suddenness of his appearances and disappearances, by his erratic movements, by his wonderful horsemanship, and by a certain air of careless bravado surrounding his proceedings. Thus far, indeed, his conduct has been suggestive in some respects of an amateur bushranger, playing rough practical jokes with the police, rather than of one who has given himself up to bushranging as a means of subsistence . . . If in the southern and western districts we have seen the law and its officers defied and successfully resisted by men of violence and blood, whose success constituted a reign of terror in the district they infested, we have, in the Northern districts, seen the law defied by way of pastime, and made as it were a laughing-stock. From the day when this man began his career in the immediate neighbourhood of Maitland, by freaks that had about them apparently more of jest than of earnest, until now, he has been illustrating what it is feared proves to a large class of young men in the colony, the attractive side of a lawless life, without raising in them qualms of disgust by resorting to bloodshed . . . The notoriety of this man is dangerous, because it is as it were a standing advertisement that the law is weak, and to be defied by any good horseman who knows the country.

Blue Cap's Gang emphasised the point with a succession of robberies across the southern districts throughout August. At one station they stayed up late into the night playing draughts with the owner. At another, they compelled a young woman to entertain them on the piano. They pressed several youngsters into their service to tend their horses. The police from stations throughout the districts were hunting for them, to no avail. Late in the month they robbed Thomas Browne, at Bundidgerie station, near Narrandera. In later life, Browne, writing under the pseudonym Rolf Boldrewood, would write the fictional bushranging saga *Robbery Under Arms*. Blue Cap's Gang gave him first-hand experience for his novel.

The gang continued to grow in number until, near the end of August, three of them – Jack the Devil, a young part-Aborigine known as Black Jemmy (who'd also worked for Marshall at Merool Creek and was accused of beating and attempting to rape Johanna Robertson at Narraburrah station) and James Smith – struck out on their own. One source later suggested they'd been kicked out due to cowardice.

The three who left didn't last long on their own. They robbed the Junee Hotel on 30 August and soon had the police on their trail. Senior Constable Usher and constables Little and White pursued the three some 130 kilometres to the hut of a widow named Sproul. Two at least surrendered without resistance. The third may have surrendered after a shot was fired at him. The three were aged seventeen or eighteen.

According to the *Yass Courier* of 11 September 1867, when they appeared in court, the crowd that gathered to see three real-life bushrangers got less than they bargained for:

> Everybody expected to see in these captives three models of strong physical build and fierce aspect; but what a surprise to the beholders to look upon three as weedy scrubbers as could well be imagined. Youths

> varying in age from eighteen to twenty years, remarkable only by their insipid expressions, simple bush untutored lads whom the wheel of circumstance would as readily turn to the path of virtue as vice. They took to bushranging simply because they happened to fall across others who had already drifted into that lawless life, rejoicing in the excitement of 'bailing-up' defenceless families, and to replenish their pocket money to buy jams and sweets where they had not the pluck to rob . . . There is nothing about them even that a romantic girl could muster a sigh upon, unless it was one of disappointment at their anti-brigand appearance.

Each of the boys entered guilty pleas to a number of charges. Each was given ten years' hard labour on each charge. It could have meant prison for life, but the sentences were made concurrent.

Blue Cap's Gang now comprised its captain, the White Chief, William Hammond and a part-Aborigine named Roberts, who was described as a lad 'who in Gilbert's time played the double game of "bush telegraph" and Government tracker alternately'.

On 10 September they spent the night at the Darlington Point Inn, while the police were 2 kilometres away at Cuba station. On 11 September the police left to search for them just before they rode in to bail up Cuba station.

Meanwhile, up in the Hunter, on 12 September, there was cause for celebration with the capture of one of Captain Thunderbolt's young accomplices. However, an exasperated *Maitland Mercury* noted: 'We hear that Thunderbolt's boy (Mason) was captured a few days since by the Tamworth police; certainly not by those of Murrurundi, who were all last week looking for lost sheep!'

Blue Cap's Gang continued their bushranging spree throughout September. On 19 September Brookong station was bailed up and a horse was taken by Hammond. It was later found drowned in Urangeline Creek, which was in flood at the time. It was thought the horse was drowned to decoy the police away from the fleeing bushrangers. However, another version of events emerged in the *Wagga Express* of 19 October:

> On Thursday last a magisterial inquiry was held on the remains, and all doubt on the matter was then cleared up. After firing at and pursuing Mr. Featherstonhaugh [sic], it is supposed that the bushrangers crossed the Urangeline Creek, which was then in flood, and that Hammond, in the darkness, missed the crossing, and his horse getting into deep water was swept with his rider, down the stream, and that both were thus drowned.

Pastoralist and later Anglican minister Cuthbert Fetherstonhaugh later wrote about his encounter with the bushrangers in his autobiography *After Many Days*. The encounter was also turned into verse in Barcroft Boake's *Featherstonhaugh*. He was also included in Rolf Boldrewood's *The Colonial Reformer* as the Reverend Herbert Heatherstone.

The gang, now down to three, continued to commit highway robberies throughout October. However, on 4 November 1867 Blue Cap was on his own, mounted on a tired horse, when he noticed three constables – Corbett, Dunlop and McGee – approaching him on the Bland Road at Humbug Creek. He hoped that, being alone, he could pass them by without his identity being suspected. Unfortunately, Corbett knew him.

'Hello, Bluey,' Corbett was later reported as saying. 'What brings you here?'

Outnumbered three to one, Blue Cap surrendered without a fight. He was taken to Young and soon faced six charges of highway robbery. It appears many of his victims had no difficulty in identifying him. The *Goulburn Herald* described his distinctive appearance:

> Any one looking at him once would recognize him again amongst

thousands. There is a leaning of the whole countenance towards the mouth which is of a sinister expression, and would make the owner not over-inviting in his appearance at any time. He is about the middle height, and seems to have a well-knit frame, though not by any means a heavy man. His weight we would suppose to be from ten to eleven stone.

He eventually received three five-year sentences, amounting to fifteen years.

After Blue Cap's capture, the White Chief continued bushranging. He gathered to his side seventeen-year-old William Brookman, 24-year-old Edward Kelly and John Payne (age unknown). That these young men should join a gang whose members were being captured within months of their commencement of bushranging and faced years in prison suggests an impulsiveness that clouded their judgement. As one of them put it when he left his job to take up bushranging, it was better than labouring for 15 shillings a week.

In the New England district, Mary Ann Ward was taken ill in late 1867. As her health faded, Captain Thunderbolt left her with friends in Muswellbrook, in the Upper Hunter. She died of pneumonia in November 1867. Not long after, Ward was romantically linked to a married woman named Charlotte Rammage, who brought him food despite her husband's opposition. She reputedly said Fred Ward could provide for her better than her husband.

For the next three weeks, the White Chief and his new gang, referred to as the Riverina Bushrangers after the capture of Blue Cap, rampaged up and down the Murrumbidgee. They robbed several stations and pubs, travellers and hawkers, and bailed up the town of Redbank. According to the *Yass Courier*:

> They had been accustomed to 'bail up' twenty or thirty men at a time – they did so at Redbank on the Lachlan, driving the imprisoned men

before them, making all kinds of sport with them – drinking, carousing, dancing, etc.; and although the men so stuck up had many opportunities of capturing Jerry and his aide-de-camp, no effort was made with that object.

On 24 November 1867, they robbed their way from Uabba station to Mossgiel station. There the White Chief and Brookman came upon Sergeant Macnamara and a constable, while Kelly and Payne were rounding up the inhabitants of some nearby shanties. Macnamara and the constable had stopped at the station for the night, while searching for sly grog carts.

The White Chief apparently challenged the sergeant, who was out of uniform, asking, 'Are you Macnamara?'

'No, I am not,' he replied.

The White Chief then turned to the other policeman to ask the same question, whereupon Macnamara pounced. In the ensuing melee, two shots were fired. One hit the constable in the arm, the other hit Brookman in the neck. The White Chief and Brookman were then taken prisoner.

Shortly after, Kelly and Payne came up (as reported in the *Argus*, 3 December 1867), 'driving before them about thirty horsemen from the shanties, but galloped off as soon as they saw the fix their mates was in'.

Edward Kelly and John Payne were subsequently arrested by a constable who was out serving summonses for the White Chief's trial when he came upon them.

Duce (the White Chief), Brookman, Kelly and Payne all faced trial early in 1868. Duce and Brookman were convicted of wounding with intent to murder and sentenced to death. Kelly and Payne were convicted of robbery under arms. Kelly was sentenced to thirty years' imprisonment, and Payne twenty years, though in a lopsided twist, Duce and Brookman subsequently had their death sentences commuted to a comparatively light fifteen years.

Some of the members of the gang, who'd been with them for earlier robberies, disappeared once the gang leaders were taken.

Thunderbolt had been active throughout 1868, robbing mails and travellers on the roads around New England and the Upper Hunter. He was sometimes on his own, at other times in company with a young apprentice. His manner was frequently courteous and a typical exchange, like one that occurred on 2 November 1868 at Yetman, on the McIntyre River, only enhanced his 'gentleman bushranger' status.

A local named Miller had camped at some yards and hobbled his horses out when a boy rode up and asked him for some tobacco. He gave it to him and the boy rode off. It was only after he was gone that Miller suspected the boy was riding one of his horses. Shortly after, while he was looking for the horse in question, he saw another traveller. Their conversation was reported in the *Maitland Mercury*.

> Miller: 'Good morning, mate. Have you seen anything of a horse (describing him) about here?'
>
> Traveller: 'Well, I expect my boy has got it.'
>
> Miller (with surprise): 'Your boy!'
>
> Traveller: 'Yes; but I suppose you don't know me – I'm Thunderbolt.'
>
> Miller: 'The devil you are. But I wish you would leave my horses alone, for I'm a very poor man, and have hard struggling to knock out a living for myself and family.'
>
> Thunderbolt: 'Well, I did not take your horse, nor did I wish the boy to take it, the young scamp. At any rate I'll find some way of returning it to you; I'll put it into one of the paddocks on the road for you.'
>
> Miller: 'Thank you. I hope you don't make a practice of robbing poor people, Mr. Thunderbolt.'

Thunderbolt: 'Do you remember me passing you yesterday afternoon, shortly before you camped? Did I rob you then! No; nor did I have any idea of doing so. I only take from them who can afford to give.

The correspondent who supplied the story to the *Mercury* went on to reflect on changes in rural society that might act to curb bushranging:

It is to be hoped, however, that the more general diffusion of the means of education now existing, even in the remotest and most obscure parts of the province, will have a salutary effect on the morals of the rising generation, and that with an increase of knowledge there will be a proportionate decrease of crime.

There was, if I remember rightly, a paragraph in your valuable journal a week or two back showing how bushrangers are made; but it only glanced at Captain Thunderbolt as a thief maker, and entirely overlooked the fact that most of the bushrangers of the last ten years were made by being kept from school when boys to go out after cattle, with men who, so far as horses and cattle are concerned, had but a very slight knowledge of 'meum et tuum' [mine and thine], and who glorified in instilling their trickeries into the minds of their young companions. I have known boys not more than eight years old, who, though they could not use a pen, were quite dexterous with a stock-whip, whose literary acquirements extended no farther than the ability to read brands, who were totally ignorant of Dr Watts, but could boldly sing a vulgar or indecent song in company, who could sit on the top rail of a stockyard and talk about 'clear skins', 'nuggets', 'sweaters', and 'soldiers', and discuss the merits and demerits of the animals in the yard with the greatest assurance.

They swore, smoked, and lied, and in many instances, instead of being reproved by those who should have taught them better, they were smiled upon approvingly, and thus encouraged to make a start on the highway at the earliest opportunity.

On 7 May 1869, 1855's gun-toting horsethief Harry Power returned to bushranging, having escaped from Pentridge Prison near the end of his fourteen-year sentence by hiding under a pile of garbage while on a prison detail to dump it outside the grounds. He robbed the mail coach near Porepunka, travellers and hawkers in the north-east of Victoria, and ventured into southern New South Wales. His success was in part due to the old bushranging resource – sympathisers. According to the *Ovens & Murray Advertiser*: 'From a certain portion of the population . . . he has received succour and information, while the police have been misled and deceived.'

George Scott was an emigrant from Ireland, a trained engineer, who had gone to the diggings in New Zealand and enlisted in a Victorian corps engaged in the Maori Wars of 1861–65. On his return he became a lay reader at a church in Bacchus Marsh, Victoria, in preparation for his being ordained a Church of England minister when the archbishop decided he was ready. In the meantime, he was referred to as 'the Minister' though he had not yet achieved the position. Among the friends in his congregation were the manager of the Union Bank at Mount Egerton and the local schoolteacher.

On the night of 8 May 1869 a masked man entered the living quarters of the bank and bailed up the manager. The manager recognised George Scott's voice and reportedly asked him if this was a suitable joke for a clergyman. When Scott threatened to shoot him the manager realised he was serious. The manager was gagged and marched over to the schoolhouse where Scott made him write and sign a note: 'Captain Moonlite has stuck me up and robbed the bank.'

They returned to the bank where 'Captain Moonlite' took £1000 in notes and coin, tied the manager up and fled.

The next morning the schoolteacher found the note, walked across to the bank and found the manager still tied up. He released him and called the police, who promptly arrested both banker and teacher. They couldn't bring themselves to believe the story that a minister of religion would turn bushranger.

The Minister, meanwhile, maintained he had nothing to do with the crime, and went so far as to provide evidence to prove his former friends' guilt. Just before he was scheduled to give evidence in their trial, he gave the first hint that he might not be as honest as the police believed. He skipped town and headed to Sydney instead. There he bought a yacht, partly with cash and partly by cheque. The vendor, however, soon discovered the cheque was worthless and called the police. Captain Moonlite was just outside Sydney Heads when the police caught up with him in a steam launch. He was sent to prison for eighteen months. By the time he was due for release, he was also facing charges for the Mount Egerton robbery, and was extradited to Victoria.

Before he got to trial he and five others managed to escape from Ballarat's newly built gaol. Four of his colleagues were immediately caught, while Moonlite and a man named Dermoodie managed to escape into the bush. When Dermoodie refused to attempt a bank robbery, Moonlite threatened to kill him. He eventually let the man go and Dermoodie was caught the next day. Moonlite was caught a week later.

He was tried for the bank robbery and sentenced to ten years' imprisonment. For good behaviour he was released early, in July 1872. He then went straight and used his former skills as a 'preacher' to make a living as an open-air lecturer in Melbourne. But he was not yet done with bushranging.

On 25 September 1869, the elusive and mercurial Moondyne Joe was finally captured, more than two years after his escape. He was caught in a wine cellar near Perth, while enjoying the libations therein. His special cell was still waiting for him. He was incarcerated, in irons, and despite petitioning to have them removed, was kept in them until the middle of 1871. He was released from prison in 1875 and went straight. He ended up wandering the streets of Perth and died in the Fremantle Lunatic Asylum in 1900. His exploits inspired escaped Irish convict John O'Reilly's 1879 novel *Moondyne*, which is available as a free e-text at Project Gutenberg.

On 16 March 1870, Robert McBean, owner of the 17 800-hectare Kilfera station that adjoined the Kelly family's paltry selection in north-east Victoria, was out on his property when he thought he saw his fifteen-year-old neighbour Ned Kelly, and a companion. When he rode up to greet them, he discovered to his shock that the companion was Harry Power, bushranger and escapee from Pentridge Prison.

Power drew a revolver and robbed McBean of his watch and horse, leaving him to walk several kilometres back to the homestead to raise the alarm. By then the pair had struck again, robbing a man named Charles Dickens of some £3. Curiously, McBean had been close enough to identify Ned but said that he was unable to see his face. Although McBean was greatly upset at the loss of his watch, a family heirloom, he may have hesitated in accusing his young neighbour. The major landowner may have disliked the smallholders on the edges of his run, but seeing them hauled off to prison was another matter. Here there's another parallel with previous bushrangers, where informants hesitated to speak up, fearing retaliation from the bushranger or his supporters.

Harry Power and Ned Kelly subsequently ranged far and wide across the north-east, covering prodigious distances while young Ned built up an intimate knowledge of bushcraft and the country both settled and wild. Their robberies were attracting plenty of attention from the police. In particular, the descriptions of the men involved in the McBean robbery had resulted in suspicion falling on Ned's uncle Jack and his son, Tom Lloyd Jnr. Tom wasn't just a relative, he was one of Ned's closest friends, so when his father was arrested and young Tom was suspected as well, the only way to clear their names was to implicate Ned or give Harry up. When the reward for the capture of Harry Power was increased to £500, the stakes were raised again.

Ned, meanwhile, was tiring of the bushranging life. Raised on the exploits of Jack Donahue, Captain Thunderbolt, Ben Hall and Dan Morgan (whose career ended just north of where Ned grew up), bushranging may have had a veneer of adventure, but the reality was days in the saddle – cold, wet and hungry – living rough while constantly hunted by police and local volunteers. Food was so scarce that at one point the pair held up a delivery boy and took his lunch. Then there was the cantankerous Power, who made matters worse by berating the lad as they travelled up and down the countryside. Fed up, Ned left him and went home.

Ned was arrested the next day, but managed to avoid prosecution. Power was betrayed by another member of Ned's family, and was sentenced to a further fifteen years in prison, of which he served fourteen before being released. He stayed out of trouble for the rest of his life, eventually drowning in the Murray River in 1890.

On 25 May 1870 Captain Thunderbolt was active on the Northern Road, bailing up travellers 6 kilometres from the town of Uralla. Soon after he'd been robbed, one of Thunderbolt's victims, Giovanni Cappasoti, got word to Uralla that Captain Thunderbolt was in the vicinity of Blanch's pub. The town's Senior Constable Mulhall and Constable Alex Walker immediately set off to investigate.

Mulhall arrived a kilometre ahead of Walker and saw two men on horseback. It's likely that one of them was in the process of having a horse taken from him by the other. In any event, one of the horsemen fired at Mulhall as soon as he came into view. When Mulhall returned fire, both men fled along a fence line. Mulhall turned back towards Uralla to link up with Walker.

'There are the bushrangers!' he reportedly shouted to the junior policeman. 'I have exchanged shots with him. Shoot the wretch.'

At this point, Mulhall probably drew back to take time to reload and Walker charged towards the bushrangers on his own. As he approached, the younger bushranger turned his horse to block him, or his skittish mount turned in fright – in any event, Walker passed him and was in pursuit of the older man, Captain Thunderbolt, at full gallop. According to the *Armidale Express*:

> The chase was kept up through the bush for nearly an hour, Ward doubling and Walker following; across gully and creek, bog and hill, full tear, the pair dashed through the bush, until at last Ward pulled up alongside a waterhole in Kentucky Creek, near the junction of Chilcott's Swamp, dismounted, and plunged into the waterhole. Walker, who was close upon his heels, with admirable prudence immediately shot the bushranger's horse, and then galloped down the creek about two hundred yards [183 metres] until he could cross it. By the time this was accomplished Ward had crossed, and throwing off his coat started to run up the creek about 100 or 120 yards [91 or 110 metres], until he came to a narrow channel about 16 feet [5 metres] wide. This he dashed across, and, when he got on the other bank, stood and faced Walker, who by this time had arrived at the edge of the creek. There was now but the creek between them.

Up to this moment, much had been made of Thunderbolt's superior horsemanship in encounters with police. However, in Constable Walker's case, he'd proved himself a match for the famed bushranger. And since the bushranging outbreak had begun, New South Wales police had been hampered by poor-quality horses, but Walker's had also been able to keep pace with Thunderbolt's.

It has been suggested that Thunderbolt's newly stolen horse wasn't up to his usual standard, but the reality is that after being ridden

6 kilometres from Uralla, Walker's mount was still fit for a chase that lasted another 10 kilometres. It was suggested in the *Armidale Express* that Constable Mulhall arrived at the encounter first because he was on the faster horse. However, it may have been that Walker was smart enough to pace his mount, conscious that a long and tiring gallop might lie ahead. In any case, having been outridden, Thunderbolt now switched tactics.

'Who the —— are you?' Thunderbolt reportedly asked.

'Never mind who I am,' the constable replied. 'Put your hands up.'

'Are you a trooper?' Thunderbolt asked.

'Yes.'

'Married?'

'Yes.'

'Well, remember your family,' Thunderbolt said, perhaps in an attempt to dissuade Walker from continuing what could be a lethal encounter.

'That's all right,' Walker replied. 'Will you come out and surrender?'

'No! I'll die first,' Thunderbolt reputedly answered. The old convict slogan 'death or liberty' still held as true as it ever did.

'Then it's you and I for it!' Walker shouted as he spurred his mount into the creek.

The *Armidale Express* reported the rest of the events:

The horse went under, head and all. At that moment Ward rushed towards Walker, evidently with the intention of pulling him off his saddle and grappling with him in the water. But at the critical moment Walker fired his last remaining shot, the ball entering under the left collar bone, near the armpit, passing through both lungs and coming out below the right shoulder blade. The effect of the shot was to make Ward fall into the water, but immediately afterwards he rose again, and endeavoured to seize Walker. Constable Walker then struck him violently on the forehead with his empty pistol, knocking him down.

> Walker then turned his horse out of the creek, and dismounting proceeded in and dragged the man out, apparently dead.

After shooting Thunderbolt, Walker was promoted to sub-inspector.

The death of Captain Thunderbolt effectively marked the end of bushranging in New South Wales – an end hastened by a number of important changes. For starters, the classic training ground for bushranging, stealing stock, dwindled after the 1866 *Brand Identification Act* made the practice more difficult. In addition, extensive fencing meant fewer stock were able to stray as easily as they had a decade earlier. The New South Wales economy was also in better shape and the improving employment situation saw fewer impoverished and idle hands turning to crime, particularly in rural areas. Even forestry had reduced the areas suitable for bushranging. But most importantly, by the end of the decade the New South Wales police force had a good number of experienced officers who were well equipped with both weapons and horses. Plus the use of trackers was widespread, as was the use of rewards to extract information from sympathetic harbourers.

However, while bushranging had been suppressed, one reality remained. Even with an experienced, well-resourced police force, Captain Thunderbolt had been captured more by good luck than good management. The police had certainly made life difficult for the average bushranger, but if Thunderbolt could remain at large for seven years, so could somebody else. It was only a matter of time.

Meanwhile, in pockets of Australia, the discontent and neglect that led young men into crime still remained. By 1870 bushranging may have become a symbol of a disappearing world, but it had not yet gone forever. And it still had the potential to become a symbol for the future.

11

The odd angry shot

1870–1877

Throughout its history, bushranging has always been entangled with politics. As governments sought to impose law and order upon the convict class, some sections of the community fell victim to unjust laws, while others demanded action and results. As convictism faded and the native-born emerged, in rural areas, farm workers were looked upon as little better than locusts. Where there weren't many votes and in consequence even fewer resources allocated, the communities themselves were held responsible when criminality surfaced. Under the circumstances, as a sense of nationalism emerged in Australia, it was understandable that the police and magistracy became the symbols of the old order imposed by government. In rural areas, they were all there was.

So while the rural sector produced a great deal of wealth, little of it was returned to the workers who generated it. As disadvantage combined with discrimination, bushranging became the inarticulate expression of discontent. The rural poor valued many of the qualities the best bushrangers embodied – splendid horsemanship, bushcraft and resourcefulness. Flawed as bushrangers might be, these would become the qualities that would eventually be extolled in stories of stockmen like the man from Snowy River, twenty years later.

Isolated incidents of bushranging still occurred, but resistance was stronger and more effective. Late in 1870 a bushranger entered a bank in Cassilis, in the Upper Hunter.

'Bail up or I'll blow your brains out!' the robber reportedly cried, brandishing a weapon.

'Will you by God!' came the teller's reply, and he jumped the counter, whereupon his assailant dropped his gun and fled. The teller chased the man up the street, the hue and cry attracting most of the small town to the chase. The robber was soon caught, but when it was discovered that the local policeman was away, the mob knocked the bushranger around before turning him loose. The gun, which turned out to be rusty and useless, was displayed in the bank where it had been dropped. The townsfolk reputedly retired to the town's two pubs for the rest of the day to celebrate their success.

In the meantime, with bushranging defeated, it was a time for complacency. Police forces were curtailed in rural districts as the need to pursue miscreants dwindled.

By 1872, the uproar over the bushranger outbreak was a distant memory for many. The atmosphere of crisis having passed, sober heads couldn't help noticing that many of the sentences handed down during the mid-1860s were far more severe than those handed down in the 1870s. For example, no one was getting a fifteen-year sentence for stealing a horse any more, but there were several people within the penal system doing fifteen years for exactly that.

The government had recognised the exceptional situation between 1867 and 1872 and discreetly shortened some sentences for good behaviour and gave other prisoners early release. However, the manner of remissions was unregulated, and prisoners gained sentence remissions more by luck than by any clear guidelines. With the scales of justice out of balance, resentment grew within the penal system.

Matters came to a head in 1872 when the sisters of Frank Gardiner petitioned the Governor of New South Wales, Sir Hercules Robinson, for a remission of his sentence on the basis that it was never intended that he serve the full thirty-two years. Gardiner having been a model prisoner, Robinson tended to agree, and thought ten years, followed by exile from the colony for twenty-two years, was more appropriate.

Normally, it was the elected government's role to intervene in prison sentences, but in non-capital cases the governor could exercise his prerogative. Apparently, Robinson believed the elected government should deal with the matter, but when he sought advice and found none forthcoming (none of the fragile elected governments wanted to touch such a political hot potato), he told Gardiner that he would exercise his power and have him released and exiled in July 1874, when his ten years were up. The negotiation wasn't public knowledge, but when it came out the reaction was to be as extreme as the consequences.

In April 1874, when news of Gardiner's imminent release finally broke, the New South Wales government became embroiled in a political crisis. In the lead-up to Gardiner's release, Justice Alfred Stephen took exception to the suggestion that he'd exceeded his authority in sentencing Gardiner to thirty-two years, and felt that the original sentence should stick. The state government also believed Governor Robinson had overstepped his authority in holding out the prospect of a pardon to Gardiner. Others felt that the arch-villain of bushranging had somehow found a way to escape justice by cunningly manipulating the justice system.

In fact, Robinson had forced politicians to confront an issue they had been avoiding for years, while young men who might still make a valuable contribution to society grew old in prison. Indeed, long after the cessation of hostilities in what would eventually come to be regarded by some as a class war, wasn't it time for the prisoners of that war to go home?

The New South Wales parliament engaged in an extended debate on the governor's decision. While some suggested the parliament had no right to question the governor's decision, others railed that pardons were the prerogative of the executive and the governor could only recommend them. However, Robinson had done precisely that two years earlier, and had been ignored.

The release of Gardiner also raised serious questions about the validity of holding a number of other bushrangers in prison. If the 'worst' of the bushrangers was to be released, what about the others? Just how many might that be? Eventually, the parliament voted on whether or not to support the governor's decision. It ended up deadlocked 26 to 26. The speaker cast his vote in favour of the governor. The date for the release was 8 July 1874.

Hercules Robinson took the unusual step of detailing the factors behind his decision in the *Sydney Morning Herald* of 26 June 1874:

> . . . the sentence of thirty-two years passed upon Gardiner was imposed at a time of great excitement and his punishment would seem to have been measured more in view of the crimes with which he was supposed to have been connected than with reference solely to those of which he was actually convicted.

In what became one of the largest legal prison breakouts in history (and possibly the only one of its kind), in the General Amnesty of 1874 a total of twenty-four well-behaved prisoners were released. Apart from Gardiner they included William Brookman, Samuel Clarke, Daniel Shea, William Willis, Alex Fordyce, Robert Cotterall, John Payne, James Jones, James Boyd, Thomas Cunningham, Charles Gough, Thomas Dargue, Henry Dargue, John Kelly, Edward Kelly (not Ned Kelly), James Smith, John Foran, John Williams, William Simmons,

William Taverner, Daniel Taylor, John Bow and John Bollard. Several of the names feature in the bushranging exploits detailed in previous chapters.

In the bushranging districts, opposition to the release was particularly strong, and monster meetings were held in the Lachlan.

Ultimately, Frank Gardiner went to America. The closing details of his life were lost in the earthquake and fire in San Francisco in 1905. He is thought to have run a saloon there. By the time of his release his partner, Kate, had run off with another man, and was later murdered in New Zealand.

12

Kelly

1878–1880

On the afternoon of 26 October 1878, 23-year-old Edward 'Ned' Kelly was a complete unknown in the annals of bushranging. To Victorian Police Sergeant Michael Kennedy and constables Michael Scanlan, Thomas McIntyre and Thomas Lonigan, he was just another petty criminal whose horse-stealing operations had been seriously curtailed by a prolonged police operation. Ned and his mates had been the bane of the region's major landholders whose immense properties were a stark contrast to the minute 'starvation blocks' where families like the Kellys struggled to make a living. Eventually a highly irregular incident saw a policeman shot in the hand and Ned's mother gaoled with two others for attempted murder. Warrants for the arrest of Ned and his younger brother Dan had been issued over the same incident, but both had been hiding out for six months with two other young horse thieves, Steve Hart and Joe Byrne. Now it was simply a question of locating Ned's mountain lair, somewhere in the foothills of the Great Dividing Range between

Mansfield and Wangaratta, and bringing them in – as some police would have it, dead or alive.

Unfortunately, among the many things the four police didn't know when they established their depot at Stringybark Creek, just north of Mansfield, was that they were just 2 kilometres from Ned's hideout. They also didn't appreciate that they'd stumbled into the backyard of a consummate bushman and horseman who'd spent most of his time on the run perfecting his skills with firearms.

Ned, on the other hand, had already been informed that the police were coming by a network of friends and sympathisers, mainly smallholders who'd endured similar intimidation and harassment by police or major landholders. He'd also been told about a second patrol that was working south from Greta, the nearest town to the Kellys' 32-hectare starvation block. The night before, Ned had seen the tracks of Kennedy's patrol and found where they'd camped. Now he was planning to add the element of surprise to the considerable advantage he enjoyed when it came to knowledge of the bush – the police only went there on patrol; for Ned, it had been his home since childhood.

Since the days of his apprenticeship with the bushranger Harry Power, Ned had matured. Despite frequent run-ins with the law, and several prison sentences, the strapping young man had become the head of his family after his alcoholic father's death. When he wasn't being harassed by police, he was diligent and hardworking – a born leader.

With one patrol nearby, and the other approaching, Ned was apprehensive that if the two patrols combined and laid siege to his hut at Bullock Creek, he and his mates would be massively outgunned. They only had a carbine, shotgun and revolver between the four of them. So he decided to strike first. He planned to ambush the patrol at Stringybark Creek, take their weapons and use the extra firepower to deal with the other party.

That afternoon, Ned took the carbine and revolver, Dan took the shotgun, and with Steve and Joe headed for the police camp. They crept as close as they were able, given that the scrub was thin around the encampment. From behind cover Ned saw two of the police in camp and mistook them for two constables he knew – Strahan and Flood (who'd had an affair with one of Ned's sisters, leading to her death in childbirth). Ned assumed the other two police were inside the tent. Covered by Dan, he started to move in.

One of the policemen was seated on a log near the fire and the other hobbling a horse when Ned reportedly shouted, 'Bail up! Throw up your hands!'

'Flood' turned, saw Ned aiming his sawn-off carbine at him and did as he was told.

The other policeman, 'Strahan', leapt to his feet and tried to run. According to a later account given by Ned, the constable dropped behind a log 6 metres from the one he'd been sitting on. When he lifted his head to fire from behind the log, Ned fired a single shot. It struck 'Strahan' in the right eye. He cried out, 'Oh, Christ! I'm shot!' and leaped out from behind the log, his hands raised to surrender. Then he collapsed and moments later, died.

Ned quickly discovered that the policeman he'd shot wasn't Strahan. It was Thomas Lonigan, who'd once 'blackballed' Ned by grabbing his testicles in a fight in the town of Benalla. And the man he took to be Flood was actually Thomas McIntyre. As for the other two police, they were out on patrol, but expected back soon.

McIntyre was to give differing accounts of the death of Lonigan in his statements and in court evidence. In one he said Lonigan was shot as he reached for his revolver, in another that he was shot while running for cover, and yet another that he was shot while behind the log. The first two versions make the killing murder. The third opens an avenue for Ned to claim that he fired in self-defence. Eventually McIntyre would say he didn't see what Lonigan was doing because he was facing Ned. He would simply say, 'I heard him fall; I did not see him fall.'

Ned later claimed that he'd known that the real Strahan, as well as Lonigan, had made bold claims before the Kelly manhunt set out.

'I won't ask him to stand,' Strahan had reputedly said. 'I'll shoot him first, like a dog.'

'If Kelly is to be shot,' Lonigan remarked, 'I'm the man who will shoot him.'

The statements may have led Ned to believe the patrols were in fact a death squad. However, immediately upon realising the man he'd shot was Lonigan, in the shock of the moment Ned's reaction gave no indication that he was aware of Lonigan's vow. According to McIntyre, he said, 'Well, I'm glad of that for the bugger gave me a hiding in Benalla one day.'

Nevertheless, Ned's search of the camp revealed a remarkable cache of weapons and ammunition. For four police there were seventy-two rounds for their revolvers, a shotgun with thirty-six shells and a large number of rounds for a Spencer repeating rifle that was with Constable Scanlan.

Later Ned would express the belief that police intended to 'riddle' him. At Stringybark he only said, 'You buggers came to shoot me, I suppose.'

Ned and McIntyre talked for about fifteen minutes, during which Ned said he would spare Sergeant Kennedy and Constable Scanlan if McIntyre could persuade them to surrender. Then they heard the approaching horses. Dan and Joe Byrne (now armed with the police weapons) took cover in the thin scrub around the camp, Steve Hart (also armed) slipped into the tent. Ned hid behind a log near the fire, telling McIntyre to sit and not try anything or he'd be shot.

McIntyre complied, and by one of his accounts called out to the approaching officers, 'Oh, sergeant. You had better dismount and surrender for you are surrounded.' However, in his first version of what happened, he didn't get a word out before Ned and the others sprang up shouting, 'Bail up! Hold your hands up!'

Despite being surprised, the two policemen reacted instinctively. Kennedy dropped forward on his horse to make his body as small a target as possible then dismounted so his horse was between him and danger. Scanlan tried to turn his horse and escape, but the animal took fright and circled instead. Scanlan had his rifle slung across his back, but with one movement he swung it under his arm and fired at Ned, the weapon still strapped to his body. The shot missed. Kennedy's first shot from his revolver, fired across the rump of his prancing horse, managed to graze Dan as he left cover and advanced.

Ned fired at Scanlan, hitting him and causing him to fall from the horse. As Kennedy's horse skittered, Kennedy gained the cover of a tree. In the confusion McIntyre leapt on Kennedy's horse and tried to escape. Ned maintains he could have shot McIntyre, who was between him and Kennedy, who was now firing from behind the tree. However, McIntyre had surrendered and Ned was reluctant to shoot an unarmed man. Now on the ground, Scanlan was still alive but wounded, struggling to unsling his rifle. Dan and Ned had their attention on Michael Kennedy. Joe Byrne was a dozen metres from Scanlan, on his right side. According to McIntyre, Scanlan tried to get up but fell on his hands and knees. In that position he was shot under the right arm.

'I saw him fall – I saw the blood spurt out from the right side as he fell,' McIntyre later said. The shooter was probably Joe Byrne.

McIntyre galloped the horse away, maintaining that he was shot at while escaping. In fact he may have been hearing the continuing gunfight between what was to become known as the Kelly Gang and the surviving police sergeant, now outnumbered four to one and armed only with a revolver.

Kennedy managed to flee, on foot, through the scrub, with Ned following him. Ned might have been able to claim he had killed in self-defence in the shootout with Lonigan and Scanlan, but in hunting Kennedy for over a kilometre, it was a different story. The policeman's flight was a terrifying scramble through unfamiliar terrain. Ned was master of the situation, moving swiftly and easily through the bush as he'd often done while pursuing kangaroos. When Kennedy tried to fire on his pursuer, Ned, absolutely lethal with his weapon, fired back and hit him in the armpit. Now wounded, Kennedy again fled in desperation through the trees. Night was falling as Kennedy realised the hopelessness of his position. There was no escaping the man who followed relentlessly on his trail. Kennedy turned again and raised his arms.

Ned later claimed that in the fading light he didn't realise Kennedy had dropped his revolver when he was shot. He thought Kennedy was about to fire at him, and so shot the unarmed man through the right side of his chest.

Reports based on accounts of the Stringybark incident obtained from friends and relatives of the Kelly Gang suggest Kennedy did not die instantly. He lingered in great pain, talking to Ned about his wife and the eleven-month-old child he'd buried just a few months before. It's possible he wrote a note to his wife and asked Ned to get it to her. Some pages were found to have been torn from his notebook, but if there was a message, it was never passed on. One account suggests that Ned, taking pity on Michael Kennedy, moved to end his suffering, but Kennedy begged him to spare his life. Ned again shot him in the chest.

Back at the police campsite the tent was set alight. The bodies of the police were robbed. Joe Byrne took a ring from Michael Scanlan's finger which he wore for the rest of his life, a grim souvenir from the man he probably murdered. The action is paralleled by serial killers taking trophies from their victims through which they're able to relive their moment of power. The other grim parallel with such killers was the body count. The police had taken three of Ned's folk when they imprisoned his mother, brother-in-law and neighbour. Now he'd taken three of theirs.

Kelly and the others assumed McIntyre was racing from the scene to raise the alarm. They realised they could no longer remain at their hideout on Bullock Creek. Now heavily armed and with the police horses supplementing their own mounts, they spent just long enough at Bullock Creek to set it alight (although the fire soon burned out) and rode away into the night. They put as much distance as they could between them and the horrific scene behind them, riding towards a future where, as the killers of three police, they would be hunted as never before.

They made their way north towards the Murray River, hoping to foil their pursuers by crossing the New South Wales border, a mode of operation they'd used when they were just simple horse thieves. Yet they knew that as news of their deed at Stringybark spread, the entire countryside would be on the lookout for them.

As it happened, it was more than a day before word reached Mansfield. Thomas McIntyre had ridden his horse to a standstill, then turned it loose and headed in a different direction, hoping to throw off the pursuers he feared were close behind. In desperation he found a wombat hole and crawled inside for the night, continuing on his way at first light. He reached Mansfield late in the afternoon of Sunday 27 October 1878 and tried to raise the alarm, but the news didn't get far because the town's telegraph office was closed on Sundays.

The Kelly Gang's flight was hampered by torrential rain. With one of Ned's cousins, Tom Lloyd, scouting ahead for them, they passed through Greta, getting dry clothes and a hot meal before proceeding through the bush, rather than risking the roads, towards Beechworth, 70 kilometres south of the border. As they rode on, however, the rain grew heavier, and the creeks and rivers began rising.

During that time the gang was spotted by Constable Hugh Bracken, who recognised Ned and Dan and knew they were wanted in relation to their crimes prior to Stringybark Creek. Word hadn't yet reached him about the murders of three of his fellow officers. Nevertheless, he tried to raise the alarm. The Kelly Gang, meanwhile, rode on to the home of Aaron Sherritt, in the Woolshed Valley west of Beechworth, where they sought assistance. Aaron, a close friend and neighbour of Joe Byrne, stood guard while the gang rested in a cave overlooking the Chinese camp where Joe, an opium addict, bought his drugs.

While the men regrouped, word of the killings at Stringybark Creek was finally spreading. On Monday, 28 October a reward for the capture of the Kelly Gang was set by the Victorian premier, Graham Berry, at a total of £800 – £200 each. Superintendent Charles Nicolson was put in charge of the manhunt.

By Wednesday, 30 October, the government had gathered sufficient detail of the events at Stringybark Creek to realise police were facing an adversary unlike any other. Ned Kelly hadn't fled the approaching police. He'd emerged from the mountains and confronted them. He and his gang had shot two, and then Ned had hunted down a third and shot him in cold blood, leaving the body to rot in the remote and lonely bush. It was a terrible and terrifying crime. The apparition of a lethal gunman stalking his victim through the bush was the stuff of nightmares. The reward was raised to £2000 – £500 for each member of the gang.

By this stage, rain was falling so heavily it was making the gang's flight almost impossible. Their hope was to get across the Murray and escape into the wide open spaces of western New South Wales, but first they had to get there. Through that day and into the next they picked their route around the floodwaters. On the Friday they called at a house where one of their horse-stealing accomplices had been arrested. William Baumgarten's wife not only told the men responsible for her husband's imprisonment where they could go, but when a police party arrived shortly after, she set them on their trail. With the police close behind, Ned and the others had no choice but to abandon their horses, take to the floodwaters and hide among the reeds.

Had the police spotted them, escape would have been impossible, but the rising waters forced the police to take a different path. Meanwhile, Ned's hopes of getting away to New South Wales were defeated by the floods, which were approaching biblical proportions. He had no choice but to return to home turf. As it turned out, it would be three days before the police pursuit really started, by which time the Kelly Gang had melted away into the heartland of their friends and relatives.

Down in Melbourne, though, the politicians seemed to think the power of legislation could fix anything. At the end of October 1878 the state parliament passed the *Felons Apprehension Act* (also known as the *Outlawry Act*), which required the Kelly Gang to surrender at Mansfield police station by 12 November. To the astonishment of few, they didn't, whereupon they acquired the legal status of outlaws – literally persons outside the normal protection afforded to all citizens by law. It meant they could be shot on sight. If previous cases related in this volume are anything to go by, making the Kelly Gang outlaws should have meant their days were numbered.

Meanwhile, in north-eastern Victoria, police patrols were coming to terms with the realities of a group of heavily armed and dangerous men with an intimate knowledge of the country and a well-developed network of support. Many police were extremely wary of blundering into another deadly ambush. Others were frustrated by their timid commanders. As weeks passed and there wasn't so much as a sighting of the gang, there was no denying that Ned had the upper hand. It wasn't long before he used it.

On Sunday, 8 December 1878, Joe Byrne rode into the modest town of Euroa and had lunch at De Boos' Hotel. There he learned that on the coming Tuesday most of the town would either be at the funeral of a local boy who'd fallen from a horse, or at a hearing of the Licensing Court. The following day, at lunchtime, the rest of the gang rode up to a homestead at Faithfull's Creek, 5 kilometres along the railway and telegraph lines from the town. Without any fuss, they drew their guns and quietly took the station hands hostage. By nightfall fourteen people were locked in a slab hut near the homestead.

The next morning they were still being held while Ned and Joe Byrne worked on letters (Ned dictating to the better-educated Joe) to Victorian MP Donald Cameron, who'd been critical of the hunt for the Kellys, and to Benalla's Superintendent John Sadleir, presenting their side of Stringybark Creek and the series of provocations that had led to it. Lunchtime came and went.

In the early afternoon, Ned, Steve and Joe left the homestead and crossed to the telegraph lines. They not only tore down the lines, they chopped down poles, smashed insulators and twisted the wires into knots, effectively isolating the town from direct outside communication.

The Kelly Gang then left Joe to guard the prisoners, assisted by a man who went by the name 'John Carson'. Ned, Dan and a lad named Becroft drove a hawker's wagon and cart into town while Steve Hart rode. They reached Euroa at around 4 p.m. All the vehicles drove into the backyard of the Euroa branch of the National Bank. Dan, Steve and Becroft remained there while Ned went to the front, knocked and said he had a cheque to cash. The bank's accountant, Bradley, opened the door slightly to say the bank was closed. When he did, Ned shoved his way inside and bailed up Bradley and a teller named Booth.

Steve Hart then entered the bank through the back door, where he found an old school friend, Fanny Shaw, ironing in the bank building's kitchen. They exchanged the usual country courtesies before Steve explained the nature of his visit and took her hostage.

Ned had by then reached the office of the bank's manager, Robert Scott, where he grabbed a revolver from his desk and shouted, 'Bail up!' Ned and Steve gathered up about £400 then turned their attention to the adjoining bank residence, home to Scott, his wife and seven children. Scott attempted to stop them, but when Steve Hart aimed two revolvers at his head, Scott's resistance evaporated.

In the residence Mrs Scott was reportedly surprised, yet impressed by the well-dressed bushrangers. While her husband continued to stall, she possibly saved him from being shot and found the key to the strong room, which yielded over £2000 in currency and gold.

The whole family, including Scott's mother, was herded out to the yard where they were loaded into their own buggy and carts and driven to Faithfull's Creek. There they found telegraph line repairer Watt, who'd been dropped off by a passing train to fix the break in the line. He'd surveyed the clearly deliberate damage to the wires and wandered over to the homestead to find out what was going on, and become another of the hostages.

At the homestead the gang, who now had thirty-seven hostages (including people who had clearly been assisting them), were in no hurry to leave. They ate dinner and let the male hostages out to stretch their legs. They herded them back into the hut when a passing train stopped and a man got out, picked up some of the broken wires and reboarded the train, which then continued on its way north to Benalla. The man was Police Magistrate Wyatt, who'd come down for the licensing hearing, noticed the broken wires when Watt had disembarked at Faithfull's Creek and had headed out on foot to investigate for himself after the hearing. Along the way he'd decided it was too far and turned back to Euroa to wait for the train that would return him to the spot anyway.

At 8.30, after treating their hostages to a display of trick riding, the Kelly Gang finally left Faithfull's Creek, riding through a night that Ned's careful planning told him would be lit by a full moon. By then Magistrate Wyatt had reached Benalla and was informing superintendents Nicolson and Sadleir that he thought the Kellys had struck at Euroa, whereupon the two boarded the train and headed in the opposite direction. They'd been fed a rumour (probably by Joe Byrne's mate Aaron Sherritt) that the gang would head for the Murray. Thus they spent the night speeding away from the scene of the crime.

When they got wind of the story, the media in Melbourne, Sydney and Victoria's north-east had a field day. 'Disgrace', 'radically wrong', 'mismanagement', they chorused. Ned, meanwhile, became the embodiment of the 'gallant', 'brave', 'valiant' bushranger of the ballads he'd grown up on. Striking from his heartland, where the police seemed powerless to touch him, he didn't simply use the bush to hide. By outsmarting and outmanoeuvring the police, and striking in such an audacious manner, he'd challenged their control over the country itself. While the Kelly mystique flourished, police morale sank.

Two days after the robbery, Chief Commissioner Captain Charles Standish travelled to Euroa to see Nicolson, only to find him exhausted from his pursuit of phantoms up to the Murray and back to Faithfull's Creek. Standish replaced him with Superintendent Frank Hare, and the police contingent in the district was increased by fifty-eight men to 217. Professional soldiers were also deployed to protect all the local banks. On 13 December the reward for Ned's capture was increased to £1000.

Then the arrests began. Detective Michael Ward identified an accomplice of the Kelly Gang at Euroa, Ben Gould, while six sympathisers were also identified and arrested for offences under the *Outlawry Act*. The problem, however, was that while the police had a good idea of who was involved, they lacked proof. So they continually applied to the court for a week's remand while the cases were prepared. In the early months of 1879 twenty-one sympathisers were arrested. They were held, without trial, for the next three months. As some commentators put it, the police strained the limits of the *Outlawry Act*. Curiously, however, the police concentrated their efforts on male sympathisers. Most of the female sympathisers remained at large, including Ned's sisters. It was also noted that after the Euroa robbery many of the sympathisers were suddenly flush with money. Ned's largesse gave those aiding him plenty of incentive to continue their support, but it was expensive for the gang.

On Saturday, 8 February 1879, in the south-western New South Wales plains town of Jerilderie, 60 kilometres north of the Murray River, Senior Constable George Devine and his wife (pregnant with their third child) were woken close to midnight. Someone outside was shouting something about a brawl in progress at Davidson's Hotel, 3 kilometres outside town. As Devine hurriedly dressed and headed out to the police station verandah, Jerilderie's other policeman, Probationary Constable Henry Richards, emerged from the office and joined him.

In front of them a man on horseback explained that the fight was serious, and that a lot of men were 'mad with drink'. Then he asked if there were only two of them to face the drunken mob. When he was told that was the case, the stranger pulled out a revolver and said, 'Move and I'll shoot you. I'm Kelly. Put up your hands.'

From both ends of the verandah, Dan, Joe and Steve appeared. The police, unarmed and completely unprepared for the Kelly Gang to cross the border and strike deep into New South Wales, had no choice but to surrender. Meanwhile, the Victorian police were scouring the Murray upstream of Corryong, 250 kilometres away, after a tip-off from an 'informant', probably Aaron Sherritt once again, that the gang was planning to cross the river there and commit a robbery at far-distant Goulburn.

Mrs Devine was terrified that her husband, the father of her children, was in danger of being shot. Ned reassured her he'd be fine if he didn't try anything. The gang then enjoyed a supper prepared by Mrs Devine, before locking the two constables into the cell, along with a drunk who'd been brought in earlier that day.

While a gang member kept watch through the night, the others slept until morning, when Ned and Dan dressed themselves in police uniforms. Then the genuine police were invited to breakfast with the bushrangers. It being a Sunday, Mrs Devine pointed out that she had to arrange the flowers in the church. Rather than have anything appear amiss, Dan went with her. Then the butcher came by with the meat for Sunday dinner. Mrs Devine answered the door, watched closely by Ned.

During the afternoon Probationary Constable Henry Richards was released and taken by Joe and Steve while they 'reconnoitred around the town'. He was told to explain to anyone who enquired that the police with him had just been assigned to the area. Joe and Steve took a particular interest in the Bank of New South Wales, housed in part of the Royal Mail Hotel's building, and the telegraph office, a short distance away on Billabong Creek.

Back at the police station, the afternoon passed uneventfully. In the evening Ned read to Mrs Devine from a letter he and Joe had been composing, which he hoped to get the Jerilderie newspaper's editor to publish. At 7500 words, it was an expanded version of the unpublished Euroa letter, although the essential points were the same. Parts of the Jerilderie Letter may have helped Mrs Devine appreciate how Ned and his family had been the victims of considerable police harassment and that this may have driven him to crime. However, the parts about disbanding the Victorian police force, deporting his enemies from Victoria and allowing him to range the lawless countryside unrestrained may have left her wondering if he'd lost his grip on reality. Not that the presence of police had been much more than an inconvenience to the wide-ranging Kelly Gang, let alone a restraint.

On Monday, 10 February 1879 the Kelly Gang started moving about Jerilderie. In police uniform, Joe and Dan revisited the telegraph office, assessed the task of destroying the telegraph lines, and returned to the police station. Ned then put on a police uniform and with Constable Richards, the now-uniformed gang walked or rode into town. Just after 10 a.m., at the Royal Mail Hotel, Richards introduced publican Charlie Cox to Ned, who promptly took him hostage. Dan and Steve gathered more hotel staff and herded them into the parlour, where Steve stood guard.

Next door at the bank Joe pretended to be a drunk and blundered in the back door. Bank accountant Edwin Living turned to throw him out when Joe produced a revolver and said, 'I am Kelly.' The teller, who was waiting out the front for the bank manager to arrive, was bailed up by Ned. From the safe the bushrangers seized £691 pounds, but the safe had an inner compartment that could only be opened by two keys. Living had one. The absent manager, John Tarleton, had the other.

Living and the teller were being herded next door when Tarleton came into the bank by the back door, and in a curious business practice, ran a bath. He was in it when Living stuck his head around the door to inform him they were being stuck up. Tarleton was incredulous until Steve Hart appeared as well, with a revolver, to confirm the story. Incredibly, Tarleton insisted on finishing his bath, and Steve let him.

Schoolmaster William Elliott called into the bank to make a deposit. It went straight into the coffers of Messrs Kelly and Co. Then William and Joe Byrne held a sack open so that a now squeaky clean Tarleton could add £1450 from the inner safe to the bandits' haul.

Shortly after, at the telegraph office, Joe a good job destroying the telegraph line. He had the telegraphist dismantle his morse key and directed some of his hostages to set about chopping down telegraph poles. As he'd done at Euroa, Ned's strategy effectively isolated the little outback town from the outside world. With its police force under lock and key, the Kelly Gang were free to take over. It was the Gilbert-Hall Gang's occupation of Canowindra all over again.

In a small town like Jerilderie, four 'new' policemen could hardly escape being noticed, and newspaper editor Samuel Gill wanted the story. He went to the police station to ask Senior Constable Devine about it, only to be met by his wife, who told him to run for his life. Instead Gill went into town and told a storekeeper named Rankin, who then told the next storekeeper Harkin, who suggested that if bushrangers were about, they should warn John Tarleton at the bank.

The bank was empty, but Ned was in the bank residence. When the men knocked on the counter he called out that he'd be there in a minute. Then it dawned on the three gentlemen that they might have walked in on the hold-up. They fled, with Ned in hot pursuit. In the ensuing scramble Rankin fell and was pounced upon by the armed Ned Kelly. He was taken into the hotel, but when Ned heard that one of the men who had escaped was the newspaper's editor, he flew into a rage and threatened to shoot Rankin. While Rankin protested that he'd only entered the bank on business, and other prisoners begged for his life, Steve Hart reportedly shouted at Ned to 'put the bugger on his knees and I'll put a bullet into him'.

It was Ned's second attempt to get his story and his cry for justice into print, and his determination is reflected by him immediately setting off in search of Gill. He eventually found Harkin, but Gill didn't stop running from what should have been the story of his life until he reached Carrah Homestead, 10 kilometres away.

Back in town, however, Gill's wife was in the newspaper office when Ned, Constable Richards and Living the accountant came in to enquire after her husband. Ned had fifty-six handwritten pages of the Jerilderie Letter that he wanted set up and printed off. He said he was prepared to pay a fair price. Mrs Gill said she didn't know where her husband was, but in any event it would be a brave printer who told Ned that if it was instant printing he was after, he'd do well to come back in about a century. Typesetting a 7500-word letter by hand (and in 1879 that was the only way it could be done) would have taken the little newspaper's typesetter at least 20 hours nonstop. Eventually Living offered to look after the letter and get Gill to print it. Reluctantly, Ned handed it over.

Back at the Royal Mail, Ned made a speech that varies with the recollections of the thirty-odd listeners, some of whom were by then quite drunk. Afterwards Ned and his gang released their hostages and headed for the police station. In town, some of the released prisoners milled about, while others set about riding to nearby towns for assistance. The town's parson, John Gribble, tried to organise a party to pursue the Kellys. He couldn't get any takers. Most of the townsfolk didn't see the need to get involved with dangerous men who had so far done them no harm. So Gribble set off in the hot afternoon sun to confront the bushrangers alone. He hoped to at least get back a small black racehorse that belonged to the daughter of the Albion Hotel's publican.

Meeting Ned, he persuaded him to at least speak to Macdougall, the publican. Ned and Steve rode back into town, but along the way Steve stole Gribble's watch. Meanwhile, once at the Albion Hotel, Ned put one of his guns on the bar and said, 'Anyone here may take it and shoot me dead, but if I'm shot, Jerilderie will swim in its own blood.' There were no takers. When Gribble came in, he told Ned Steve had his watch, whereupon Ned made his gang member return it. He then had a last drink at the pub while his gang assembled on the outskirts of town. By some accounts they may have galloped up and down the main street shouting, 'Hurrah for the good old times of Morgan and Ben Hall.'

When at last Ned arrived he told the rest of his gang that bank manager Tarleton and accountant Living had ridden for the police. The gang set off in pursuit, but soon gave it up and turned their horses towards the Murray. That night heavy rain washed out all signs of their passing. Once again, though, thanks to Ned's careful planning, a full moon lit their way.

As it turned out there wasn't even the possibility of a police pursuit until 7.30 that night. Jerilderie's two police constables were locked in the cells with the men from the telegraph office. Senior Constable Devine's wife had the key, but in obeying Ned's instructions to the letter, she ensured that her husband, whose life she'd begged the bushrangers to spare, couldn't get himself into any danger.

When news of the extraordinary hold-up broke, it caused a sensation. Despite the immense manhunt for them, the Kelly Gang appeared able to strike at will. And the manner of their crimes was nothing short of spectacular. They'd now struck in three locations, hundreds of kilometres apart. With police seemingly incapable of doing anything to contain the fast-moving bushmen of the Kelly Gang, an entire region extending across the rugged north-east of Victoria into the rolling plains of southern New South Wales appeared to be at their mercy. In towns, farmhouses, the big homesteads and on every lonely bush road, law-abiding citizens were haunted by the spectre of Ned Kelly. He was the ultimate embodiment of bushranging – seemingly invincible in the wilderness he had made his domain.

As Jerilderie was in New South Wales, the state government decided to top up the Victorian rewards, increasing the reward for the gang's capture to a staggering £8000 – £2000 for each member – this at a time when a police sergeant's annual income was £50. As for Ned, yet another of his elaborate plans had worked successfully. However, it was anything but flawless. It failed in its objective of getting the Jerilderie Letter published. And the duration of the crime had grown longer. Euroa had lasted thirty-two hours from start to finish, Jerilderie forty-four. It may have been a classic power-trip scenario, but lengthier hold-ups also increased the scope for things to go terribly wrong.

Once again, security in banks far and wide was stepped up. The Kelly Gang had taken some £2000 at Jerilderie, enough to support them in comfort for some time, or to fund their flight far beyond the reach of the Victorian police. They chose instead to return to the safety of their support base.

Not surprisingly, the sensation caused by Jerilderie soon saw copycat crimes in several locations. Immediately after Jerilderie Thomas Gorman, Charles Jones, William Kaye and William Hobbs (Hoppy Bill) began bushranging between Balranald and Ivanhoe in western New South Wales. They surrendered after a brief shootout that saw one policeman wounded. All four men were sentenced to death but their sentences were commuted to life imprisonment.

The Victorian police, meanwhile, attempted to tighten their grip on 'Kelly Country'. The Victorian government accepted a Queensland offer of an elite squad of trackers, led by Sub-Inspector Stanhope O'Connor. The six young men were the best of the best, but the Victorian media pounced on their ethnicity and promptly labelled them cannibals, hastening to add that O'Connor would not permit them to eat Ned and his gang. As for the Victorian police, Commissioner Standish had been forced to accept the Queensland offer by the Victorian government. Superintendent Hare also thought the Queensland team was nothing special and didn't deploy it effectively.

Consequently, the trackers' potential threat to the Kellys was neutralised due to a mix of racism, politics and incompetence. They may, however, have had a psychological impact on the gang, who were aware of their capabilities and were consequently more cautious in their movements. In his *History of the Australian Bushrangers*, Boxall refers to Kelly describing them as 'six little black devils' and wanting to shoot them if he got the chance.

The following month Superintendent Hare was removed from the hunt for the Kelly Gang after injuring his back when his horse jumped a fence. Nicolson was reappointed. Standish used the opportunity to save the cash-strapped Victorian government some money and cut the force at Nicolson's disposal by thirty-one, and also reduced the military guard on banks.

Over the ensuing months, what had become known as the Kelly Outbreak descended into stalemate. The cautious police patrols couldn't track down the gang in the remote and uninhabited mountain ranges, and the gang couldn't rob the well-guarded banks. With the proceeds of the Jerilderie job, they didn't need to, but neither did they act on the threats contained in the as-yet unpublished Jerilderie Letter: 'I give fair warning to all those who has reason to fear me to sell out . . . and do not attempt to reside in Victoria. Neglect this and abide by the consequences.'

Despite this, for nearly eighteen months after the Jerilderie hold-up the Kelly Gang was silent.

Not so the copycats. At 9 p.m. on 5 November 1879, the Australasian Bank at Moe, in Gippsland, was stuck up. After a struggle that saw a single shot fired, the would-be bushrangers fled empty-handed. The next morning two brothers – Robert and James Shanks – were located at the train station, waiting for a train. Revolvers were found in their bags. White hoods were spotted nearby. They were both convicted of attempted robbery.

Down in Melbourne, George Scott, the one-time Captain Moonlite, had been making his living since his release in March 1879 by lecturing passers-by. Former preacher Scott may have wanted to go straight, but with the fame of the Kelly Gang spreading, the temptation to turn bushranger grew.

In the middle of the afternoon on 15 November 1879, Moonlite led five young men – James Nesbitt, Thomas Williams, Augustus Wernicke, Thomas Rogan and Graham Bennett – to the McDonald family's Wantabadgery station, near Wagga Wagga in New South Wales. They bailed up the homestead and rounded up the McDonald family and up to a dozen people from around the property, holding them in the dining room of the main house. While the bushrangers were looting the station's store, a visitor from a neighbouring station and the local schoolteacher rode up. They were bailed up, but the schoolteacher refused to surrender. The young bushrangers threatened to shoot him.

When Moonlite arrived on the scene he pulled the schoolteacher off his horse. 'You —— old fool,' he reportedly said to him. 'Get down and do as you're told. I'm Moonlite.'

In the evening, the station manager, Baynes, returned to the homestead and was bailed up as well. The bushrangers then sat down to dinner, taking turns while some stood guard. After dinner, drinks were served all round. The aging Mr McDonald was allowed to go to bed, but everyone else remained in the dining room all night, sleeping at the table. The bushrangers took turns on guard while others slept. The bushrangers were still at the station at breakfast time. This was clearly not simply a robbery. The apparent objective was to emulate the Kellys, or outdo them.

When station manager Baynes remarked to one of Moonlite's men, 'This is bad work', Moonlite overheard him and went into a rage. He accused him of attempting to corrupt his men and would have shot him but for the intercession of the women on the station.

As more people arrived at Wantabadgery, they were bailed up and held with the others. One of them arrived with a young horse that took Moonlite's fancy. However, when he tried to mount the filly, she shied away. Moonlite lost his temper with the creature and ordered it to stand or he'd shoot it. The animal continued to rear and Moonlite proved as good as his word, putting a bullet in the unfortunate animal's head.

He then had a buggy brought around and took Mr McDonald with him while he stuck up the nearby Australian Arms Hotel. He took the publican's children hostage in the buggy and ordered the publican and his wife to walk to Wantabadgery.

On his way back there he stuck up everyone along the way, taking them prisoner as well.

At the station, when he caught sight of manager Baynes, Moonlite realised he'd left a potential enemy unguarded. He again threatened to kill him, this time by hanging him from a tree. Again the women of the station saved the man's life, calming the erratic bushranger, who had upwards of thirty-five hostages.

Moonlite now patrolled the station boundary, adding to the population under his reign of terror, when he came upon a man riding over from the neighbouring station, Eurongilly.

'Where are you going with that pistol?' Moonlite reputedly challenged him.

'To fight the bushrangers,' the man answered.

'By God you've found them,' Moonlite cried as he bailed the man up. He took him back to the station and put him on trial for unlawfully carrying firearms. Moonlite was the judge, two of his men and two station hands were the jury. Fortunately, after the case was heard, the jury found the man not guilty. Moonlite told the man if the verdict had gone the other way he'd have sentenced him to death and executed him immediately. The bushrangers then turned their attention to lunch.

During the afternoon, Mr McDonald managed to escape from the bushrangers. Considering the number of hostages they now had, they may not have noticed him go. He got a horse and rode to Wagga Wagga, 35 kilometres to the west, for the police. Constables Howe, Hedley, Williamson and Johns immediately set out for Wantabadgery. A telegraphic message was sent to Gundagai, 42 kilometres east of Wantabadgery, and five more police set out from there as well. The Wagga Wagga police arrived at Wantabadgery at 4 a.m. the following morning. The bushrangers were still there, thirty-six hours after they'd arrived. The Gundagai police, mounted on fresh horses obtained from a station along the way, arrived shortly after. The nine police then prepared to attack.

When the shooting started, the bushrangers allowed their hostages to leave the homestead. The hostages got up onto a ridge to watch the gunfight, and were joined by several hundred spectators from the surrounding district.

In the ensuing gunfight, Constable Bowen from Gundagai was shot (he died a few days later), one bushranger (23-year-old James Nesbitt) was shot and killed, and two bushrangers (nineteen-year-old Augustus Wernicke and twenty-year-old Graham Bennett) were wounded before the others surrendered. Wernicke also died of his wounds within days of the gun battle.

Moonlite, Rogan, Bennett and Williams were convicted of the murder of Constable Bowen, but the jury recommended mercy in the cases of the three young bushrangers because of their ages (all were nineteen or twenty) and because they'd been led astray by the 37-year-old Moonlite. However, the Kelly Outbreak ensured there was little mercy to be found in the justice system. Moonlite and Rogan were executed in Darlinghurst Gaol, while the other two were sentenced to imprisonment for life.

On 15 December 1879, another copycat attempted to turn bushranger. George Gustave de Thenar bailed up Holy Plains station, in Victoria's Gippsland. After robbing the place he fled into the bush. However, a fortnight later, he turned himself in. The supposed son of the Count de la Thenar reportedly said he'd 'had enough of the bush' and that having done wrong he was prepared to pay the penalty.

As 1879 rolled into 1880, the Kelly story appeared to be growing cold. However in the autumn of 1880 things started happening. On 22 March there was a report that mouldboards – steel plates from ploughs – were being stolen from farms within the immediate vicinity of Greta in Victoria. Then came a rumour from police informers that armour was being made.

Former Greta schoolteacher Daniel Kennedy, codenamed 'Denny', and 'the Disease Stock Agent' (the Kelly Gang being the diseased stock), wrote to Superintendent Nicolson on 20 May 1880 that 'missing portions of cultivators described as jackets are now being worked and fit splendidly. Tested previous to using and proof [presumably against gunfire] at 10 yards [9 metres]'. He also commented that 'a break out may be expected as feed is getting scarce'.

With the hard months of winter approaching, the Kelly Gang was being spurred into activity by a growing cash-flow crisis. Meanwhile, Detective Michael Ward had begun playing Aaron Sherritt as bait. The young friend of Joe Byrne had been 'assisting' the police with their inquiries, although he'd actually planted rumours that sent police on false trails. Now Ward made out that the relationship had become cosier, fanning suspicions. Ned had already spelt out what he'd do to informers in the Jerilderie Letter:

> Any person aiding or harbouring or assisting the Police in any way whatever or employing any person whom they know to be a detective or cad or those who would be so deprived as to take blood-money will be Outlawed, And declared unfit to be allowed human buriel [sic] their property either consumed or confiscated And them theirs and all belonging to them exterminated off the face of the earth, the enemy I cannot catch I shall give a payable reward for.

It's bloodthirsty stuff from a man who insisted he wasn't a murderer. It also assumes a position of authority over the territory that he can almost be forgiven for considering his own. Indeed, the letter concludes, 'I am a widow's son outlawed and my orders must be obeyed.' Ned clearly saw himself as a leader, relatively secure within his domain, police patrols notwithstanding. There's a story that Ned intended to declare north-east Victoria an independent republic, and that handbills were printed to that end. Unfortunately, if they existed none of the handbills can be located in private or public hands. Yet the reality was that the bush that he ranged had come to be known as Kelly Country anyway. For police it was hostile territory that began on the outskirts of the towns – the combination of sympathisers in settled districts and the uninhabited mountains where the Kelly Gang lurked made pursuit in either potentially lethal.

By June 1880, Sherritt's bush shack was being watched at night by four police officers, who then sheltered in the cramped hut during the day. Given the history of sympathisers who had eventually turned bushrangers in, the Kelly Gang may have been right to suspect Sherritt had decided their race was run and it was time to cash in. He probably wasn't the only one, but he was certainly the most exposed.

Rumours continued to circulate that the Kelly Gang was about to make a move. On Friday, 25 June 1880 the Disease Stock Agent informed the man who was back in charge of the Kelly hunt, Superintendent Hare (he'd replaced Nicolson on 2 June), that the Kellys were now completely broke, that they had bullet-proof armour, that they were about to do something 'that would cause the ears of the Australian world to tingle'.

Hare, with Superintendent Sadleir present, promptly sacked the agent. He was so contemptuous that he remarked to Sadleir that with agents like this it was no wonder he and Nicolson hadn't caught the Kellys. Yet he failed to notice that the date suggested for imminent action happened to coincide with a night when the moon was full. It had been full when the Kelly Gang escaped from Euroa and Jerilderie, lighting their way as they fled into the trackless bush after their daring robberies.

At approximately 6.30 the following evening, one of Aaron Sherritt's neighbours, Anton Wick, knocked at the door of Aaron's hut and called out that he was lost. Aaron unlocked his door and opened it to tell Anton that his house was where it always was. He didn't notice that Anton was handcuffed. Then Joe Byrne emerged from the darkness beside Anton, levelling the shotgun taken from Sergeant Michael Kennedy at Stringybark Creek at his best friend. He blasted a hole in his throat and another through his body.

Aaron died at the feet of his distraught young wife Ellen and her mother, Mrs Barry. In the bedroom, the four police were fumbling with their guns. Joe fired into the flimsy partition and challenged the men to come out. When they didn't, he sent Ellen in to make them come out. They refused. After a second attempt they kept Ellen with them, so Joe sent Mrs Barry in. She too was detained by the cowering constables. Joe was joined by Dan, and the pair threatened to burn the place down. After two hours, during which they attempted to set the place alight, they rode off into the night.

Meanwhile, 40 kilometres away Ned Kelly and Steve Hart were preparing to ride down into the town of Glenrowan. They put their newly made body armour on beneath their oilskin coats, left four saddle horses and a packhorse carrying a drum of explosives in the bush south of the town, and after the 9 p.m. train of Saturday, 26 June 1880 puffed past on its way north to Wangaratta, they made their move.

Just past the now darkened railway station they tried to lift the train lines on the Wangaratta side of town, using tools they'd brought for the purpose. They soon found they couldn't budge the fish plates that held the rails, so they went to some nearby workers' tents to get some help. Six railway men got out of their tents, but their boss, Louis Piazzi, had a woman with him, and only vacated the tent after a gunshot interrupted his coitus. Piazzi then told Ned he was out of luck. He and his men weren't railway workers; they were quarrymen and lacked both the tools and knowledge to lift the rails. Ned moved on to the Glenrowan Inn, 70 metres from the tents, and bailed up the publican, Ann Jones, her fourteen-year-old daughter and four young sons. Ned then roused John Stanistreet, the stationmaster, and told him to show the quarrymen how to sabotage the railway line. Stanistreet didn't have a clue, but suggested local platelayers James Reardon and Dennis Sullivan might be more help.

While Ned went to get them, Dan and Joe arrived fresh from the bloodshed at the Woolshed Valley. When Ned returned with the two platelayers, he learned that phase one of his plan had, literally, been executed. Phase two, derailing the trainload of police that would rush to the scene when the news broke, was proving more difficult. After that, the gang was supposed to descend on the now defenceless Benalla and plunder all the banks there.

Ned took James Reardon to the site of the planned derailment (accompanied by his wife, eight children and their lodger) but it was only when they got there that Reardon remembered that he needed a crowbar. Steve Hart went to fetch it and eventually, despite the stalling of labourers, stationmaster and platelayers, the job was done. An operation that should have taken a few moments had taken half the night.

As with the previous Kelly robberies, most of the hostages were then escorted to the local pub, the Glenrowan Inn, where fires were kindled in the predawn chill. Some of the women and children went to the stationmaster's house, guarded by Steve Hart. The gang then settled down to await the arrival of the speeding train and the ensuing carnage among the hated police.

Remarkably, Glenrowan's sole policeman that night was left unmolested. Constable Hugh Bracken was in bed with gastric flu. The town's other three police, also ill as a consequence of watching the Kelly house in cold weather, were absent from town. Glenrowan's other publican and his family from the rival McDonnell's Hotel, sympathisers with the Kellys, were escorted to the Glenrowan Inn, if only for appearances. Other sympathisers tended the horses while more joined the 'hostages'. Glenrowan was, after all, just 10 kilometres from Greta – the very heart of Kelly Country, with the larger centres of Benalla 20 kilometres south and Wangaratta a similar distance north.

As the morning wore on, and there was still no train, the number of hostages grew. At 11 a.m. schoolteacher Thomas Curnow, his wife

Jean and their baby, his sister Catherine and brother-in-law David Mortimer were bailed up by Ned. The women went to the stationmaster's house, Jean carrying the infant. Thomas and David joined the people in the Glenrowan Inn.

Thomas Curnow was twenty-five, the same age as Ned, and had lived in the town for four years, studiously avoiding taking sides when the Kelly Gang tested the loyalties of everyone in the district. On the verandah of the inn, where the drink was starting to flow freely, Thomas learned of the sabotage of the railway line and Dan and Joe confirmed 'we're going to send the train and its occupants to hell'.

There was still one problem: no train. By midday the day after Aaron Sherritt had been shot, the four policemen still hadn't managed to report the killing. The police response perfectly illustrates why their efforts to apprehend the Kelly Gang had met with such abject failure. The four constables had been afraid to venture out in Kelly Country until daylight, twelve hours after the cold-blooded murder of Aaron Sherritt. Then, rather than expose themselves to danger by going into Beechworth themselves, the police tried to send locals to raise the alarm. Initially, an over-eager Kelly sympathiser, Paddy Byrne, turned the locals back.

Word of Aaron Sherritt's murder finally reached Beechworth at 1 p.m. on Sunday 27 June. There Detective Michael Ward tried to pass the news to Superintendent Hare in Benalla, but the telegraph operator couldn't get through. Eventually, Hare got the news at 2.30 p.m. Hare, who had a contingent of mounted police, two local trackers and a special police train at his disposal, had everything he needed to get rolling. He didn't move. Instead he telegraphed Police Commissioner Standish in Melbourne and awaited instructions.

Standish got Hare's message at 4.30 p.m., whereupon he went to see Queensland Sub-Inspector O'Connor to find out if he and his Queensland trackers, who'd been sacked and were about to take ship back to Queensland, would rejoin the hunt. O'Connor sent a message to Queensland for permission. The answer was no. He was pressed to send a second request. Eventually, after several hours, permission was granted. Standish, one of the men who'd regarded the Queensland trackers with contempt, waited patiently while the men he supposedly had no time for were made available.

Back at Glenrowan, the hours passed slowly. In the afternoon, Ned organised various sporting contests and entertainments, revelling in the role of master of ceremonies. As the sun began to dip towards the western horizon, more than sixty hostages waited in and around the inn and stationmaster's house.

At Glenrowan, as evening fell, a bonfire was lit behind the inn's kitchen and there was dancing. Still there was no train, and now an entire day had passed. Ned began releasing some of the prisoners he trusted. When he decided he should take Constable Bracken prisoner, Thomas Curnow asked to be released. He told Ned he was with him heart and soul. After taking Bracken prisoner, while dressed in his armour, Ned let the schoolteacher and his family go.

As Thomas drove his wife and sister to his mother-in-law's, he told them he was going to try to warn the train, whenever it finally did arrive. His wife Jean would have none of it. She refused to stay at her mother's home, so Thomas drove her home and put her to bed. When she finally went to sleep, he set about his plan to warn the train. He got a candle, matches and a red scarf then set out to ride along the line to Benalla to raise the alarm. It was just after 2 a.m. on Monday 28 June when he started out from his home, on the Benalla side of town. Almost immediately he heard the sound of a train approaching at speed.

The special train from Melbourne had finally got under way at 10 p.m. It was delayed and slightly damaged when it struck a railway gate which, it being a Sunday, was closed because trains didn't run on Sundays. It reached Benalla at 1.30 a.m. There O'Connor, five trackers (one had died while assigned in the colder Victorian climate) and a media contingent were joined by Hare, seven troopers and a civilian volunteer. The train, pulled by a new engine, left Benalla at 2 a.m. on Monday morning, speeding north with the damaged locomotive travelling ahead as a pilot.

The pilot engine was 2 kilometres from Glenrowan when the driver saw what he took to be a burning log up ahead. A little closer, he realised someone was signalling. He applied the brakes and as he passed, called out, 'What's the matter?'

Thomas Curnow shouted, 'The Kellys!'

The driver sounded three warning blasts on his whistle. When the pilot engine stopped, the guard jumped down. Curnow explained that the line had been sabotaged on the other side of Glenrowan and the Kellys had taken over the town. The guard headed back down the line to warn the special train. Before he left, Curnow begged him not to reveal his informant, fearing reprisals against himself and his family.

Back at Glenrowan what had become a party was in full swing. The remaining people from the stationmaster's house, including women and children, had been brought to the inn. As they grew tired, some of them went home, while others remained at the pub drinking and singing into the night. Finally, Ned decided to let almost all of his hostages go, after he'd given them a little talk.

It was in the midst of his discourse that Joe Byrne came running back to the inn and cried out, 'The train's coming!'

Rather than let the forty or so remaining hostages go, Ned ordered them to stay in the pub. The Kelly Gang went into the dining room and started putting on their armour, followed by their coats. Ned and Joe were dressed first and went outside, where Ned saw the train halted in a cutting near the approach to town. In the clear moonlight, the pilot engine was now coupled to the special train, its lights doused.

Back in the Glenrowan Inn, Ned also ordered the lights to be extinguished. Things were clearly not going to Ned's elaborate plan. Worse still, there didn't seem to be any alternative scheme in case things went wrong. Those in the Glenrowan Inn watched and hoped that the train, which was clearly moving with much more caution than Ned's plan anticipated, would continue on through the town. But it would only get a short way past the station before it would be stopped by the torn-up line. While those in the Glenrowan Inn looked on, the train chugged slowly forward. It pulled into Glenrowan Station and stopped.

At this pivotal moment, Ned had few options. He could stand and fight, and probably succumb to the superior numbers of police. He could admit his plan had failed and take flight. In reality, he probably had no choice at all. He could no longer afford the loyalty of his harbourers and sympathisers. If he fled with his tail between his legs, he wouldn't get far.

There was an appropriate symbolism in his having torn up the train tracks outside Glenrowan. For the Kelly Gang, and for bushranging in general, it was the end of the line. All that remained was the old slogan: 'death or liberty!'

On the platform Superintendent Hare turned to the only civilian present and reputedly said, 'What had we better do?'

The volunteer, Charles Rawlins, who knew the town well, suggested they see the stationmaster. Hare sent him with three constables. There a terrified Mrs Stanistreet told them her husband was one of the prisoners of the Kellys at the Glenrowan Inn.

'How many are there?' Rawlins asked.

'Forty,' she answered.

In the inn, Bracken was quietly warning the hostages to get down as low as they possibly could. Outside, Ned was watching as the train sat puffing in the station. Then the sound of horses being unloaded carried far in the cold night air. Bracken chose his moment, slipped out of the hotel, and ran. It was only a short distance down a slight incline to the platform.

Hare assumed the Kellys would flee (the same error police had made at Stringybark Creek) and he would pursue on horseback, but when Bracken reached the station, he gasped out, 'Over there. The Kellys. Not five minutes ago. Stuck us all up. The four of them, quick, quick!'

Hare and those who had their weapons (about half of the fourteen-odd police and Aboriginal trackers present, plus *Argus* reporter Joe Melvin), abandoned the horses and started to run to the Glenrowan Inn. By then all four of the Kelly Gang were standing in the shadows of the verandah, watching the police running towards them in broad moonlight.

A turnstile allowed pedestrians to pass through the railway fence one at a time into the sloping ground that lead up to the Glenrowan Inn. Hare charged through in the lead, wielding a shotgun, oblivious to the men on the verandah. Ned aimed a rifle and fired at Hare at a range of 30 metres, hitting him in the wrist. The superintendent reportedly cried out, 'Good gracious! I am hit the very first shot.'

The rest of the gang unleashed a volley that sent the rest of the police scattering for cover – which comprised a few trees and a ditch in the railway reserve. At first they only managed a sporadic return fire and Ned, emboldened, moved out into the moonlight. One of the constables, Charles Gascoigne, fired two shots from his .45 Martini Henry rifle. One shot passed through Ned's bent left forearm then through his upper arm. The other hit his right foot, the bullet shattering bone and tearing flesh from toe to heel.

A few moments later all the police began directing their fire at the Glenrowan Inn, causing havoc as the thin walls gave no protection from the hail of bullets and sprayed the occupants with splintering wood. Despite lying on the ground, Jack Jones, the thirteen-year-old son of publican Ann Jones, was hit in the hip. The bullet sliced upwards through his body, leaving the boy screaming in agony, blood running from his mouth. Another bullet grazed his sister Jane's forehead as she and her mother carried him towards the kitchen at the back of the inn and put him near the brick chimney for what little protection it could give. Then a labourer, Neil McHugh (no known relation to the author), realising the boy was going to die if he didn't get medical attention, carried him out past the police to the house of platelayer James Reardon. The boy died anyway, later that day.

One of the quarrymen, George Metcalf, died when a bullet hit him in the eye. Then line repairer Martin Cherry, who'd gone to the pub to be part of the story of a lifetime when he heard the Kellys were there, found the floor uncomfortable. When he got up onto a bed in the kitchen he was hit in the groin, the bullet causing massive internal injuries. Those around him tried to do what they could for him as bullets, splinters of wood and broken glass tore through the air around them.

Despite Ned's injuries, the Kelly Gang returned almost as much gunfire as they took. Then, in the midst of the volleys, two rockets were fired into the sky from the vicinity of McDonnell's Hotel, on the other side of the railway line. Who had fired them, and to whom or what they were signalling, was a mystery to the police. However, it may have been a call to Kelly sympathisers to rise up and throw the police out of Kelly Country once and for all.

Finally, amid the hail of gunfire, a voice cried out that there were women and children in the hotel and to stop shooting. There was a pause, during which all the women and children, led by the wounded Jane Jones, ran from the building. The Reardons and their eight children, including a baby, weren't quick enough. Trailing behind the other non-combatants they were challenged as they approached the police lines. When they said they were women and children, the police heard male voices (those of the father and older boys) and opened fire. Three of the children ran onwards to safety. The rest ran back to the Glenrowan Inn.

The police were now deployed at the front (south) and left (west) of the inn, but lacked the manpower to surround the building. While the women and children were escaping, one of the constables reportedly heard Ned and Joe talking. Ned asked Joe to help him reload his weapon. Joe said he thought his leg was broken.

Having reloaded, Ned emerged from the breezeway at the back of the hotel separating the main building from the kitchen. He fired at the police who fired back. Still exchanging gunfire with the police, and hit several times in the body with no effect, he made his way towards the back fence of the inn. Bleeding profusely from the wound to his arm, he tried to staunch it using a cap he'd been wearing under his helmet. He reached the back fence, where he had a horse saddled and waiting for him. Despite his injuries, he climbed up and rode out of Glenrowan. There are suggestions, based on the oral histories of descendants of those involved, that Ned, seeing his grand plan for Glenrowan going awry, went to warn sympathisers converging on the scene not to get involved. Another possibility is that he simply ran away.

Shortly after, two policemen, constables Kelly and Arthur, found Ned's blood-soaked cap dropped on the ground, and his rifle. Constable Kelly was now the officer in charge, the injured Hare having managed to extract himself from in front of the inn. He was soon on his way to Benalla to seek medical attention while his men continued the deadly fire-fight with the Kelly Gang.

Constable Kelly was attempting to create the impression that he had the place surrounded, but Ned's cap and rifle suggested the gang could slip away to the safety of their refuges in Kelly Country, even if they were severely injured.

At least word of the siege was spreading quickly. Superintendent Sadleir was already on his way from Benalla with thirteen reinforcements. In Wangaratta, 20 kilometres north, Sergeant Arthur Steele had been alerted by telegram, and when Constable Bracken arrived to say the gang were still at Glenrowan, Steele set out on horseback with five constables.

By 6 a.m., some thirty-five police were deployed around the Glenrowan Inn. Some later stated that in approaching the inn they must have passed extremely close to Ned, who may have been lurking somewhere outside their cordon. Nevertheless, before dawn, the remaining members of the gang were effectively surrounded, outnumbered and outgunned by twelve to one. And the police knew that by this time, at least, Ned (wherever he was) and Joe had serious gunshot wounds.

Ned may have managed to slip outside the police lines, but there was little hope of escape for the others, even if the gang's armour could protect them in a last desperate shootout. Ned could have left them to their fate, but it appears that he either returned to the vicinity of the inn, or had remained there after escaping. His situation hopeless, completely outgunned, it was when the first faint glimmer of dawn lit the eastern horizon that Ned, in the vicinity of the Inn's back fence, made a move. In full armour, including his roughly welded helmet, he struggled to his feet and despite his wounds began walking slowly back towards his mates at the Glenrowan Inn.

As he advanced, Margaret Reardon tried once again to get herself and her remaining children clear. Dan let them go and when they got into the yard in front of the inn, Margaret screamed at the police not to shoot. Sergeant Steele told them to put up their hands or he'd shoot them like dogs. She and her eldest son Michael, seventeen, did the best they could as Margaret held a baby and Michael led a child by the hand.

Despite this, Margaret maintained that Steele started shooting. Margaret kept going. Michael's courage failed him and he turned back. She managed to escape, perhaps because Constable Arthur shouted to Steele that if he fired at her again, he'd shoot Steele himself.

Steele reloaded and fired two shots at Michael Reardon, just as he reached the inn. One bullet hit him, deflecting off his shoulder and stopping behind his breastbone. As he collapsed, his father, who hadn't dared try leave, helped his son inside.

Unnoticed, Ned reached the back of the inn, where he saw Joe pouring himself a whisky in the bar. Joe Byrne saluted his leader with a toast, 'Many more years in the bush for the Kelly Gang.'

Just then another volley of police bullets tore through the building. Joe paid dearly for not keeping low. Despite his armour, a bullet tore through his groin. With blood pouring from the wound, he collapsed. Moments later he was dead.

Ned went out onto the verandah and challenged the police. They made no reply, so he turned back indoors to gather his remaining men. In the murky building, strewn with the dead, the injured and those still trapped alive, he did not see his brother and Steve Hart. Assuming they'd made a break for it, he decided to take on the police alone. He walked out the back again and saw seven or eight police nearby. None fired as he made his way up the paddock to the horses. It was only there that Constable Gascoigne realised he was trying to escape and called out to the police on the other side of the inn to stop him. One of the horses broke through a sliprail and galloped away. The rest were shot in the yard by the police.

Seeing Dan and Steve's horses, Ned may have realised the pair were still inside the Glenrowan Inn. Oral histories suggest sympathisers may have told him they hadn't made it out. In any case, Ned Kelly turned once more, and despite his injuries and body armour that at 50 kilograms was equivalent to half his own bodyweight, he staggered towards the police lines.

The figure that emerged from the mists and hanging gun smoke walking down the slope to the north of the Glenrowan Inn was never to be forgotten by those who saw it – police, journalists and sketch artist Thomas Carrington. In full armour, a cloak thrown over his shoulders, helmet accentuating his height so that he seemed larger than any ordinary man, Ned Kelly slowly moved forward. The police lines were now threatened by a figure some likened to the headless ghost of Hamlet's father.

Constable Arthur thought it was a prankster until Ned raised his right arm from within the folds of his cloak and using his left hand to support it aimed a revolver. Arthur fired first, hitting the helmet at close range. The armour stopped the bullet, but the force caused Ned to lurch to one side. He then raised his revolver again and fired. His arm, however, was crippled and the bullet hit the ground a metre in front of Arthur. Arthur fired again, hit Ned again, but only caused him to lurch once more. Other police nearby started firing, too, with little effect. One heard Ned say, 'Fire away you buggers. You cannot hurt me.'

From 10 metres away constables Healy and Mountiford fired at Ned with shotguns. He laughed. As the police continued shooting, Ned slowly advanced.

At first Sergeant Steele couldn't see what the other police were firing at. Then, in the growing light, he saw what he took to be a tall black man wrapped in some kind of rug. He called on his men to cease firing at the stranger – a remarkable move since he'd had no qualms about shooting women and children earlier in the morning. Ned then clarified his identity by calling to Steve and Dan, who rallied inside the inn and came to the back and started firing at the tree Steele was using for shelter.

Ned moved forward, the way ahead of him opening as police fled. Yet they closed in on the left, right and behind, firing constantly, the shots causing Ned to stagger first one way, then another. To the artist Thomas Carrington the figure was moving as if drunk. In a clump of three small trees 100 metres from the northern side of the inn, Ned rested for a moment amid the crossfire. At that moment, despite all the shooting, Joe Byrne's mare Music approached him. The animal may have sensed Ned's distress, but while the police feared he might mount and ride off, such athleticism was beyond Ned at this moment. The horse moved away and was promptly shot, though not fatally, by the police.

Ned's revolver was out of ammunition, so he drew a second. It was promptly shot from his hand, the bullet ripping through flesh and bone in the process. Nevertheless, he drew a third revolver, the last weapon he was carrying.

Sergeant Steele was now at risk of being caught between Ned and the inn, where Dan and Steve were still firing from the breezeway at the back of the building. Hoping Ned was trying to reload, Steele charged the trees where Ned had sunk to his knees. From cover, Ned fired as the sergeant approached. Steele dived low, dirt from the shot spraying into his eye. Other police gave their sergeant covering fire, Constable Healy again hitting Ned's hand, severing a finger. It may have been the pain that spurred Ned to action. He rose and staggered on, veering towards a large fallen tree that lay in the direction of the train station.

Behind the tree, a railway guard from the special train, Jesse Dowsett, found the monstrous apparition of Ned Kelly heading straight for him. He aimed his railway-issue Colt revolver and fired half a dozen shots. They all bounced off. The figure kept coming.

Ned made it to the tree and slumped against it, exhausted. Dowsett suggested he surrender, but Ned would have none of it. So Dowsett shot him in the head.

'How do you like that, old man?' Dowsett reputedly asked.

But thanks to the armour the bullet bounced off, and Ned replied, 'How do you like this?' as he fired back, narrowly missing the railway man.

Behind Ned, Sergeant Steele had closed in. He realised that the armour only extended to Ned's thighs, and prepared to take a shot that would bring him down. Then the mare Music intervened again.

She charged back into the midst of the action, turning Ned's attention towards Steele. To no avail. The policeman fired, the shot hit Ned in the right knee. Ned fought to stay on his feet as Steele charged him and fired again, the shot tearing through his hip, thigh and groin. Finally, Ned fell forward, crying, 'I'm done. I'm done.'

He was still gripping his revolver when Steele leapt on him. With blood spurting from his wounded hand Ned tried to bring the gun over his shoulder to fire. Guard Dowsett and Constable Kelly dived onto Ned as well, the mass of bodies flailing as Ned fought to the last. Dowsett grabbed Ned's wrist, trying to tear the gun away. A shot rang out, the gun going off beside Steele's face, just missing him. Finally, Ned was disarmed. At last they were able to pull away the helmet to discover that they had caught Ned Kelly. He was alive, but only just.

As Ned lay on the ground, pale and near death, others converged on the scene, trigger-happy and fired by the bloodlust of the capture. For a few moments it seemed the police who'd been terrorised by Ned Kelly for over two years and at last had him at their mercy would shoot him where he lay. Then Dowsett started shouting, 'Take him alive!'

Constable Hugh Bracken, Ned's hostage the day before, stood over Ned with a shotgun and stated emphatically, 'I'll shoot any bloody man that dares touch him.'

They were only 100 metres from the inn, and as they tried to bear Ned away, Dan and Steve kept a constant fire trained upon them. They seemed determined that none of the gang would be taken alive. Police returned fire, especially at Dan, who had ventured outside the building. He was hit in the leg before being forced to retreat. Ned was eventually taken to the stationmaster's house, where he gave newspaper reporters the first of several versions of the intended plan at Glenrowan. After wrecking the train, the gang was to ride to Benalla, blow up the railway line from Melbourne, and with the town thus isolated they would plunder the Bank of New South Wales.

At the inn there was a standoff until 10 a.m., when Superintendent Sadleir (who had arrived on one of the many trains filled with more police and the plain curious who raced to the scene as news of the siege spread) negotiated the release of the roughly thirty remaining prisoners. There was a rush for safety, made more terrifying by some police threatening to shoot those who were trying to flee. Some, like Michael Reardon, received medical attention that may have saved their lives. Martin Cherry, still bleeding from the wound to his groin, couldn't be helped from the inn. He remained inside, near the kitchen, where the only others left were Dan Kelly and Steve Hart.

There was some talk with Ned about getting his men to surrender, but he doubted his ability to sway them. Around lunchtime a priest suggested a man of the cloth might be trusted. Ned thought the priest would be suspected of being a policeman in disguise, and shot. As the afternoon wore on, the stalemate continued, except that the police began to note the gathering of Kelly sympathisers in McDonnell's Hotel, on the other side of the railway tracks. Emotions were running high, but it would have been an extraordinary step if the Kelly sympathisers, more used to raising crops, cattle and kids, raised hell with the cops instead.

Sadleir, meanwhile, requested an artillery piece to be sent from Melbourne, a decidedly drastic approach to resolving the situation. Then Senior Constable Charles Johnston suggested setting the inn ablaze. Sadleir agreed, and at 3 p.m. police fired volleys into the building to cover Johnston as he approached with straw and kerosene. By this stage over a thousand people were involved in or watching the unfolding drama, among them the Kelly sisters Maggie, Kate and Grace. Police tried to get them to call on their brother and Steve to surrender, even as the preparations for burning the boys out were finalised. Maggie refused, but Kate agreed. The inn may have already been alight when she approached. A photo of the scene shows a woman outside the building as smoke billows from its eaves.

As the building burned more fiercely, the priest, Dean Gibney, ignored police warnings and approached. He was joined by Superintendent Sadleir on the verandah, where they were confronted by a wall of fire. Despite this, Gibney walked into the burning building where he found Joe Byrne's body. He then leapt through a burning doorway to find Dan and Steve's bodies in one of the bedrooms. He took one of their hands and formed the opinion that they'd been dead for some time. The siege was over.

Police managed to carry Joe's body from the scene before the flames engulfed it, but the fire all but incinerated Dan and Steve. Martin Cherry was found, still alive, near the kitchen, but died of his wounds shortly after. Police, media and sightseers swarmed over the scene, some of them scavenging for souvenirs. Any fires of rebellion were quenched in the scenes of mourning at the station, to which the bodies were taken, and at the stationmaster's house, where Ned remained alive despite nearly thirty bullet and shotgun wounds.

Amid the tumult of emotion surrounding Dan and Steve, the police capitulated and allowed the Kelly sympathisers to remove their bodies. Later attempts to recover them for an inquest met with such threats and intimidation that they were eventually buried by their families and friends without a full examination. Joe's body was taken to Benalla, where the following day it became a macabre freak show, tied to a door of the gaol for a 'photo opportunity'.

The media initially celebrated the capture of the Kelly Gang, but even as the smoke around the ruins of the Glenrowan Inn was clearing, they began counting the cost. The focus was the police action in firing with reckless disregard for life at a building full of innocent people. Three hostages had died. A number of others suffered serious gunshot wounds. The post mortem then moved on to the failings of the police throughout the hunt for the Kelly Gang. The unseemly manoeuvring for credit (and for the significant reward money that was about to be distributed) and the widely differing accounts of who fired at innocent people such as Michael Reardon were raised.

Ned, meanwhile, had been rushed by train to Melbourne, ostensibly for urgent medical attention, but conveniently getting him far away from the heartland of his support base, from where it was feared a rescue attempt might be launched. For one of the features of the Kelly Gang was that it may have comprised only four men, but it seemed to the police that it included the population of the entire countryside.

Ned was taken to Melbourne Gaol where his captors took the task of healing him particularly seriously. They had to keep him alive long enough to stand trial, and should he be found guilty, to hang. As it happened, his mother was interred in the woman's section of the same prison, and while he was recovering she was permitted to see him.

The lead-up to Ned's trial demonstrated that the threat from the Kelly Country remained a matter of concern for the authorities, as the government actively prevented the land of sympathisers being mortgaged to pay for Ned's defence. He nevertheless enlisted fiery MP William Zincke to represent him at his committal hearing in Beechworth. However, when he added Zincke's political rival David Gaunson to his team, Zincke walked out on the night before the hearing, leaving Gaunson to pick up the pieces. Needless to say, Ned was committed to trial on the single charge of the murder of Constable Lonigan. The trial was initially set down for Beechworth, but once again, fears for the safety of the jury saw the case moved to Melbourne.

The problems for Ned's defence continued. The cost of a barrister was quite simply beyond him and his hard-pressed sympathisers – £50 for the first two days and £10 a day after that. The man David Gaunson suggested for the job, Hickman Molesworth, suggested a delaying tactic while the Kellys raised the cash. His junior, Henry Bindon, would appear and admit that he was completely ignorant of the case (which was true). He would then ask for an adjournment until he was sufficiently briefed to properly conduct the defence, which would open the door for Molesworth to conduct the case. Before Judge Redmond Barry in the Central Criminal Court on Monday 18 October 1880, he had the trial postponed until the 28th.

The increasingly desperate defence sought help from the Crown. It provided £7. Further efforts to raise money were an abject failure, and on the 28th, when it became clear there weren't enough funds to hire Molesworth, the woefully inexperienced Bindon was flung before the court to defend Ned Kelly, having been handed the case only two days earlier. To the charge of murder of Thomas Lonigan Ned pleaded not guilty.

The court, with Judge Barry presiding, heard evidence for two days, during which the prosecution sought to have a copy of the Jerilderie Letter tendered. It was a curious action. In modern times Ned's supporters regard the document as a testament to his innocence. Neither the prosecution nor Ned's own lawyer Bindon saw it that way. Bindon objected to the letter being admitted on the grounds that it wasn't written in Ned's hand. The author, and therefore the only person who could reliably be said to hold the letter's opinions, was the deceased Joe Byrne. It seems both the prosecution and defence in Ned's trial looked upon the letter as incriminating. Perhaps they'd read it in its entirety, not just selectively.

The evidence was concluded on the afternoon of the second day of the trial, the defence having made little headway against the flimsy recollections of Constable McIntyre in particular (it was only thirty-three years later that Superintendent John Sadleir admitted in his book *Recollections of a Victorian Police Officer* that McIntyre's initial statement, given three days after Stringybark Creek, largely substantiated Ned Kelly's version of the shooting of Lonigan). In his summing up, Judge Barry dismissed Ned's assertion that he'd shot Lonigan in self-defence. Barry contended that no one had a right to challenge police when they're acting to maintain the peace. However, the real question was whether the police were upholding the law or were an execution squad.

The jury retired at 5.10 p.m. on 29 October and took just thirty minutes to arrive at a verdict. When they returned to the court the foreman, a dairyman named Samuel Lazarus, rose to his feet and when asked for his verdict replied, 'Guilty.'

Ned was then given an opportunity to speak. He thought the court had got it wrong. 'Nobody knows about this case except myself,' he said, 'And I almost wish now that I had spoken – and I wish I had insisted on being allowed to examine the witnesses myself. I am confident I would have thrown a different light on the case.'

As he prepared to deliver sentence, Redmond Barry felt compelled to disagree. 'No circumstances that I can conceive could have altered the result of your trial,' he said.

To which Ned replied, 'Perhaps if you had heard me examine the witnesses, you might understand. I could do it.' He added, 'It is quite possible for me to clear myself of this charge if I liked to do so. If I desired to do it, I could have done so in spite of anything attempted against me.'

It was too much for Barry. 'The facts against you are so numerous and so conclusive,' he said, 'not only as regards the offence which you are now charged with, but also for a long series of criminal acts which you have committed during the last eighteen months, that I do not think any rational person could have arrived at any other conclusion. The verdict of the jury is irresistible.'

He was right of course, up to a point. Had Ned been tried on every charge that could have been brought against him, even his façade of fighting for liberty and justice might have crumbled. Did he expect anyone to believe he had pursued Sergeant Michael Kennedy for 2 kilometres through the bush in order to shoot him in self-defence? Was there a point during the killing of two other police (Thomas

Lonigan and Michael Scanlan), robbing two banks, taking dozens of hostages and robbing many of them at gunpoint, executing Aaron Sherritt, attempting to kill a trainload of police and using dozens of hostages as human shields resulting in the deaths of thirteen-year-old Jack Jones, George Metcalf and Martin Cherry (plus fellow gang members Steve Hart, Joe Byrne and his brother Dan) when his claim of police provocation was no longer justified?

Ned appeared to expect the justice system to look at everything from his perspective and declare him innocent of any and all crimes. It was never going to happen. Redmond Barry sentenced Ned to death and the Victorian government acted with almost unseemly haste in setting the date for his execution for 11 November 1880, less than a fortnight after the sentence was handed down. In the few days that followed, thousands rallied to plead for clemency and a petition collected over 30 000 signatures.

Despite the pressure that was brought to bear, the Victorian government refused to commute the sentence. Far from the eucalypt-scented air of his mountain haunts, Ned was hanged within the dank confines of Melbourne Gaol on the morning of 11 November 1880. Just a few metres away, in the women's section of the gaol, his mother was excused work detail. As with so many aspects of Ned's life, there are several versions of his last words. Unlike the harangues of other bushrangers detailed in this volume, Ned's summation was as accurate as it was succinct: 'Such is life.'

After his execution, a death mask was made, then the body was decapitated and the brain removed, for study by practitioners of the now discredited science of phrenology. The body was then made available for dissection by medical students – a modern interpretation of quartering. What remained was buried in an unmarked grave in the prison grounds. At the time of his death, Ned Kelly was twenty-five years old.

The justice system had in no way let Ned walk free. However, shortly after his death, it took a long hard look at his case from his perspective. A royal commission into the Kelly Outbreak was announced to examine police conduct throughout the period that Ned was at large. Not surprisingly it found serious deficiencies in a range of areas and a number of officers. Indeed, in exposing the open warfare between senior officers, it was itself a showcase of all that was wrong in the Victorian police.

Meanwhile, the image of the armoured Ned Kelly had already seized the imagination of a nation. The apparition of the iron-helmeted man that loomed out of the morning mists of 27 June 1880 differentiated Kelly from every other bushranger and ensured he would hold a unique place in Australian history. Coupled with Ned's politics and the approach of Australian nationhood, when the nation broke free of the English yoke at last, it made Ned a symbol of Australian identity that has endured to this day. For all his crimes, he was and is Australia's greatest self-made hero.

A NOTE ON REFERENCES

In preparing this volume, consideration was given to the inclusion of references and an index. However, due to the large extent of the text, which resisted most efforts to pare it back, preference was given to it, rather than to many pages of material of only passing interest to most readers.

Sufficient detail is contained in the text to identify nearly all the newspaper articles, most of which can be found in the invaluable online resource trove.nla.gov.au/newspaper.

Readers requiring further assistance with references are welcome to write to the author care of Penguin Australia.

read more
my penguin e-newsletter

Subscribe to receive *read more*, your monthly e-newsletter from Penguin Australia. As a *read more* subscriber you'll receive sneak peeks of new books, be kept up to date with what's hot, have the opportunity to meet your favourite authors, download reading guides for your book club, receive special offers, be in the running to win exclusive subscriber-only prizes, plus much more.

Visit penguin.com.au/readmore to subscribe